Y0-BRJ-233

THE MEDIEVAL
CONSOLATION OF PHILOSOPHY

GARLAND MEDIEVAL BIBLIOGRAPHIES
(VOL. 7)

GARLAND REFERENCE LIBRARY
OF THE HUMANITIES
(VOL. 1215)

GARLAND MEDIEVAL BIBLIOGRAPHIES

THE MEDIEVAL
CONSOLATION OF PHILOSOPHY
An Annotated Bibliography

Noel Harold Kaylor, Jr.

GARLAND PUBLISHING, INC. • NEW YORK & LONDON
1992

© 1992 Noel Harold Kaylor, Jr.
All rights reserved

Library of Congress Cataloging-in-Publication Data

Kaylor, Noel Harold, 1946–
    The medieval Consolation of philosophy : an annotated bibliography /
by Noel Harold Kaylor, Jr.
        p.   cm. — (Garland medieval bibliographies ; vol. 7) (Garland
reference library of the humanities ; vol. 1215)
    Includes bibliographical references.
    ISBN 0-8240-5548-9
    1. Boethius, d. 524—Translations—Bibliography. 2. Boethius, d. 524.
De consolatione philosophiae—Bibliography. 3. Philosophy and
religion—Early works to 1800—Bibliography. 4. Happiness—Early
works to 1800—Bibliography. I. Title. II. Series. III. Series: Garland
reference library of the humanities ; vol. 1215.
Z8106.3.K38   1992
[B659.Z69]
016.189—dc20   92-459
                                                                                            CIP

Printed on acid-free, 250-year-life paper
Manufactured in the United States of America

016,189
K 23 m

Für Karl Heinz und Jutta,

in herzlicher

Dankbarkeit

CONTENTS

vii

PREFACE

Boethius was one of the most important literary and philosophical figures during the Middle Ages. His influence extended into almost every area of medieval intellectual and artistic life. Of primary importance for this study are the numerous vernacular translations of his last work, the **Consolation of Philosophy.** The titles collected in this annotated bibliography represent the scholarship generated by the translations which were produced in medieval England, France, and Germany. An attempt has been made to make the entries as complete as possible to 1990, and some titles from 1991 and 1992 have been included.

Separate chapters are devoted to the **Consolatio** traditions of medieval France and Germany. Because the Old and Middle English traditions are separated by a hiatus, each has been given its own chapter. All chapters dealing with one of these four **Consolatio** traditions are subdivided into two sections. Section I is devoted to the major translation in the tradition, that is, the translations by King Alfred, Notker, Jean de Meun, and Chaucer; Section II is devoted to the other translations in the linguistic tradition.

An introductory chapter at the beginning of the bibliography provides a general discussion of Boethian scholarship. The Introduction, unlike the later chapters which treat the individual vernacular traditions, does not include an exhaustive bibliography. It simply introduces the life and works of Boethius, indicating the various directions Boethian scholarship has taken and mentioning the more important studies which help to define those sundry areas of research.

Each of the four chapters which comprise the main body of this bibliography is designed to stand as an autonomous unit. Thus, viewed as a whole, the work is a bibliography and study of the European tradition of **Consolatio** translations, but viewed on a chapter-by-chapter basis, it is a collection of independent bibliographies on the individual vernacular traditions. The lists of relevant titles accompanying each section of the chapters and the bibliography at the end of the book are arranged

ix

alphabetically by author, but the articles and books by individual authors are arranged chronologically, from earlier to later works.

I wish to thank Dr. Hans Schulz of Vanderbilt University for his advice and hours of assistance when this study was still becoming a dissertation; I could have worked with no other advisor as effectively. I am grateful to Professor Dr. Karl Heinz Göller for his generous assistance and encouragement during several years of my research at the University of Regensburg in Bavaria. He, more than anyone else, provided me with direction when I was beginning my work as a medievalist.

I owe a debt of gratitude to the Vanderbilt University Library for its assistance in locating materials essential to the completion of this work, and to the library of the University of Regensburg, Germany, for performing miracles in locating the German dissertations and other rare articles which I needed. I am also indebted to Southeast Community College of Kentucky, and particularly to Mr. Robert Pafford, for the hours of computer time required in producing an early draft of this bibliography.

Among my colleagues in Boethian studies who have been so helpful, I am very grateful to Professors Keith Atkinson and Glynnis Cropp for their ceaseless encouragement during the several years when this work was in progress. They sent me their offprints, they alerted me to articles and works which had escaped my notice, and occasionally they consoled me philosophically and spiritually when I became discouraged in my work.

I appreciate the help of my friends and students at the University of Northern Iowa who volunteered their services as proofreaders of my manuscript: Linda Bingham, Keith Bockoven, Dan Geers, Anne-Françoise Le Lostec, Frederick Walthour, and Dr. Richard Utz.

Finally, I am indebted to Mr. Peter Giunta of Cambridge, Massachusetts, for urging me toward the completion of this bibliography and for giving me the technological advice and support which made possible the production of a final text. Without his help, this book might never have reached the publisher's desk.

Noel Harold Kaylor, Jr.
University of Northern Iowa
March, 1992

The Medieval

Consolation of Philosophy

CHAPTER I

INTRODUCTION
THE MEDIEVAL TRADITION OF
THE CONSOLATION OF PHILOSOPHY

The tradition of medieval translations of the **De Consolatione Philosophiae** by Boethius extends from c. 900 A.D., the date of King Alfred's work, to the end of the fifteenth century. It includes nearly twenty translations of varied quality and importance, and among these, the French tradition alone consists of about thirteen translations, which are listed by Richard Dwyer in his book, **Boethian Fictions** (Dwyer 1976). The relative obscurity of the **Consolatio** in our post-Renaissance world belies the fact that its influence upon medieval thinkers and writers was third only to that of the Bible and the works of St. Augustine.

In the **Consolatio**, through five books, comprising thirty-nine prose passages alternating with an equal number of meters, Boethius creates a narrative fiction in which Lady Philosophy visits and instructs a prisoner in his prison cell. The work is a confession or spiritual autobiography in that the prisoner ostensibly is Boethius himself, in his prison cell in Pavia. It differs from such works as the **Confessions** of St. Augustine, however, because it is not a memoir. The reader observes the prisoner's "present tense" development as Lady Philosophy instructs him. Boethius begins:

Carmina qui quondam studio florente peregi,

3

> Flebilis heu maestos cogor inire modos.
> Ecce mihi lacerae dictant scribenda Camenae
> Et veris elegi fletibus ora rigant.
>> [Stewart, Rand and Tester 1978 (**Consolatio**, I, 1-4), 130]

The present tense verbs help to give the text its sense of immediacy, an effect which could not be achieved without the fictional framework. Overcome by the arbitrariness and injustice of being wrongly accused of treason and imprisoned, Boethius has allowed himself to indulge in self-pity resulting from his loss of wealth, position, power, fame, and pleasure. He has temporarily abandoned the teachings of philosophy, the values he has followed throughout his life, and for that reason, he has lost his identity. The Socratic dialogue between the prisoner and his mentor develops step-by-step a propositional system which begins with the premise that the universe is rationally ordered. The perennial problems of human existence are discussed and given solutions: what constitutes true human happiness, why must good people suffer while the bad prosper, and how is it that man is subject to the vicissitudes of chance and fortune? Ultimately, aided by Lady Philosophy's instruction, Boethius transcends his unhappiness, reawakening to a consciousness of eternal philosophical verities which cannot first be distributed and then rescinded by Fortune's inconstant whims. He has not been consoled in his misfortune, however, as the title suggests; his attention has been lifted, rather, out of Fortune's realm of constant change into Philosophy's domain of permanent, absolute values. Boethius, the prisoner, has been re-educated into the philosophical knowledge which he had forgotten.

      Near the opening of Book I of the **Consolatio**, Lady Philosophy enters Boethius' prison cell, finding him surrounded by poetic Muses who are reinforcing his self-pity and unhappiness: they are prompting him to further indulgence in self-pity by urging him to express his sadness in poetry. George Saintsbury says, interestingly, that medieval literary criticism really begins here, when Lady Philosophy dismisses the Muses, calling them deceitful "strumpets and Mermaidens" (Saintsbury 1900, vol. 1, 390). With their eviction accomplished, Lady Philosophy begins her diagnosis of the "patient," Boethius. She assures him that his problem is curable, that he has simply forgotten his true nature and his proper understanding of the universe. He has strayed, Lady Philosophy says, out of the "Civitas Philosophiae," and her job is to help him return. She then reminds him of the all-important first premise of the philosophical system he must reconstruct: the universe is rational and orderly.

Lady Philosophy begins Book II dramatically, assuming the persona of Lady Fortuna in order to explain Fortune's activities to Boethius. Fortune's nature consists in change; to ask that it be otherwise is to ask that she cease to be Fortune. To trust in Fortune is, therefore, to invite disappointment. Boethius should have something solid upon which to build his happiness, and Lady Philosophy suggests that this solid foundation is self-knowledge. Boethius must put aside his remorse and learn from his misfortune, becoming aware again that, in spite of any adversity, the universe is not chaotic and random, and that love binds all the diverse elements into a unified system.

Book III is devoted to differentiating true felicity from the many distractions of the world. Lady Philosophy discusses wealth, high office, power, fame, and pleasure, pointing out that each has failed to provide him with the lasting happiness he desires. He had chosen to allow his life to be ruled by Fortune; he must now choose to leave caprice behind and be guided by reason. After a brief prayer to the philosopher's God, the Primum Mobile, there is a long section of close logical argument in which Lady Philosophy induces Boethius to understand again that the Good is the end of all universal activity. The evil which Boethius fears is an illusion: God is the substance all good participates in, and evil is insubstantial. With this insight gained, Boethius must never look back upon his false values, or he, like Orpheus, might again lose that which he holds most dear.

The problem of good and evil and the possibility of free will are treated extensively in Book IV. If God is good, why do the righteous suffer while wrong-doers seem to prosper? Lady Philosophy shows this paradox to have no real foundation: those who do evil have ceased, like Ulysses' crew on Circe's island, to be human; the prosperity of wrong-doers is a false happiness, and its enjoyment is to be pitied rather than envied. Next, Boethius wonders how men can have free will in a universe ruled by an omniscient God--it would seem God's foreknowledge of men's deeds necessitates events and precludes any possibility of their resulting from human agency. Again, the answer to such a question requires a shift in perspective: from man's point of view, on earth, living in time, it appears that free will must be an illusion; but from God's point of view, beyond time, in eternity, man is seen to have free will even though God knows his actions before they take place. The Divine

Mind manifests itself in two ways. In eternity, it has its pure form as Providence, but in time, it appears as Fate. God rules the universe with love and directs its course toward the Good. Hence, all fortune is ultimately good fortune. Boethius must try to understand his misfortune from God's point of view. "Earth overcome grants you the stars."

Lady Philosophy finishes her instruction in Book V by showing that even seemingly random events, which we call chance occurrences, are part of the rational structure of the universe. Man must strive for a holistic view, though he can never attain the total simplicity of God's perspective. In a universe ruled by such an all-knowing God, it is best to intend the Good because the Good is, ultimately, the end of all activity. Any imagined justification for sorrow which Boethius earlier may have conjured up in poetry has now vanished: Lady Philosophy has forced him to reaffirm the values he had briefly forgotten, and holding them again, he cannot be unhappy.

The most immediate literary context in which to consider the **Consolatio** is that of the Boethian corpus. In the second commentary to the **De Interpretatione**, Boethius stated his hope to translate for the Latin world as many of the works of Plato and Aristotle as possible and to show that their philosophies could be reconciled. Most of the Boethian canon seems to support such an agenda. His plan was never fully realized, but considering the political responsibilities he accepted during the reign of Theodoric and his early death, he finished a surprisingly large body of work. For the study of the quadrivium, a word which he himself seems to have coined, he produced the **De Institutione Arithmetica** (in two books) and the **De Institutione Musica** (in five books), which are still extant. A Boethian text on geometry is attested to by ancient authorities, but his work cannot be identified among the several works on geometry which survive from the period. It is also probable that he wrote a book on astronomy, the fourth study in the quadrivium, but any such work is now completely lost. The **De Arithmetica** and the **De Musica** are both theoretical in approach, and of the two, the latter has proved the most influential in later centuries.

An article, "The **De Institutione Arithmetica** and the **De Institutione Musica**" (Caldwell 1981), is a good introduction to Boethius' work on Arithmetic and Music. "Boethius' Geometry and Astronomy" (Pingree 1981) discusses problems relating to Boethius' contribution to these areas of study. "Boethius in the Medieval

Quadrivium" (White 1981) gives an assessment of Boethius' importance to the "upper division curriculum" of the Middle Ages. "The Scholar and his Public" (Kirkby 1981) gives information on the general condition of scholarship at the time of Boethius.

To the medieval library on logic, Boethius added several volumes. He began his work on this subject by writing a commentary on Vitorinus' Latin translation of Porphyry's **Introduction to the Categories** (the **Isagoge**). Later, probably dissatisfied with Vitorinus' work, he made his own translation and wrote another commentary (in five books).

Of Aristotle's Organon, he translated the **De Interpretatione (Peri hermēneias)**, in two books. He then wrote a simple commentary (in two books) and later an advanced commentary (in six books). He also translated the **Categories (Praedicamenta)**, following it up with a commentary based on Porphyry (in four books). This last work is one which can be dated fairly accurately; he was writing it during the year of his consulship, 510 A.D. Concerning any other works on logic, a translation of Aristotle's **Topics** can be attributed to him with certainty. Translations of the **Prior** and **Posterior Analytics** as well as the **De Sophistica Elenchis** have been at times granted and at times denied Boethian origin by various critics. It is particularly the attribution of the **Posterior Analytics** which has found little support among the authorities.

Boethius' remaining works on logic include a commentary on Cicero's **Topics** (in five books) as well as five original treatises: **De Syllogismis Categoricis** (in two books), **De Syllogismis Hypotheticis** (in three books), **De Divisione, De Differentiis Topicis**, and the **Prolegomena (Antepraedicamenta)**. Boethius' importance for the discipline of logic is seen primarily in his preserving its study in Latin for the early medieval period.

The dating of Boethius' works on logic is discussed in two articles, "On the Chronology of Boethius' Works on Logic I" (Rijk 1964, I) and "On the Chronology of Boethius' Works on Logic II" (Rijk 1964, II). The importance of Boethius as a preserver of the discipline of logic is treated in "Boethius and the Study of Logic" (Barnes 1981). The influence of Boethius' work on the medieval study of logic is discussed in "Boethian Logic in the Medieval West" (Lewry 1981).

Four of the **Opuscula Sacra** or theological works can now be attributed to Boethius with some certainty, which has not always been the case. These four works are the **De Trinitate (Tractate I)**, two shorter pieces, the **Utrum Pater et Filius et Spiritus Sanctus (Tractate II)** and the **Quodmodo Substantiae (Tractate III** or the **De Hebdomadibus)**, and the **Contra Eutychen et Nestroium (Tractate V)**. Another work, the **De Fide Catholica (Tractate IV)**, is sometimes attributed to Boethius, but it, unlike the other works, is not mentioned in ancient sources. Occasionally, critics place it among the five or six other works believed to have been falsely attributed to Boethius. The **Opuscula Sacra**, too, were often included in medieval curricula more for the quality of their argument and Latin eloquence than for their value to theology. They are the basis for claims that Boethius was Christian, but the **Consolatio**, his final statement to the world, offers no certain evidence for such an assertion.

Two general, introductory articles on these important works are "The Text of the **Opuscula Sacra**" (Mair 1981) and "The **Opuscula Sacra** in the Middle Ages" (Gibson 1981). Together, they form a good introduction to these works.

Finally, in the Boethian corpus, there is the **De Consolatione Philosophiae**, Boethius' last book and manifesto on the rational foundation of the universe and the importance of philosophy in human life. It was produced during the author's period of imprisonment at Pavia, c.523-24. It is unique among Boethius' writings because it is neither an academic treatise or commentary nor a translation of a learned Greek text. It is a very personal expression of one man's understanding of himself as part of a rational universe, and in its fictional framework, using verse alternating with prose, the **Consolatio** is formally literary. It is this uniqueness in content and form which allowed the **Consolatio** to enjoy a tradition in the Middle Ages which developed separately from that of the writer's other works.

One book, **Prison Books and their Authors** (Langford 1861), and an article, "Imprisoned English Authors and the **Consolation of Philosophy** of Boethius" (Dolson 1922, "Imprisoned English Authors"), place the **Consolatio** in the context of prison literature. "Literary Design in the **De Consolatione Philosophiae**" (Crabbe 1981) gives a general introduction to the problems of genre in the work. On a somewhat related topic,

"Illustrations in Manuscripts of Boethius' Works" (D.K. Bolton 1981) provides information on the subject suggested by the title. For information on one of the Meters of Boethius preserved, complete with musical notation, in a medieval manuscript, see the article, "The Boethian Metrum 'Bella bis quinis': a new Song from Saxon Canterbury" (Page 1981).

Between 524 and the end of the eighth century, the **Consolatio** remained obscure. The first person north of the Alps to show its influence was Alcuin, "the educator of Charlemagne's empire"; and the oldest Latin manuscript of the work dates from the early Carolingian period, from about 800 (Parks 1981). Discussing this early Latin tradition, Jacqueline Beaumont concludes:

> In all cases, use of the text was eclectic, literary and moralizing. It was not Boethius in himself who was important. It was not an understanding of his work which was required, but the application, piecemeal and out of context, of thoughts, images and elegant phrasing which gave added point to the work of the moment. (Beaumont 1981, 282)

The **Consolatio** was first used, therefore, in the schools as a manual of Latin phrasing and literary allusions rather than as a work important in itself. Seventy-six Latin manuscripts remain from the ninth, tenth, and eleventh centuries, and of these, sixty are glossed in various ways, indicating the major concerns of readers and copiers of the text.

The oldest vernacular translation is in Old English. It is an all-prose version, which is generally accepted as the work of Alfred the Great. Later an alliterative verse translation of most of the meters appeared, but the verses are not assigned with any certainty to King Alfred. Interestingly, one manuscript does exist in which the alliterative meters have been substituted for the corresponding passages in the prose translation, yielding a text which mirrors the alternating verse and prose form of the Latin original (see Godden 1981). Thus the process of manuscript revision which is seen in the Old English tradition and in the preparation of this unique manuscript indicates two divergent attitudes among the medieval translators of the **Consolatio**: on the one hand, to render into the vernacular the content of the work, and on the other, to do justice to the form.

Boethius was a master of both prose and verse in the **Consolatio,** and his craftsmanship did not escape the notice of his medieval translators. Among the translations there was some disagreement, however, as to how to deal with the mixture of genres in the work. For example, in England Chaucer produced an all-prose translation, but within half a century of its appearance, John Walton answered it with an all-verse rendering. In Germany Notker III wrote an all-prose translation, but Gustav Ehrismann has noted that some of his prose renderings of the meters have metrical qualities (Ehrismann 1932, 430). In France, Jean de Meun produced a prose translation, but a later editor borrowed his preface and put it at the beginning of a hybrid work in mixed prose and verse.

In the translations, the choice of either prose or verse is an index of the translator's intentions. Generally, an all-prose rendering, such as Chaucer's or Notker's or Jean de Meun's, is a utilitarian work in which the emphasis is on the **prodesse** rather than on the **delectare** aspect of the work. An all-verse translation, such as John Walton's, emphasizes the **delectare** aspect of the work. For the tradition as a whole, it may be noted that there was a development from the early all-prose, through the intermediary all-verse renderings, toward the later mixed, verse-prose translations.

Another general characteristic of the **Consolatio** tradition which affected the form of the translations was the incorporation into the body of the text of various amounts of extraneous material, which consisted sometimes of short glosses and sometimes of long narrative digressions. As an extreme example of this development, there is the prose translation by Pierre de Paris of about 1309. It contains a veritable encyclopedia of lengthy interpretations and stories from mythology; Pierre, it would seem, created his own commentary and presented it as part of the text. This "commentary" was later extracted from the translation and offered as a separate Latin text, one manuscript of which survives in France (Thomas and Roque 1938, 449). A mid-fourteenth-century French translation (referred to as the "Anonymous of Meun") in 12,340 verses appeared and in it whole episodes had been developed to expand the Boethian text (Dwyer 1976, 51-65). Even the relatively concise renderings by Jean de Meun and Chaucer evidence this medieval habit of expanding the translations with glosses, some of which, such as Chaucer's gloss on the word **tragedy**, have become noteworthy in their own right. The tendency to enrich the **Consolatio** translations with added material continued to the Renaissance.

Although they represent an important part of the medieval tradition, the commentaries on the **Consolatio** are not specifically a part of the present study, but they deserve mention because they were the source of much of the extraneous material incorporated into the translations. They also form indirect links between certain of the translations. For example, there is no direct connection between the vernacular translations of Alfred the Great and Chaucer, but Chaucer had consulted Trevet's commentary while preparing his prose rendering, and Trevet had consulted Alfred's translation while preparing his commentary.

The history of the Latin commentaries and their importance in the **Consolatio** tradition is studied at length by Pierre Courcelle in an article and later in his book, La Consolation de Philosophiae **dans la tradition littéraire: antécédents et postérité de Boèce** (Courcelle 1939; Courcelle 1967). An article by Jourdain discusses some of the unedited commentaries (Jourdain 1862). In a less comprehensive study, "Aspects of the Medieval French and English Traditions of the **De Consolatione Philosophiae**," Alastair Minnis gives thorough consideration to the importance of the commentaries for the French **Consolatio** tradition (Minnis 1981). The commentaries form an important link in the complex and continuous fabric of the medieval **Consolatio** tradition.

The philosophy expressed in the **Consolatio** was welcomed by most medieval thinkers. Boethius discusses the nature of good and evil, the foreknowledge of God, and the possibility of free will, and he integrates these complex ideas into a seemingly consistent, theistic world view. The disdain expressed in the work for worldly vanities and the trappings of wealth and high position were at least compatible with medieval monastic attitudes.

The prose translations in particular attest to the existence of a vernacular audience receptive to Boethian ideas, and that audience was Christian. The problem of Boethius' theology, or his attitude toward Christianity, is related to the subject of his philosophy. Concerning

Boethius' actual stand on Christianity, Henry Chadwick summarizes the
view accepted by most critics today:

> The author [Boethius], it is true, wrote some pages on Christian
> theology which are of greatest consequence. But he did not write
> them as a theologian in the ordinary sense of the word; he is
> addressing himself only indirectly to a pastoral or "political"
> situation in the church, as a logician who thought there was
> some tidying up to be done in the ecclesiastical garden.
> (Chadwick 1981, 1)

In the Middle Ages, however, there was a strong tendency to read the
Consolatio as a Christian text. In the Latin work, Boethius' deity is
that of the philosophers, the Primum Mobile, and not the God of
Christianity. But medieval translators and commentators attempted to
equate or reconcile this deity with the Christian God, and some of the
philosophical content of the work was "medievalized" or made to seem
more Christian. We see an attempt to bring Boethius' phrasing closer to
Christian constructions even in Chaucer's rather close translation. Early
in the **Consolatio**, Lady Philosophy uses the image of the city as a
metaphor for her kingdom of philosophy and reason; she tells the prisoner
Boethius that his confusion indicates that he has strayed from this city,
which is his native land. In Chaucer, we read:

> For yif thow remembre of what cuntre thow art born, it nys nat
> governed by emperoures, ne by governement of multitude, as
> weren the cuntrees of hem of Atthenes; but o lord and o king,
> and that is God, that is lord of thi cuntre, whiche that rejoisseth
> hym of the duellynge of his citezeens, and nat for to putten hem
> in exil . . . . (Benson 1987, **Boece**, I, prose 5, 405)

This English, although close to the Latin, refers unmistakably to the City
of God rather than to the City of Philosophy. Gibbon is right when he
says, "The senator Boethius is the last of the Romans whom Cato or
Tully could have acknowledged for their countryman" (Gibbon 1909, vol.
4, 211), but Boethius' classical ideas become mixed with medieval values
even in the better translations.

The happy combination in the **Consolatio** of an acceptable
philosophy and Latin eloquence prompted Notker to produce the first

continental translation of the work as a gloss upon the Latin text. Notker wanted to teach his students good Latin through meaningful texts, and he chose the **Consolatio** as one of the vehicles. The work's philosophy in this instance helped to justify its study as a significant example of Latin used well. For further general information on the **Consolatio** tradition in Germany, see the article, "Latin and Vernacular in the Northern European Tradition of the **De Consolatione Philosophiae**" (Palmer 1981).

The historical and biographical dimension of the work also impressed medieval translators. The story of Boethius, a man capable of articulating the profound ideas one finds in the **Consolatio**, who is unjustly imprisoned, sentenced, and executed, is, in ways similar to that of Christ scourged and put to death, compelling. Richard Morris, echoing a passage from Milton, was able to say of Boethius: "No philosopher was so bone of the bone and flesh of the flesh of the Middle-age writers as Boethius" (Morris 1886, ii). It was as much because of medieval sympathy for the circumstances of his life and execution as because of medieval receptivity to the philosophy itself that this statement is true.
Boethius discusses his imprisonment in Book I, and readers of the **Consolatio** could not be unaware of the writer's ultimate fate, a fate, of course, not mentioned in the text. Dramatic irony is thus established which involves the reader in a unique way. Just beyond the philosophical triumph described in the course of the work stands the historical tragedy of Boethius' death, and this tragic end shares the reader's attention as he follows the arguments developed by Lady Philosophy.
The medieval reader would not have been so likely as we today to distinguish the prisoner Boethius in the **Consolatio** from the historical Boethius who authored the work. Boethius' description of his treatment by Theodoric would have been taken as fact, and his suffering and death at the hands of Theodoric, an Aryan who was also responsible for the death of a pope, John I, was interpreted as martyrdom. Gibbon, in his eloquence, is again worth quoting:

> While Boethius, oppressed with fetters, expected each moment the sentence or the stroke of death, he composed in the tower of Pavia the **Consolation of Philosophy**: a golden volume not unworthy of the leisure of Plato or Tully, but which claims

incomparable merit from the barbarism of the times and the
situation of the author.   (Gibbon 1909, vol. 4, 215)

The historical and biographical dimension of the **Consolatio**, presenting
such an image of Boethius falsely condemned and awaiting execution,
contributed much to its popularity in the Middle Ages. It is perhaps also
a reflection of our twentieth-century lack of interest in religious
martyrdom that the **Consolatio** has become a relatively obscure work.

The importance of the vitae, or lives of Boethius, deserves
mention here. Most of the **Consolatio** translations are prefaced by
information on the life and times of Boethius, and these prefaces form a
tradition of their own, almost independent of the **Consolatio** itself. The
various translators borrowed information from earlier prefaces, they used
information from the commentaries, and they extracted material from the
Consolatio itself. The resulting mixture of information and
misinformation entered the vitae. In that tradition, Boethius was
generally viewed as a Christian martyr; he was even acknowledged as a
saint in some parts of Italy. However, Theodoric, elsewhere referred to as
Theodoric the Great, became an arch-villain. An article by Edmund Reiss,
"The Fall of Boethius and the Fiction of the **Consolatio**
Philosophiae" (Reiss 1981), calls attention to the fact that the vitae
continue to influence readings of the **Consolatio** even today.

The end of the medieval tradition is signaled by such Renaissance
Consolatio translations as that by Queen Elizabeth I [(Pemberton 1899)
(see Grafton 1981)]. Her work seems to have been achieved
independently, directly from a Latin manuscript without reference to the
earlier translations, the commentaries, or the vitae. Elizabeth attempted a
close rendering of the **Consolatio**, both in its content and its form.
During the Middle Ages, such careful attention to textual details was not
generally a priority. As pointed out above, the medieval translators felt
the need to incorporate explanations and interpretations into the text,
bringing the accumulated wisdom of the earlier authorities into their
work. The Renaissance desire to understand ancient texts on their own
terms, a desire which is seen in Elizabeth's translation, brought an end to
the long medieval tradition. The year 1500 is the terminal date for
translations considered in this study, a time when the conventions of the
medieval tradition cease to characterize the translations.

Some general studies of the medieval **Consolatio** tradition and of the life and importance of Boethius are available and are helpful as introductions. Hugh Fraser Stewart's book, **Boethius: An Essay** (Stewart 1891) focuses more on the **Consolatio** and Boethius' theological works than on his academic works. Stewart's book is a significant beginning for any study of Boethius. When it was written, it represented a fresh consideration of Boethius and his importance. A book by Howard Rollin Patch, **The Tradition of Boethius: A Study of His Importance in Medieval Culture** (Patch 1935), is also a good source of general information, but this work, too, pays but slight attention to Boethius' more academic works. A. van de Vyver's article, "Les Traductions du **De Consolatione philosophiae** de Boèce en littérature comparée" (van de Vyver 1939), gives a valuable list of the early European translations of the **Consolatio**, and it is fairly complete. Each entry is accompanied by a short description of the translation, giving some manuscript information and an indication of its affinities with other translations. The article offers a good, concise overview of the entire European **Consolatio** translation tradition. The early Spanish and Catalan translations of the **Consolatio** are the subject of an article by Ronald Keightley (Keightley 1987); he describes all of the translations as well as a translation into Spanish of Trevet's commentary. In conjunction with this article, see also an article by Clovis Brunel (Brunel 1955) which describes a fragment of a Catalan **Consolatio** translation. In the context of these general studies, I must mention in passing the dissertation which represents the original version of this annotated bibliography (Kaylor 1985).

A book which achieves a comprehensive appreciation of the many facets of Boethius' work and influence is a collection of articles edited by Margaret Gibson, **Boethius: His Life, Thought and Influence** (Gibson 1981). The collection attempts to bring together factual and critical data on just about every aspect of Boethius' importance. It was compiled to commemorate the fifteen hundredth anniversary of Boethius' birth, and it is a worthy memorial for that occasion, accessible and interesting to the specialist and non-specialist alike. Many of the articles mentioned above are contained in that volume. Another book, **The Medieval Boethius: Studies in the Vernacular Translations of the** De Consolatione Philosophiae, edited by Alastair J. Minnis (Minnis 1987), is a companion piece to

Gibson's book. It brings together articles which fill in certain gaps left in the earlier collection of essays.

As to the biography of Boethius, the general studies mentioned above offer essential information. Helen M. Barrett's book, **Boethius: Some Aspects of His Times and Work** (Barrett 1940), has the advantage, however, of referring constantly to original sources on the life of Boethius, something which the more general works do not do. On the special problem of the Christianity of Boethius, see M. Cappuyns' article, "Boèce" (Cappuyns 1937), which gives fairly objective consideration to both the positive and negative aspects of the argument. For very general information on the life of Boethius, see the article, "Boethius, Anicius Manlius Severinus," in the **Verfasserlexikon** (Rädle and Worstbrock 1978); see also articles by Matthews and Minio-Paluello [(Matthews 1981) (Minio-Paluello 1970)].

Finally, as to the manuscripts and the Latin text, a Latin **Consolatio** edited by Rudolphus Peiper (Peiper 1871) is an early critical edition from which most subsequent editions of the **Consolatio** stem. Ludwig Bieler's edition (Bieler 1957), made for the Corpus Christianorum, Series Latina, is a respected text (for an earlier edition, see Migne n.d.). The new edition of the Loeb Classical Library's **Boethius: Tractates, De Consolatione Philosophiae** (Stewart, Rand, Tester 1978) also deserves consideration as a critical edition. The older edition for Loeb contained faulty translations, but the new volume, with the **Consolatio** translated by S.J. Tester, corrects those errors. Cooper Lane's **A Concordance of Boethius: the Five Theological Tractates and the Consolation of Philosophy** (Cooper 1928) is, of course, important as part of the scholarly apparatus on Boethius.

A cautionary and informative article, "The Vulgate Tradition of the **Consolatio Philosophiae** in the Fourteenth Century" (Kottler 1955), points out for students of the medieval translations the limitations of all critical editions of the Latin text. Kottler indicates that by the fourteenth century, scribal error and faulty emendation had produced several distinct varieties of the Latin text. Before medieval translators are credited with errors, these variations in the tradition of the Latin text should be considered.

List of Relevant Titles

1. Barnes, Jonathan. "Boethius and the Study of Logic." In **Boethius: His Life, Times and Influence**, edited by Margaret Gibson, 73-89. Oxford: Basil Blackwell, 1981.

   Barnes divides Boethian works on logic into three types: 1) translations, 2) commentaries, and 3) treatises. Each type is discussed. The critic's analysis shows that Boethius was not an original logician; his importance lies in his having preserved the discipline for the Latin world.

2. Barrett, Helen M. **Boethius: Some Aspects of His Times and Works.** Cambridge: n.p., 1940. Reprint. New York: Russell and Russell, 1965.

   Barrett gives a fairly complete picture of Boethius' life. The original source material is referred to directly. Particular emphasis is given to circumstances surrounding the death of Boethius.

3. Beaumont, Jacqueline. "The Latin Tradition of the **De Consolatione Philosophiae**." In **Boethius: His Life, Thought and Influence**, edited by Margaret Gibson, 278-305. Oxford: Basil Blackwell, 1981.

   Beaumont considers the Latin reception of the **Consolatio**, primarily through the Latin commentaries on the work. Remigius' commentary and its revisions are described at length. William of Conches is the last commentator to be discussed--the culmination of the earlier Carolingian attitudes toward the **Consolatio**. The thirteenth century brought new attitudes to commentaries.

4.   Benson, Larry D., ed. **The Riverside Chaucer**.
      3rd ed. Boston: Houghton Mifflin, 1987.

      This is the most recent of the critical editions of
      Chaucer's works.

5.   Bieler, Ludwig, ed. **Boethii Philosophiae
      Consolatio**. Corpus Christianorum, Series
      Latina, no. 94. Turnholti, Belgium: Typographi
      Brepols Editiones Pontificii, 1957.

      This is a widely used critical edition of the
      Consolatio, based on early manuscripts.

6.   Bolton, Diane K. "Illustrations in Manuscripts of
      Boethius' Works." In **Boethius: His Life,
      Thought and Influence**, edited by Margaret
      Gibson, 428-37. Oxford: Basil Blackwell, 1981.

      Bolton adds updated and additional information on
      illuminations identified and described by Courcelle
      (1967).

7.   Brunel, Clovis. "Fragment d'un ms. de la
      traduction Catalane de la **Consolatio** de Boèce."
      Romania 76 (1955): 522-4.

      As the title suggests, this short article describes a
      fragment of a Catalan **Consolatio** translation.

8.   Caldwell, John. "**De Institutione
      Arithmetica** and the **De Institutione
      Musica**." In **Boethius: His Life, Thought
      and Influence**, edited by Margaret Gibson, 135-
      54. Oxford: Basil Blackwell, 1981.

      Caldwell discusses possible sources of Boethius'
      work: Boethius probably derived much of the **De
      Arithmetica** from Nicomachus of Gerasa and the

De Musica from the Pythagoreans. The De
Musica was written for a sophisticated audience.
Boethius was probably not a performer, but an
important sixth-century theorist.

9.   Cappuyns, M. "Boèce." In **Dictionnaire**
     d'histoire et de géographie
     ecclésiastique. Vol. 9, 347-80. Paris: Librairie
     Letouzey et Anê, 1937.

     This is primarily a description of problems related
     to the Christianity and possible martyrdom of
     Boethius.

10. Chadwick, Henry. "Introduction." In **Boethius:**
     His Life, Thought and Influence, edited by
     Margaret Gibson, 1-12. Oxford: Basil Blackwell,
     1981.

     Chadwick gives a picture of a complex intellectual
     who is neither a Christian theologian nor a pagan
     apologist. He discusses the wide range of
     Boethius' thought. Quite rightly, he views the
     Consolatio as his most celebrated work.

11. Cooper, Lane. **A Concordance of Boethius:**
     the Five Theological Tractates **and the**
     Consolation of Philosophy. Mediaeval Academy
     of America Publication, no. 1. Cambridge, Mass.:
     Mediaeval Academy of America, 1928.

     This is a concordance to Latin concepts; it is
     useful for anyone involved in Boethian studies. It
     has not been superseded by more recent studies.

12. Courcelle, Pierre. "Étude critique sur les
     commentaries de la **Consolation** de Boèce (IXe-
     XVe siècles)." **Archives d'histoire**

doctrinale et littéraire du moyen âge 4 (1939): 5-140.

This study presents work which is preliminary to Courcelle's book, cited below (Courcelle 1967).

13. ----------. La Consolation de philosophie dans la tradition littéraire: antécédents et postérité de Boèce. Paris: Études Augustiniennes, 1967.

This is the standard study of the Latin commentaries on the Consolatio, as well as of the influence of the commentaries on the translations. It is accurate except for some details which have been questioned by more recent critics.

14. Crabbe, Anna. "Literary Design in the De Consolatione Philosophiae." In Boethius: His Life, Thought and Influence, edited by Margaret Gibson, 237-74. Oxford: Basil Blackwell, 1981.

Neo-Platonists are shown to have influenced Boethius' imagery and metaphors, but the primary influences on literary design are found to be Ovid, Cicero, Seneca, and Augustine. The article gives a particularly lengthy discussion on Augustine's influence, which is shown to have been substantial.

15. Dolson, Guy Bayley. "Imprisoned English Authors and the Consolation of Philosophy of Boethius." American Journal of Philology 43 (1922): 168-9.

As the title suggests, this article treats English authors who suffered imprisonment and discovered a kindred spirit in Boethius.

16.   Dwyer, Richard A. **Boethian Fictions: Narratives in the Medieval French Versions of the** Consolatio Philosophiae. Mediaeval Academy of America, no. 83. Cambridge, Mass.: Mediaeval Academy of America, 1976.

       Among other things, Dwyer describes the digressions found in the "Anonymous of Meun" verse translation of the **Consolatio**.

17.   Ehrismann, Gustav. "Notker III (Labeo) von St. Gallen." In **Handbuch des deutschen Unterrichts in höheren Schulen**. Vol. 6, pt. 1, **Die althochdeutsche Literatur**, 416-58. Munich: C.-H. Beck'sche Verlagsbuchhandlung, 1932.

       This article gives information on Notker who, in his prose **Consolatio** translation, appears to have attempted to capture some of the metrical quality of the Boethian meters.

18.   Gibbon, Edward. **The History of the Decline and Fall of the Roman Empire**, edited by J.B. Bury. Vol. 4. London, 1909. Reprint. New York: AMS, 1974.

       This is still one of the best introductions to the historical period in which the **Consolatio** was written. It captures the political atmosphere of the time.

19.   Gibson, Margaret, ed. **Boethius: His Life, Thought and Influence**. Oxford: Basil Blackwell, 1981.

       This book is an anthology of articles on all aspects of Boethian scholarship. The headings of

the main sections are: 1) "Boethius: Life and
Circumstances," 2) "The Scholastic Writings," 3)
"The **De Consolatione Philosophiae**," 4)
"Epilogue: Boethius in the Renaissance." Unlike
earlier general studies, this one reflects the whole
spectrum of Boethius' thought and influence. All
articles in the book are mentioned either in this
introduction or elsewhere in this annotated
bibliography.

20.   ----------. "The **Opuscula Sacra** in the Middle
         Ages." In **Boethius: His Life, Thought and
         Influence**, edited by Margaret Gibson, 214-34.
         Oxford: Basil Blackwell, 1981.

         This is a study of the reception of the **Opuscula
         Sacra** in the Middle Ages through Latin MSS and
         commentaries. The study concludes that the same
         theological work was done better by Augustine,
         but that the **Opuscula Sacra** became important
         school texts on applied logic.

21.   Godden, Malcolm. "King Alfred's Boethius." In
         **Boethius: His Life, Thought and
         Influence**, edited by Margaret Gibson, 419-24.
         Oxford: Basil Blackwell, 1981.

         This article gives a summary of information on
         and problems concerning the **Consolatio**
         translation by Alfred.

22.   Grafton, Anthony. "Epilogue: Boethius in the
         Renaissance." In **Boethius: His Life,
         Thought and Influence**, edited by Margaret
         Gibson, 410-15. Oxford: Basil Blackwell, 1981.

         This is a short study of the reception of Boethius
         in the Renaissance. The Humanists had the task
         of separating Boethius' **Consolatio** from the

medieval additions--they had to recover the text from the glosses and interpolations which writers had inserted.

23. Jourdain, M. Charles. "Des Commentaires inédits de Guillaume de Conches et de Nicolas Triveth sur **La Consolation de la philosophie** de Boèce." **Notices et extraits des manuscrits de la Bibliothèque Nationale** 20 (1862): 40-82.

As the title indicates, this article treats certain unedited commentaries on Boethius' **Consolatio**. It can be read as preliminary to the work done on the commentaries by Courcelle, which is listed above.

24. Kaylor, Noel Harold, Jr. "The Medieval Translations of Boethius' **Consolation of Philosophy** in England, France, and Germany: An Analysis and Annotated Bibliography." Ph.D. diss., Vanderbilt University, 1985.

This dissertation is an earlier, unpublished version of this present annotated bibliography.

25. Keightley, Ronald G. "Boethius in Spain: A Classified Checklist of Early Translations." In **The Medieval Boethius: Studies in the Vernacular Translations of** De Consolatione Philosophiae, edited by Alastair J. Minnis, 169-87. Woodbridge, Suffolk: D.S. Brewer, 1987.

In this article, Keightley describes the early Spanish and Catalan translations of the **Consolatio,** as well as a Spanish translation of Trevet's commentary.

26.   Kirkby, Helen. "The Scholar and His Public." In
        Boethius: His Life, Thought and
        Influence, edited by Margaret Gibson, 44-69.
        Oxford: Basil Blackwell, 1981.

        Kirkby calls into question any possible sixth-
        century Renaissance in the West. She compares
        the intellectual work of Cassiodorus and Boethius,
        examining their audience. Boethius is seen as an
        aristocratic intellectual of a traditional Roman
        type.

27.   Kottler, Barnet. "The Vulgate Tradition of the
        Consolatio Philosophiae in the Fourteenth
        Century." **Mediaeval Studies** 17 (1955):
        209-14.

        Kottler suggests that the text of the **Consolatio**
        had developed into several divergent families of
        erroneous texts by the fourteenth century.

28.   Langford, John Alfred. **Prison Books and**
        Their Authors. London: William Tegg, 1861.

        Consideration is given to Boethius (as well as to
        Cervantes, John Bunyan, and others) as an author
        of prison literature.

29.   Lewry, Osmund. "Boethian Logic in the Medieval
        West." In **Boethius: His Life, Thought and**
        Influence, edited by Margaret Gibson, 90-134.
        Oxford: Basil Blackwell, 1981.

        Lewry carefully follows the career of Boethius'
        works on logic through all the great schools of the
        Middle Ages, from the Carolingian awakening
        through the 1500s. Meticulous attention is given
        to sources and medieval reception.

30.   Mair, John. "The Text of the **Opuscula Sacra.**"
        In **Boethius: His Life, Thought and
        Influence**, edited by Margaret Gibson, 206-13.
        Oxford: Basil Blackwell, 1981.

        Mair gives a study of the contents of Boethius'
        theological works and the circumstances
        surrounding their writing. He concludes that
        critical editions are inadequate and more extensive
        studies of sources are needed.

31.   Matthews, John. "Anicius Manlius Severinus
        Boethius." In **Boethius: His Life, Thought
        and Influence**, edited by Margaret Gibson, 15-
        43. Oxford: Basil Blackwell, 1981.

        Matthews places Boethius in the social and
        political traditions of late Antiquity. He contrasts
        the more practical Cassiodorus with the idealistic
        Boethius. Boethius is seen as representative of the
        ancient senatorial tradition of leisured scholars.

32.   Migne, J.P., ed. **Boetii, Opera Omnia.**
        Patrologiae Latinae, nos. 63-64. Turnholti,
        Belgium: Typographi Brepols Editiores
        Pontificii, n.d.

        This is a critical edition of the Latin text of the
        Consolatio of Boethius.

33.   Minio-Paluello, Lorenzo. "Boethius." In
        Dictionary of Scientific Biography. Vol.
        2, 228-36. New York: Charles Scribner's Sons,
        1970.

        Minio-Paluello reviews the problems related to
        authenticating and dating Boethius' works. He
        discusses the possibilities of spurious ascriptions.

34.   Minnis, Alastair. "Aspects of the Medieval French
        and English Traditions of the **De Consolatione
        Philosophiae**." In **Boethius: His Life,
        Thought and Influence**, edited by Margaret
        Gibson, 312-61. Oxford: Basil Blackwell, 1981.

        Attention is given here to Jean de Meun, Chaucer,
        and John Walton. Minnis gives a detailed study of
        these translators' use of earlier commentaries and
        translations in preparing their own translations.
        He reveals the importance of the commentary
        tradition for the individual translations.

35.   ----------, ed. **The Medieval Boethius:
        Studies in the Vernacular Translations
        of the** De Consolatione Philosophiae.
        Woodbridge, Suffolk: D.S. Brewer, 1987.

        This is a companion to the book edited by
        Margaret Gibson (Gibson 1981). It fills in
        information on certain points not covered in the
        earlier work.

36.   Morris, Richard, ed. **Chaucer's** Boece **Englisht
        from Boethius's** De Consolatione
        Philosophiae. Chaucer Society, no. 76 (first
        series). London: N. Trübner, 1886.

        This is one of the two editings of Chaucer's
        Boece which were prepared for the Chaucer
        Society.

37.   Page, Christopher. "The Boethian Metrum 'Bella
        bis quinis': a new Song from Saxon Canterbury."
        In **Boethius: His Life, Thought and
        Influence**, edited by Margaret Gibson, 306-11.
        Oxford: Basil Blackwell, 1981.

Page reports on a Boethian metrum which exists complete with musical notation.

38.   Palmer, Nigel F. "Latin and Vernacular in the Northern European Tradition of the **De Consolatione Philosophiae**. In **Boethius: His Life, Thought and Influence**, edited by Margaret Gibson, 362-409. Oxford: Basil Blackwell, 1981.

Palmer concentrates on the German **Consolatio** tradition of the late Middle Ages. The vernacular renderings are seen as important "cribs" for understanding the Latin **Consolatio**.

39.   Parks, M.B. "A Note on MS Vatican Bibl. Apost., lat. 3363." In **Boethius: His Life, Thought and Influence**, edited by Margaret Gibson, 425-27. Oxford: Basil Blackwell, 1981.

This is a description and history of one of the earliest surviving **Consolatio** manuscripts.

40.   Patch, Howard Rollin. **The Tradition of Boethius: A Study of His Importance in Medieval Culture**. New York: Oxford University Press, 1935.

This is one of the essential general studies on Boethius and the **Consolatio**. The chapter headings are 1) "Tradition and Legend," 2) "Medieval Thought," 3) "Translations of the **Consolatio**," 4) "Imitations and Influence." Although the title promises a comprehensive study on Boethius, most of the emphasis is on the **Consolatio**.

41.   Peiper, Rudolfus. **Anicii Manlii Severini Boetii** Philosophiae Consolationis, **Libri**

Quinque, accendunt eiusdem atque
incertorum Opuscula Sacra. Lipsiae: Aedibus
B.G. Teubneri, 1871.

This is one of the earlier, good critical editions of
the Consolatio and other works by Boethius.

42.   Pemberton, Caroline, ed. Queen Elizabeth's
        Englishings of Boethius, De Consolatione
        Philosophiae; Plutarch, De Curiositate;
        Horace, De Arte Poetica (part). Early English
        Text Society, no. 113. London: Kegan Paul,
        Trench, Trübner, 1899.

        This is the critical edition of Queen Elizabeth I's
        Consolatio translation.

43.   Pingree, David. "Boethius' Geometry and
        Astronomy." In Boethius: His Life,
        Thought and Influence, edited by Margaret
        Gibson, 155-61. Oxford: Basil Blackwell, 1981.

        Pingree discusses manuscript problems for the
        Geometry and the impossibility of assigning any
        of the fragmentary Latin texts to Boethius. No
        book by Boethius on astronomy has been attested.

44.   Rädle, Fidel and F.J. Worstbrock. "Boethius,
        Anicius Manlius Severinus." In Die deutsche
        Literatur des Mittelalters:
        Verfasserlexikon, edited by Kurt Ruh, et al.
        Vol. 1, 908-28. Berlin: Walter de Gruyter, 1978.

        This is a concise general survey of the major
        issues in Boethian scholarship.

45.   Reiss, Edmund. "The Fall of Boethius and the
        Fiction of the Consolatio Philosophiae."
        Classical Journal 77 (1981): 37-47.

Reiss argues against historical/biographical readings of the **Consolatio**. Boethius created a fiction in the work, so primary consideration should be given to that fact.

46.   de Rijk, L.M. "On the Chronology of Boethius' Works of Logic, Part I." **Vivarium** 2 (1964): 1-49.

This is the first part of a two-part article on the dating of Boethius' works on logic.

47.   ----------. "On the Chronology of Boethius' Works of Logic, Part II." **Vivarium** 2 (1964): 125-62.

This is the second part of the article by de Rijk listed above.

48.   Saintsbury, George. **A History of Criticism and Literary Taste in Europe**. Vol. 1, **Classical and Medieval Criticism**. New York: Dodd, Meade, 1900.

In this study, brief mention is made of Boethius' place at the beginning of medieval literary criticism.

49.   Stewart, Hugh Fraser. **Boethius: An Essay**. London: 1891. Reprint. New York: Burt Franklin, 1974.

This is one of the important general studies on the entire Boethian tradition. The chapter headings are: 1) "A Glance at the Controversy on Boethius," 2) "Boethius and Theodoric," 3) "The **Consolation of Philosophy**," 4) "The Philosophy of the **De Consolatione**," 5) "The Theological Tracts," 6) "On Some Ancient Translations of Boethius' Last Work," 7)

"Boethius and the Scholastic Problem." Stewart
summarizes prior scholarship, but also adds fresh
information and insights.

50.   Stewart, Hugh Fraser, E.K. Rand, and S.J. Tester,
        eds./trans. **Boethius: Tractates, De
        Consolatione Philosophiae.** Cambridge,
        Mass.: Loeb Classical University Press, 1978.

        This is one of the more useful critical editions,
        complete with an English translation facing the
        Latin text.

51.   Thomas, M. Antoine and Mario Roques.
        "Traductions françaises de la **Consolatio
        Philosophiae** de Boèce." In **Histoire
        littéraire de la France** 37 (1938): 419-506 and
        542-7.

        Among other things, this article gives a good
        introductory discussion of the Pierre de Paris
        Consolatio translation.

52.   van de Vyver, A. "Les Traductions du **De
        Consolatione philosophiae** de Boèce en
        littérature comparée." **Humanisme et
        Renaissance** 6 (1939): 247-73.

        Van de Vyver lists all of the European
        Consolatio translations, giving brief
        descriptions for each entry.

53.   White, Alison. "Boethius in the Medieval
        Quadrivium." In **Boethius: His Life,
        Thought and Influence,** edited by Margaret
        Gibson, 162-205. Oxford: Basil Blackwell, 1981.

        This is a study of the reception by medieval
        scholars and theorists of Boethius' books on the

four mathematical arts. Boethius' works are
primarily on theory, not practice. White
concludes that Boethius' lasting value in this area
is with the cosmologists rather than with the
scientists.

CHAPTER II

THE OLD ENGLISH TRADITION

Alfred's **Consolatio** Translation

Alfred, the only English king to be honored with the addition of "Great" to his name, lived from 849 to 899. His was a critical period in English history, when the Anglo-Saxons were occupied with fighting off invasions by the Danes. Oddly enough, it was also a time for preserving knowledge and making it available to an English speaking audience.

Scholars are fortunate because Alfred's contemporary, his Welsh mentor Asser, left a biography of the king (Stevenson 1959). Asser's account is the basis for much of the factual information we have on the life and times of Alfred, and it gives insight into the plans leading to his **Consolatio** translation. We know that the period of Alfred's active interest in translation from Latin sources extended only from 887 until the end of his life, but it is not known for certain whether he personally made all of the translations credited to him or simply commissioned them. However, the **Consolatio** translation is generally accepted as his own work.

Alfred is reported to have formulated a plan for promoting education in his realm by giving his Anglo-Saxon subjects a small library of Latin works translated into English. This basic library consisted of: Bede's **Ecclesiastical History**, Orosius' **Universal History**,

Gregory's **Pastoral Care** and **Dialogues**, Augustine's **Soliloquies** (sometimes referred to in the criticism as the "Blooms" of Augustine), and Boethius' **Consolatio**. This, then, is the canon that forms the immediate context of Alfred's **Consolatio** translation. George Brown's **King Alfred's Books** contains a description of the texts of all of Alfred's translations, historical notes, and lengthy quotations (Browne 1920), but it lacks, as Fr. Pompen noted (Pompen 1923), an index. The chronology and description of the library created by Alfred is given by Dorothy Whitelock (Whitelock 1966). She also discusses Alfred's methods of translation. The background and history of Alfred's translations are the subject of a short article by Ian Jack (Jack 1971); he takes an unusual, iconoclastic view, suggesting that Alfred's accomplishments are highly over-rated, and that much of his reputation depends upon the completion of his projects by his successors. Most critics, however, have praise for the work with which Alfred traditionally is credited.

The European tradition of **Consolatio** translations begins c.900 with the Old English version by Alfred the Great. Although the Old English tradition comprises but a single translation, it has prompted a sizable body of criticism. The problems dealt with in this criticism are divided in this chapter into five categories: 1) editions, 2) general studies, 3) textual studies, 4) studies of commentaries possibly used by Alfred, and 5) influence studies. These will be treated in this order.

Editors have only two manuscripts and a fragment which attest to Alfred's **Consolatio** translation. A manuscript from the beginning of the twelfth century [Bodl. 180, or sometimes Bodl. NE. C. 3. 11(B)] contains the version generally accepted as the original text, and it is an all-purpose rendering. The other manuscript (BM Otho. A. VI), from either the beginning or the middle of the tenth century, contains a prose text mixed with alliterative renderings of the **Meters of Boethius**. A. Napier discovered a fragment of the Alfred translation, which had been written in a tenth-century hand, on the back page of another manuscript (Bodl. 86). The description first appeared in an article (Napier 1887) in which Napier gives a full transcription of the fragment, with lacunae filled in by readings from the other Old English **Consolatio** manuscripts.

Interest in editing Alfred's translation first led to a transcription of the text, primarily from Bodl. 180, but containing alternate readings from BM Otho. A. VI., made by Franciscus Junius in the seventeenth century. Using this transcription as a base text, Christopher Rawlinson produced the first printed edition of both the prose text and the **Meters** (Rawlinson 1698). His edition became, in turn, the basis for the second printed edition, prepared by J.S. Cardale (Cardale 1829), which also contains both the prose text and the **Meters**, but with a Modern English rendering of each. In 1858, translations of all of Alfred's works were printed in a two-volume set: **The Whole Works of Alfred the Great** (Giles 1858). The first volume contains the translations, which are of uneven quality, and the second contains essays on Alfred and his times. The year 1864 saw the publication of a third editing of Alfred's translation, **King Alfred's Anglo-Saxon Version of Boethius'** De Consolatione Philosophiae **With a Literal English Translation, Notes and Glossary,** by Samuel Fox (Fox 1864). Finally, there appeared the critical edition of the translation which is still used today: Walter Sedgefield's edition (Sedgefield 1899). His rendering of the Old English text into Modern English appeared separately (Sedgefield 1900). But Sedgefield's work has not escaped some revision. Fr. Klaeber published a few notes suggesting corrections to Sedgefield's edition of the text as well as to his Modern English rendering (Klaeber 1903). O. Arngart, on the other hand, has noted several Latin words and expressions which Alfred either mistranslated or altered in meaning in the process of translating the Latin **Consolatio** (Arngart 1947), small problems which had escaped the notice of both Sedgefield, who edited and translated the work, and Schmidt, whose dissertation gives a detailed analysis of Alfred's work (Schmidt 1934).

Another article pertains only peripherally to the problem of editing Alfred's works. J.E. Wülfing published two letters, correspondence between Cardale and Bosworth in the first and between Bosworth and Fox in the second (Wülfing 1897); the letters give no new information about Alfred's **Consolatio,** but they do give some insight into the relationship between the early scholars who worked with the translation.

Alfred's **Consolatio** translation is described in the general studies of the **Consolatio.** Stewart's **Essay** is especially relevant in its attention to the nature of the many additions and alterations which Alfred incorporated into his version (Stewart 1891). Stewart divides these interpolations into four categories: the historical, geographical, mythological, and Christian.

Friedrich Fehlauer included in his dissertation (Fehlauer 1908) and its subsequent printed version (Fehlauer 1909) a section on Alfred's **Consolatio**, but his book is basically a list of translations, offering little new information other than a European context for the various translations. It must be classified, therefore, among the general works which summarize previous criticism. Guy Dolson's dissertation is remarkable for its breadth (Dolson 1926, dissertation). It attempts a comprehensive study of all English translations of Boethius' **Consolatio** as well as a list of all works in English influenced by it. This study includes, of course, Alfred's work. Biographical information is given for each author, and examples are presented from their writings; no in-depth studies of individual texts are attempted.

Two other works of general interest to Boethian studies should be mentioned here. One is the book-length work done by Howard Patch, **The Tradition of Boethius** (Patch 1935). It presents a survey of many aspects of Boethian influence in the medieval period, and one section is devoted to Alfred's translation. A. van de Vyver's article (van de Vyver 1939) must also, for the sake of completeness, be mentioned. It places Alfred's translation into the broader context of all the European translations of the **Consolatio**; that is, it puts the translation in the broadest possible context which would be of interest to students of comparative literature. The article is, however, a list of translations without analysis.

Articles which relate specifically to the text of Alfred's translation will be classified in the following paragraphs; works which mention Alfred's **Consolatio** translation only in passing are excluded, as are studies of Boethian influence upon **Beowulf** and other Old English works influenced by the Latin **Consolatio** rather than by Alfred's rendering.

Kurt Otten's **König Alfreds Boethius** (Otten 1964) remains the most comprehensive study of Alfred's **Consolatio** to date. Otten comments on Alfred's use of commentaries and on his style. He was the first critic to indicate a basis of the discrepancy between the Latin and the Old English texts: he maintains that Alfred's emphasis was on freedom while Boethius' was on fate or determinism.

Alfred's adaptation of Boethius is the thesis of Anne Payne's book. She writes:

> There are a number of themes thrown into the foreground by Alfred's various alterations, which are comprehensive enough to be subjected to extensive analysis. The most important of these alterations is his substitution of a theory which is based on the idea of freedom for one which is based on the idea of order. (Payne 1968, p. 16)

She then proceeds to discuss these differences in detail.

Katherine Proppe wrote a reply to Anne Payne's argument. She claims that Payne's work overemphasizes freedom, a single element in a much broader complex of thought. She states that her own purpose is not

> to point out petty inconsistencies but to show the semi-emergent Roman conception of Christianity, rationality, humility and renunciation lying side by side with tenacious old Anglo-Saxon emotion. (Proppe 1973, p. 648)

Her article, however, is a bit harsh on Payne's thoughtful book.

W.F. Bolton, in an article, also takes exception to Anne Payne's thesis, maintaining that Alfred's translation represents an epitome of Anglo-Saxon interest in the **Consolatio.** He concludes: "The Alfredian version, though it does not wholly recapture the original, does what it set out to do: it crowns a century [the ninth century] of Boethius scholarship in Europe and in England" (W.F. Bolton 1986, 163-4).

The earliest important textual study of the translation itself is Sedgefield's introduction to his edition (Sedgefield 1899). He covers such topics as the relationship of the translation to the Latin original, the dialect of the text, and the problem of date and authorship. This introductory material, though brief, is a compendium of information gathered about the text up to the time of publication. Alfred Krawutschke's dissertation deals specifically with the language of Alfred's **Consolatio** (Krawutschke 1902). It analyzes the syntax, grammar, and dialect, and it serves as an aid to reading the Old English text. In a short article, E. Koeppel shows that Alfred's version of the **Consolatio** had to have been produced after the Orosius (Koeppel 1908). He points out that the name of the Gothic king Raedgota was first translated in the Orosius; then it appeared in the **Consolatio** translation but not in the Latin original; and finally it reappeared in the alliterative **Meters.** He is also careful to point out that this bit of insight came from one of his students of Old English.

Another study of the language of King Alfred's **Consolatio** translation is Otto Exter's dissertation (Exter 1911). Exter develops the theory that the word **wesen** is used for concrete meaning and that **beon** is used for abstract meaning. This work, too, is an aid to reading the text, differentiating the use of two terms which are practically synonyms, both meaning **to be.**

Karl Heinz Schmidt produced a general study of Alfred's text (Schmidt 1934) in which he gives a book-by-book summary of the translation and evaluates certain of the alterations Alfred made in the content of the **Consolatio.** His study of the relationship between the Old English and the Latin original is detailed.

A book by Ludwig Borinski (Borinski 1934) offers a very detailed analysis of Alfred's style based on a complex model of narrative theory.

Two works by Jerold C. Frakes raise the study of Alfred's translation from a semantic to a conceptual level. In his dissertation (Frakes 1982), he discusses the concept of **fortuna** in Boethius' **Consolatio** and then as it appears in Alfred's and Notker's translations. Later, in an article, he discusses the neo-Platonic cosmological order as it is described by all three writers. He concludes:

> Die dualistische Metaphysik der **Consolatio** wurde also in den Bearbeitung ihrer ersten Übersetzer zum pragmatisch-christlichen System des Gradualismus bei Alfred, der stark von der angelsächsischen **Bekehrungsmentalität** beeinflußt wurde, und zum unfreiwilligen Gerüst des Augustinismus des 11. Jahrhunderts bei Notker. (Frakes 1984, 74)

In the work produced by Frakes, criticism has thus shifted to the level of ideas.

The study of Alfred's use of commentaries began in 1895 with an article by G. Schepss (Schepss 1895). He identifies a group of commentaries, which he designates KY, as a source of Alfred's

Christianizing additions to the **Consolatio** text. He mentions no possible author for the source manuscript of group KY, but he suggests that Asser would be a highly unlikely candidate. In his conclusion, he says:

> Das . . . steht als Resultat absolut fest, daß Alfred ältere
> lateinische Vorlagen benutzt hat, und daß seine vornehmste
> Quelle identisch ist mit unserer Kommentargruppe KY.
> (Schepss 1895, p. 159)

Karl Heinz Schmidt's article identifies the KY group treated by Schepss as the work of Remigius of Auxerre. In his argument, he makes the following observation:

> Alfred und Remigius sind Zeitgenossen im engsten Sinn. Die
> Boethius-Erklärung des Remigius muß also überaus schnell den
> Weg zum englischen Hof gefunden haben, wenn auch Alfred's
> Übersetzertätigkeit, zumal die Bearbeitung der **Consolatio**, in
> die letzten Jahre seines Lebens fällt. Wir sind aber zu der
> Annahme berechtigt, daß Alfred zu den westfränkischen Klostern
> und ihren Gelehrten in näherer Beziehung gestanden hat.
> (Schmidt 1934)

Pierre Courcelle produced a thorough study of all the commentaries on the **Consolatio** (Courcelle 1939; Courcelle 1967), treating their influence upon all the medieval vernacular translations. Brian Donaghey, basing his ideas on findings by Courcelle, Schepss, and other critics (but completely independent of Schmidt), maintains that Remigius of Auxerre was the author of the commentaries of group KY (Donaghey 1964). But he observes that Remigius died in 908 and that he wrote his commentary in c.901 (or 902)--that is, after Asser had used a commentary to help Alfred. He concludes that both Alfred and Remigius probably used the same earlier commentary, possibly the commentary referred to as the Anonymous of St. Gall. Courcelle had also suggested this possibility, but the method of influence offered in Donaghey's article is much simpler than Courcelle's model, cutting out some intermediary steps suggested by Courcelle. The information contained in the article by Donaghey should be consulted in conjunction with information in the book by Kurt Otten, published the same year (Otten 1964). Otten deals extensively with Alfred's use of commentaries, as well as with many other topics. Joseph S. Wittig, in an article (Wittig 1983), maintains that none of the commentaries existing at the time Alfred wrote would have given him all the material he incorporated into his text; therefore, much more knowledge of Antiquity and many more books were available in ninth-century England than is generally assumed.

Basing her study on the commentaries available to scholars in medieval England, Diane Bolton indicates that the Anglo-Saxons took a much more strongly patristic or conservative view of the **Consolatio** than did the contemporary continental scholars (D.K. Bolton 1977). Hers is a basic reception study of the **Consolatio**, concentrating on the history of ideas and the effect of personalities upon events.

We know now that Alfred's **Consolatio** version and Chaucer's **Boece** are only indirectly connected by way of Trevet's commentary: Trevet had read Alfred's translation before preparing his work, and Chaucer had read Trevet. Brian S. Donaghey has studied Trevet's use of Alfred's translation in an article (Donaghey 1987), discussing fully all aspects of his reading. Two critics have compared Alfred's and Chaucer's renderings. Peggy Faye Shirley's dissertation (Shirley 1977) compares the two translations, discovering that Alfred's interest was in the education of his audience while Chaucer's was in accuracy of translation. In 1979, Olga Fischer compared the rendering of Latin philosophical terms into Old English and Middle English, finding that Alfred's language was adequate as a vehicle for Boethian concepts (Fischer 1979).

The influence of Alfred's **Consolatio** translation upon subsequent works was not extensive. In an article, Frank G. Hubbard studies the "Blooms of King Alfred," a work which is included in the **Beowulf** manuscript (BM Cotton Vitell. A. xv.) . He offers parallel passages to show the resemblance between certain of the "Blooms" and passages from Alfred's **Consolatio** translation. He concludes:

> all the evidence that has been produced to prove the king to be
> the translator of **Boethius** becomes evidence that he is the
> author of the "Blooms," and, on the other hand, all the evidence
> that goes to show that he is the author of the "Blooms" has
> weight to prove that he made the translation of the **De
> Consolatione Philosophiae**. (Hubbard 1894, p. 340)

Studying a collection of "Sayings of Cato" [sic] (**Sammlung von Cato-Sprüchen**, ed. Nehab. Berlin, 1879), Max Förster showed that Alfred's translation was not completely unknown to the England of the Middle Ages (Förster 1901). The collection of sayings contains some additions from Alfred's **Consolatio** which were probably written down by the compiler from memory. The quotations are not exact, but they greatly resemble Alfred's work.

Guy Bayley Dolson's dissertation (Dolson 1926, dissertation) needs to be mentioned in the context of these articles on influence. It is not specifically on the influence of Alfred's work, but it is a comprehensive study of all English works that show any influence from the **Consolatio**.

Murray Markland gives evidence for the direct influence of Alfred's **Consolatio** translation upon the Old English "Deor" (Markland 1968/1969). The linguistic evidence seems to support such a view. W.F. Bolton, in an article (W.F. Bolton 1971/1972) responds to Markland's argument, pointing out some of its weaker points. It undermines much of the force of the earlier article, but it is not totally conclusive in denying the possibility of influence upon the "Deor" of Alfred's **Consolatio**. In another article, Bolton presents evidence of the influence of Alfred's **Consolatio** upon Aelfric's "Lives of Saints" (W.F. Bolton 1972). Kevin Kiernan maintains that the **Consolatio** translation by Alfred is, indeed, an intermediary influence between the Latin work by Boethius and the "Deor" (Kiernan 1978). Such a theory helps to explain certain problems in the "Deor" text.

A very recent article on the **Consolatio** translation by Alfred is by Malcolm Godden (Godden 1981). The author adds nothing new to the scholarship on this problem, but he does reiterate one important point which critics have been aware of for many years and which is mentioned above: Trevet, in preparing his commentary on the **Consolatio**, had referred to Alfred's translation during the course of his work.

King Alfred's **Consolatio** has not generated a vast quantity of scholarship, but it has stimulated work in the five areas discussed above, all of which still leave questions unanswered. For example, Alfred's possible motivation for translating Boethius has been examined, but detailed reception studies are lacking, and this is due perhaps to a lack of documents for study. It has been suggested that Asser first introduced Alfred to the **Consolatio**, but there is no proof, so any implications of that fact cannot be discussed. The problem of which commentaries Alfred might have used is unresolved. Alfred's work represents a large area of research on the European **Consolatio** tradition, and much remains there for future investigation and speculation.

List of Relevant Titles

1. Arngart, O. "Three Notes on King Alfred's Boethius." **English Studies: A Journal of English Language and Literature** 28 (1947): 74-80.

    Arngart makes no unified argument, but he 1) points out an error in Sedgefield's 1900 translation of Alfred's **Consolatio** version, 2) indicates mistranslations of the Latin by Alfred, and 3) gives etymologies of certain problematic Old English words used in Alfred's rendering.

2. Bolton, Diane K. "The Study of the **Consolation of Philosophy** in Anglo-Saxon England." **Archives d'histoire doctrinale et littéraire du moyen âge** 64 (1977): 33-78.

    Bolton's study contains a very thorough examination of commentaries on the **Consolatio** available in medieval England. The conclusions indicate that the Anglo-Saxons took a very conservative (patristic) view of the text, as opposed to the more literary, humanistic, and Neoplatonic view among continental commentators. Alfred, in his translation, shows himself to be one of the most conservative of the Anglo-Saxon writers. The article contains two appendices: 1) a list of Anglo-Saxon **Consolatio** manuscripts, and 2) a list of mythological glosses in Remigius of Auxerre manuscripts.

3. Bolton, W.F. "Boethius, Alfred, and Deor Again." **Modern Philology: A Journal Devoted to Research in Medieval and Modern Literature** 69 (1971/1972): 222-7.

   Bolton assesses errors in Markland's article (Markland 1968). The argument here greatly weakens but does not destroy Markland's argument for an "Alfredian link" between the Old English "Deor" and its source in the **Consolatio**. Bolton shows that such a link is unnecessary: the connection with the **Consolatio** was probably direct.

4. ----------. "The Alfredian Boethius in 'Ælfric's **Lives of Saints** I.'" **Notes and Queries** 217 (1972): 406-7.

   Bolton argues for the direct influence of Alfred's **Consolatio** translation upon Ælfric's **Lives of Saints**. Four parallel texts are used to present the case, and the texts are allowed to argue for themselves.

5. ----------. "How Boethian is Alfred's **Boethius**?" In **Studies in Earlier Old English Prose**, edited by Paul E. Szarmach, 153-68. Albany: State University of New York Press, 1986.

   Bolton argues against Anne Payne's thesis (Payne 1968) that Alfred's translation represents a personal statement to his Anglo-Saxon subjects. He maintains that Alfred's translation with its many interpolations represents a culmination of important Boethian scholarship in the ninth century.

6.   Borinski, Ludwig. **Der Stil König Alfreds:**
       Eine Studie zur Psychologie der Rede.
       Leipzig: Bernard Tauchnitz, 1934.

       Borinski presents in this book a detailed analysis
       of Alfred's style based on a complex model of
       narrative theory.

7.   Browne, George Forest. **King Alfred's Books.**
       London Society for Promoting Christian
       Knowledge. New York: Maxmillian, 1920.

       The collection includes a translation of Alfred's
       Consolatio. The introduction gives a very
       general picture of Alfred's interest in translation
       and scholarship.

8.   Cardale, J.S. **King Alfred's Anglo-Saxon**
       Version of Boethius' De Consolatione
       Philosophiae. London: n.p., 1829.

       This is one of the earliest editions of Alfred's
       translation, based on the Rawlinson edition of
       1698. It is a parallel-text edition, containing both
       the Old English and Modern English.

9.   Courcelle, Pierre. "Étude critique sur les
       commentaires de la **Consolation** de Boèce (IXe-
       XVe siècles). **Archives d'histoire doctrinale**
       et littéraire du moyen âge 4 (1939): 5-140.

       This material was later incorporated into
       Courcelle's book (Courcelle 1967).

10.   ----------. La Consolation de philosophie **dans la**
       tradition littéraire: antécédents et
       postérité de Boèce. Paris: Études
       Augustiniennes, 1967.

The book surveys the medieval commentaries on
Boethius; it is important here for the light it sheds
on those commentaries which critics have
suggested as sources for Alfred's translation.
Courcelle suggests here that Alfred and Remigius
both made use of the Anonymous Commentary of
St. Gall.

11.   Dolson, Guy Bayley. "The **Consolation of
       Philosophy** in English Literature." Ph.D. diss.,
       Cornell University, 1926.

       This is an essential work in Boethian studies. It
       gives brief, summary information about Alfred's
       prose translation, and it includes references to all
       Boethian influence the author could account for in
       English literature. Because of its general
       approach, however, it does not treat the
       controversial issues in any depth.

12.   Donaghey, Brian S. "The Sources of King Alfred's
       Translation of Boethius's **De Consolatione
       Philosophiae**." **Anglia: Zeitschrift für
       englische Literatur** 82 (1964): 23-57.

       Donaghey concerns himself with the use of
       Commentaries in the preparation of Alfred's
       Consolatio translation.

13.   ----------. "Nicholas Trevet's Use of King Alfred's
       Translation of Boethius, and the Dating of His
       Commentary." In **The Medieval Boethius:
       Studies in the Vernacular Translations
       of the** De Consolatione Philosophiae, edited by
       Alastair J. Minnis, 1-31. Woodbridge, Suffolk:
       D.S Brewer, 1987.

       Donaghey reconstructs Trevet's preparation of his
       commentary, indicating that he would have

finished it before 1300. He also gives as parallel
quotations the various passages in the commentary
which show evidence of Alfredian influence. One
passage indicates that Trevet may have used the
version of Alfred's translation containing the
alliterative meters.

14.   Exter, Otto. **Beon und Wesen in Alfreds
        Übersetzung des Boethius, der Metra und
        der Soliloquien.** Ph.D. diss., Christian-
        Albrechts-Universität zu Kiel, 1911. Kiel: H.
        Fiencke, 1911.

To attain a more exact reading of Alfred's version
of the **Consolatio,** Exter shows that the use of
wesen as an indicator of concrete meaning and
beon as an indicator of abstract meaning signify
necessary distinctions in the text.

15.   Fehlauer, Friedrich. **Die englischen
        Übersetzungen von Boethius'** De
        Consolatione Philosophiae. Ph.D. diss., Albertus-
        Universität zu Königsberg, 1908. Königsberg:
        Hartungsche Buchdruckerei, 1908.

In this study, Fehlauer lists the English
Consolatio translations and gives lengthy
summary information on Alfred's prose
translation. No new findings or interpretations are
presented.

16.   ----------. **Die englischen Übersetzungen
        von Boethius'** De Consolatione Philosophiae.
        Berlin: Emil Felber, 1909.

This is the printed version of the dissertation listed
above (Fehlauer 1908).

17. Fischer, Olga. "A Comparative Study of Philosophical Terms in the Alfredian and Chaucerian Boethius." **Neuphilologus** 63 (1979): 622-39.

Fisher studies the philosophical terms used by Alfred and Chaucer in their respective translations of the **Consolatio,** indicating that Alfred had an adequate supply of native terms into which to render the Latin concepts of the original text. Chaucer, on the other hand, had to make use of nearly fifty percent French loan words in his **Consolatio** translation. The study proves that the pre-conquest Anglo-Saxons were not as linguistically rudimentary as some critics might lead us to believe.

18. Förster, Max. "Zum altenglischen Boethius." **Archiv für das Studium der neueren Sprachen und Literaturen** 106 (1901): 342-3.

The author identifies certain additions to a collection of the "Sayings of Cato" [sic] (ed. Nehab, Berlin, 1879) as paraphrases of Alfred's **Consolatio** translation. In addition to this, ideas and views similar to those of Alfred are shown to stem from the same time and area as the **Consolatio** translation.

19. Fox, Samuel. **King Alfred's Anglo-Saxon Version of Boethius** De Consolatione Philosophiae **With a Literal English translation, Notes, and Glossary.** London, 1864. Reprint. New York: AMS, 1970.

This is the third published editing of Alfred's **Consolatio** translation.

20.   Frakes, Jerold Coleman. "**Fortuna** in the
       Consolatio: Boethius, Alfred and Notker."
       Ph.D. diss., University of Minnesota, 1982.

       This dissertation consists in a semantic
       investigation of **fortuna** in Boethius'
       Consolatio and in Alfred's and Notker's
       translations of the work. It seeks definitions for
       the term in the context of the cosmological order
       given in each work.

21.   ----------. "Die Rezeption der Neuplatonischen
       Metaphysik des Boethius durch Alfred und
       Notker." **Beiträge zur Geschichte der
       deutschen Sprache und Literatur** 106
       (1984): 51-74.

       Frakes studies the neo-Platonic dualism of
       Boethius' work as it is received by Alfred and
       Notker in their translations.

22.   Giles, J.A. **The Whole Works of Alfred the
       Great**. 2 vols. London, 1858. Reprint. New
       York: AMS, 1969.

       Volume one presents translations into Modern
       English of Alfred's works; volume two contains
       essays on the life and times of Alfred.

23.   Godden, Malcolm. "King Alfred's Boethius." In
       **Boethius: His Life, Thought and
       Influence**, edited by Margaret Gibson, 419-24.
       Oxford: Basil Blackwell, 1981.

       This is a concise but thorough review of the
       scholarship on Alfred's translation of the
       Consolatio. It treats most of the major areas of
       controversy. It gives good summary and
       introductory materials on Alfred's text.

24.   Hubbard, Frank G. "The Relation of the 'Blooms
        of King Alfred' to the Anglo-Saxon Translation of
        Boethius." **Modern Language Notes** 9 (1894):
        161-71.

        Hubbard uses parallel passages to show that the
        author of the Anglo-Saxon prose translation of the
        Consolatio also wrote the "Blooms of King
        Alfred."

25.   Jack, R. Ian. "The Significance of the Alfredian
        Translations." **Australasian Universities
        Language and Literature Association** 13
        (1971): 348-61.

        Jack claims that much of the praise heaped upon
        Alfred ("Father of English Prose") is misplaced.
        He initiated much, and fortunately for his place in
        history, his successors (such as Edward the Elder)
        saw his work on through to completion.

26.   Kiernan, Kevin S. "Deor: the Consolations of an
        Anglo-Saxon Boethius." **Neuphilologische
        Mitteilungen** 79 (1978): 333-40.

        Kiernan maintains that the **Consolatio**
        translation by Alfred is intermediate between the
        Boethian original and the Old English "Deor."

27.   Klaeber, Fr. "Notes on Old English Prose Texts."
        Modern Language Notes 18 (1903): 241-7.

        Under the heading "I. Boethius" there is a series of
        suggested improvements to Sedgefield's edition of
        Alfred's **Consolatio** (1899) and translation into
        Modern English (1900).

28.   Koeppel, E. "Zur Chronologie der Übersetzungen
        des Königs Alfred." **Anglia: Zeitschrift für**

englische Philologie (Beiblatt) 19 (1908):
330-3.

Koeppel offers evidence that Alfred's **Consolatio**
translation (as well as the alliterative **Meters**)
was written later than the Orosius translation.

29.   Krawutschke, Alfred. **Die Sprache der**
       Boëthius-Übersetzung des Königs Alfred.
       Ph.D. diss., Friederich-Wilhelms-Universität zu
       Berlin, 1902. Berlin: Julius Driesner, 1902.

The author maintains that Alfred was the translator
of both the prose **Consolatio** and the alliterative
Meters. He presents a study of the language used
by Alfred in his texts.

30.   Markland, Murray F. "Boethius, Alfred, and
       Deor." **Modern Philology** 66 (1968/1969):
       1-4.

Markland strongly suggests that there is direct
influence between Alfred's **Consolatio**
translation and the Old English "Deor."

31.   Napier, A. "Bruckstücke einer altenglischen
       Boethiushandschrift." **Zeitschrift für**
       deutsches Altertum und deutsche
       literatur 31 (1887): 52-4.

Napier transcribes a fragment of the Alfredian
translation of the **Consolatio** written in the hand
of a tenth-century scribe. It was found on the last
sheet of MS Junius 86 of the Bodleian Library.

32.   Otten, Kurt. **König Alfred's Boethius.**
       Studien zur englischen Philologie, no. 3 (neue
       Folge). Tübingen: Max Niemeyer Verlag, 1964.

This is the most comprehensive study which
exists on Alfred's **Consolatio**. Otten sees
system in Alfred's alterations of Boethius. Unlike
Boethius, but like Augustine and Gregory the
Great, Alfred views the universe not as indifferent
but as operating according to a system of justice
in the distribution and denial of goods.

33.   Patch, Howard Rollin. **The Tradition of
        Boethius: A Study of His Importance in
        Medieval Culture.** New York: Oxford
        University Press, 1935.

        Patch covers all aspects of Boethian influence
        during the Middle Ages. He includes some general
        information on the Old English occurrences.

34.   Payne, F. Anne. **King Alfred and Boethius:
        An Analysis of the Old English Version
        of the** Consolation of Philosophy.
        Madison/Milwaukee: University of Wisconsin
        Press, 1968.

        Payne concentrates on the differences in world
        view presented in Alfred's **Consolatio**
        translation and its Latin original. Where Boethius
        was concerned with fate, Alfred was concerned
        with freedom; where Boethius looked to
        philosophy, Alfred looked to wisdom for dealing
        with reality.

35.   Pompen, Fr. A. Review of **King Alfred's
        Books,** by Bishop G.F. Browne. **English
        Studies** 5 (1923): 130-32.

        This early review of **King Alfred's Books** is
        generally favorable, but Pompen complains of the
        lack of an index.

36.   Proppe, Katherine. "King Alfred's **Consolation of Philosophy.**" **Neuphilologische Mitteilungen** 74 (1973): 635-48.

This is a response to Anne Payne's book, **King Alfred and Boethius** (Payne 1968). Proppe maintains that the translation represents a "semi-emergent Roman conception of Christianity, rationality, humility, and renunciation lying side by side with tenacious old Anglo-Saxon emotions."

37.   Rawlinson, Christopher. **King Ælfred's** Consolation of Philosophy. Oxford: n.p., 1698.

This is the earliest edition of Alfred's **Consolatio** translation, based on a transcription of the prose text and variant readings made by Franciscus Junius.

38.   Schepss, Georg. "Zu König Alfreds 'Boethius.'" **Archiv für das Studium der neueren Sprachen und Literaturen** 94 (1895): 149-60.

This is one of the early articles which note the importance of the commentaries for the production of the medieval **Consolatio** translations. It indicates the importance of a particular group of commentaries (designated as KY) to the process of Alfred's Christianizing of Boethius.

39.   Schmidt, Karl Heinz. **König Alfreds Boethius-Bearbeitung.** Ph.D. diss., Georg-August-Universität zu Göttingen, 1934. Göttingen: University Press, 1934.

Schmidt offers a book-by-book commentary on Alfred's **Consolatio** translation. He clarifies in his introduction some earlier criticism on Alfred's use of commentaries by indicating that Alfred had used Remigius of Auxerre's commentary.

40.   Sedgefield, Walter John, ed. **King Alfred's Old English Version of Boethius** De Consolatione Philosophiae. 1899. Reprint. Darmstadt: Wissenschaftliche Buchstellschaft, 1968.

This is now the standard critical edition of the prose translation of the **Consolatio** by Alfred the Great (as well as of the **Meters**, which are included). It contains an introduction and a glossary.

41.   ----------, trans. **King Alfred's Version of the** Consolations of Boethius **Done into Modern English, With an Introduction**. Oxford: n.p., 1900.

Scholarly opinion holds this translation to be free and often unreliable.

42.   Shirley, Peggy Faye. "Fals Felicite and Verray Blisfulnesse: Alfred and Chaucer Translate Boethius's **Consolation of Philosophy**." Ph.D. diss., University of Mississippi, 1977.

In this comparative study, Alfred's translation is shown to focus upon the enlightenment of his audience: his Anglo-Saxon subjects. Chaucer focuses, on the other hand, upon the accuracy of the translation.

43.   Stevenson, William Henry, ed. **Asser's Life of Alfred: Together With the Annals of Saint Neots**. Oxford: Clarendon Press, 1959.

This work is included here because it is a biography of Alfred by his contemporary and mentor, Asser.

44.   Stewart, Hugh Fraser. **Boethius: An Essay.** London: 1891. Reprint. New York: Burt Franklin, 1974.

The short portion of this essay which is devoted to Alfred is an appreciation of the King's accomplishment of making a difficult and formally demanding Latin work into a vehicle for his own Christian outlook and educational aims.

45.   van de Vyver, A. "Les Traductions du **De Consolatione philosophiae** de Boèce en littérature comparée." **Humanisme et Renaissance** 6 (1939): 247-73.

This critic puts Alfred's translation into the context of all European **Consolatio** translations. The article is primarily a list of the translations; no new information is presented.

46.   Whitelock, Dorothy. "The Prose of Alfred's Reign." In **Continuations and Beginnings: Studies in Old English Literature**, edited by Eric Gerald Stanley, 67-103. London: Nelson, 1966.

This article offers a comprehensive view of the translations ascribed to Alfred, their chronology, and their significance.

47.   Wittig, Joseph S. "King Alfred's **Boethius** and its Latin Sources: A Reconsideration." **Anglo-Saxon England** 11 (1983): 157-98.

Wittig argues against Georg Schepss' opinion (Schepss 1895) that Alfred relied primarily on Latin commentaries on the **Consolatio** for his many interpolations into the text. None of the commentaries examined by Wittig contains all of the material which Alfred incorporated into his version. Wittig's conclusion is that more books from Antiquity were available in Alfred's day than most scholars assume.

48.   Wülfing, J.E. "Zum altenglischen Boethius: zwei Briefe von Cardale an Bosworth und von Bosworth an Fox." **Anglia: Zeitschrift für englische Philologie** 19 (1897): 99-100.

Wülfing transcribes letters from Cardale (editor of Alfred's **Consolatio** translation, 1829) to Bosworth and to Fox (a translator of the Old English work into Modern English). The article sheds light on the interaction among early scholars concerned with Alfred's translation.

The Old English
Meters of Boethius

The Old English **Meters of Boethius** have been of
considerable critical interest, and the scholarship they have generated will
be examined below in three categories: 1) the manuscripts and editions of
the **Meters**, 2) the problem of authorship, and 3) textual studies.

The alliterative **Meters** are preserved in only one source, the
BM MS Cotton Otho A.vi. This manuscript contains Alfred's prose
translation of the **Consolatio**, but in this case most of the Old English
prose which corresponds to the Latin meters has been replaced by
alliterative verses. The manuscript was damaged by fire in 1731, and for
this reason, it lacks meters 1, 2, 3, 4, and 22 as well as the alliterative
proem. Fortunately for later scholars, however, the fire occurred after
Franciscus Junius had made his transcription of Alfred's prose translation.
His transcription, which exists only in manuscript form, contains the
prose text of the Bodleian manuscript, but alternate readings and the
Meters from the Cotton manuscript were included. A dissertation by
Susan Ford [Wiltshire] on the Latin **Meters of Boethius** (Ford 1967)
contains background information on the Latin sources of the Anglo-Saxon
translations, information essential to any approach to the problem of the
Old English **Meters**.
    The standard general studies should also be consulted for
background information on the Old English **Meters**: Howard Patch's
**The Tradition of Boethius: A study of His Importance in
Medieval Culture** (Patch 1935); Hugh Fraser Stewart's **Boethius:
An Essay** (Stewart 1891); and A. van de Vyvers' "Les Traductions du
De Consolatione Philosophiae de Boèce en Litterature Comparée"
(van de Vyver 1939).
    Nine meters of the Latin **Consolatio** are not among the Anglo-
Saxon **Meters**. The prose translation leaves six of them untranslated (I:
3, 4; II: 1; and V: 1, 2, 3). In the Cotton manuscript, three of the
remaining meters are left in their prose versions (I: 6; II: 2; IV: 7); these

are the three meters which had not been given the usual rubrics in the prose work. To the meters is added an alliterative proem and a rendering into verse of Alfred's historical introduction to the prose translation. This historical introduction is usually counted as meter number one.

Rawlinson's edition of Alfred's translation was drawn primarily from the transcription made by Junius, and it contains the **Meters** (Rawlinson 1698). Cardale's edition contains some, but not all, of the **Meters** (Cardale 1829). Samuel Fox published the first separate edition of the **Meters** (Fox 1835), which includes a rendering of the Anglo-Saxon verses into modern English prose. Fox's edition of the complete **Consolatio** translation of Alfred also contains the **Meters**, but the prose renderings into the modern idiom, found in the earlier edition, have been replaced by the verse translation of Martin F. Tupper (Fox 1864). Christian W.M. Grein printed the **Meters** as part of his anthology of Anglo-Saxon poetry (Grein 1858). Bruno Assmann published the **Meters**, but as part of an anthology of Anglo-Saxon poetry (Assmann 1898). Walter Sedgefield printed the **Meters** at the end of his 1899 edition of Alfred's translation (Sedgefield 1899), Krämer published the **Meters** along with a thorough textual and linguistic study (Krämer 1902), and finally, the edition entitled **The Paris Psalter and the Meters of Boethius** by George Krapp appeared (Krapp 1932). Grein's article, "Zur Textkritik der angelsächsischen Dichter" (Grein 1865), is relevant here; in this short study, the author suggests improvements in his own dictionary of Anglo-Saxon poetry, which includes, of course, the **Meters**.

Critics who concern themselves with the problem of the authorship of the **Meters** concentrate their attention on two groups of two elements in the texts: the prose translation and the alliterative **Meters** on the one hand, and the prose and verse prefaces on the other. The prose proem has been compared to Alfred's proem for the translation of Gregory's **Cura Pastoralis**, and the verse proem and **Meters** to the only other alliterative verses surviving from Alfred's pen, those from the beginning and end of the **Cura**.

Items mentioned below do not include literary histories and works not specifically concerned with Alfred's translation, even though the problem first surfaced in a literary history: Thomas Wright denied Alfred's authorship of the **Meters** in his **Biographia Britanica**

Literaria I (Wright 1842). Before Wright's time, critics had simply assumed the assignment of the **Meters** to Alfred to be valid.

The year 1882 saw two independent responses to Wright's statement. Martin Hartmann (Hartmann 1882) begins with a review of opinions held by all the editors and literary historians prior to 1842, and he offers generous quotations from their works. He then presents counter-arguments to the issues raised in Wright's comments. One of the more interesting points Hartmann makes is this: Wright argues that the alliterative **Meters** are of poor quality--unworthy of King Alfred; Hartmann counters by saying that the **Meters** should be assigned to Alfred precisely because they lack the finesse of a practiced poet.

Although Otto Zimmermann's dissertation (Zimmermann 1882) responds to Wright's work of 1842, his purpose is not primarily to attack Wright, but rather to prove that Alfred wrote the **Meters**. Among other things, he presents the thirty lines of verse from the **Cura Pastoralis**, showing that Alfred consistently lacked genius in writing alliterative poetry. He also defends Alfred's exclusive use of the prose translation instead of the Latin text as the source for his **Meters**. The dissertation gives more textual analysis than Hartmann's article, especially in comparing the alliterative verses to their corresponding prose passages.

Alfred Leicht published Part I of a two-part article in which he responds to Hartmann's work of the previous year (Leicht 1883). Leicht is very positive in his denial of Alfred's authorship of the **Meters**. He points out that, but for two relatively short instances, the **Meters** show no originality, depending entirely for their content upon the prose source.

Part II of Leicht's article (Leicht 1884) sets about the task of proving his point that Alfred did not write the alliterative verses by comparing the Latin **Meters** to their Anglo-Saxon prose equivalents and these Anglo-Saxon prose renderings to their equivalent alliterative verses. One of the major obstacles to a proof that Alfred did not write the alliterative **Meters** is the statement in the two prefaces that he did. In order to maintain the opinion on the authorship of the verses which Leicht does, it is also necessary to attack the authorship of the prefaces. This is Leicht's motivation in this particular article.

Ernst Krämer again raised the question of authorship in the introduction to his edition of the alliterative **Meters** (Krämer 1902). On linguistic grounds, he comes to the conclusion that Alfred did, indeed, write the **Meters**.

Fehlauer provides a good summary of the various arguments for and against Alfred's authorship in his dissertation, and its later published version, which discusses in summary form all the English translations of the **Consolatio** (Fehlauer 1908; Fehlauer 1909). The work is primarily a list of translations, however, offering little new information. Kenneth Sisam also summarizes the main points on this problem (Sisam 1953). He casts his vote for Alfred's authorship of the prose proem, and, consequently, for the **Meters** themselves. He defends his view using historical and linguistic evidence, chiefly exterior to the text.

The problem of authorship has often been reopened since 1842, and opinions on this point still remain inconclusive. As several critics have pointed out, the evidence, if it is valid, is on the side of Alfred's own authorship. The burden of proof seems to be upon those critics who would argue against his authorship of the **Meters**. Malcolm Godden, in his recent article (Godden 1981), summarizing the scholarship on King Alfred's **Consolatio** translation, says that the evidence now points to Alfred as the author of the **Meters**.

Relatively little textual scholarship exists on the Anglo-Saxon **Meters**. Martin Cohn studied syntactical and grammatical aspects of the alliterative **Meters** as well as degrees of sound change (Cohn 1922). Because the **Meters** can be fairly accurately dated to c.900, they are invaluable for dating other surviving examples of Anglo-Saxon poetry.

A short article by J.H. Kern comments on the meanings of words and the problems of authorship of the alliterative **Meters** (Kern 1923). It, too, must be considered in any comprehensive study of the **Meters**.

John W. Conlee's article (Conlee 1970), building on some earlier work by Larry Benson on Anglo-Saxon formulaic poetry, finds that the poet of the **Meters** used formulaic phrases whenever possible, and like the author of the prose translation, tended to add dialectic material to the text he was rendering into verse.

Allan Metcalf's dissertation (Metcalf 1966) compares the poetic vocabulary used in the **Meters** with that of Alfred's prose version. Metcalf points out the unique place the **Meters** have in Anglo-Saxon prose equivalent. He later revised and published his work (Metcalf 1973). In another article (Metcalf 1970), he counters arguments from critics who charge the poet of the **Meters** with lack of originality. Metcalf maintains that the **Meters** were written as integral parts of the whole

Consolatio text, so too much "originality," that is, too much deviation from the Old English prose, would have led to inconsistency. In his book (Metcalf 1973), he studies the vocabulary of the **Meters**, comparing the frequency of words repeated in the prose translation of the **Consolation** and in other Old English poetic works. He maintains that a charge of lack of originality is not valid criticism. Anglo-Saxon prose and Anglo-Saxon verse are two separate realms of diction.

Naomi Myrvaagnes' dissertation (Myrvaagnes 1970) compares the style of the **Meters of Boethius** to that of **Beowulf**. As might be expected, the **Beowulf** is found to be a superior example of Anglo-Saxon alliterative verse. Daniel Donoghue, in an article (Donoghue 1986), attempts to show, through stylistic analysis, that the alliterative **Meters** do have significant poetic value.

As pointed out above, the problem of authorship for the **Meters** has been one of the most fascinating areas of **Consolatio** criticism for scholarly speculation. Arguments have been offered on both sides of the issue, and results remain open to further debate. The **Meters** have also been useful in studies of the development of the English language. Even for textual studies, the **Meters** have proved surprisingly important, producing the long-standing controversies mentioned above.

List of Relevant Titles

1.   Assmann, Bruno. **Die Handschriften von Exeter, Metra des Boethius, Salomo und Saturn, die Psalmen.** Bibliothek der angelsächsischen Poesie, no. 3. Leipzig: n.p., 1898.

      This is one of the early editions of the alliterative **Meters of Boethius.**

2.   Cardale, J.S. **King Alfred's Anglo-Saxon Version of Boethius'** De Consolatione Philosophiae. London: n.p., 1829.

      This is one of the earliest editions of Alfred's **Consolatio** translation containing the **Meters.**

3.   Cohn, Martin. "Die Rolle der **Metra des
      Boethius** im Streit um die Datierung der
      Denkmäler der angelsächsischen Poesie." Ph.D.
      diss., Schlesische Friedrich-Wilhelms-Universität,
      Breslau, 1922.

      Cohn's article is a thorough syntactical and
      grammatical study of the **Metra** as well as a
      source of information on English sound changes.
      The **Metra** can be dated fairly accurately at c.900
      AD and their position in the development of Old
      English poetry becomes a point of reference for
      dating the other Old English poetry.

4.   Conlee, John W. "A Note on Verse Composition
      in the **Meters of Boethius.**"
      Neuphilologische Mitteilungen 71 (1970):
      576-85.

      This is a study of the use of the Old English oral
      formulaic tradition entered into by the poet of the
      Meters. The poet, like the author of the prose
      version, often adds extraneous didactic material to
      the text.

5.   Donoghue, Daniel. "Word Order and Poetic Style:
      Auxiliary and Verbal in **The Meters of
      Boethius.**" **Anglo-Saxon England** 15
      (1986): 167-196.

      Donoghue views the alliterative **Meters** as a
      versification of the prose renderings found in the
      Anglo-Saxon **Consolatio** translation. They
      were probably made without reference to the Latin
      originals. His conclusion is that the **Meters**
      succeed technically in bringing significant poetic
      value to the prose.

6. Fehlauer, Friedrich. **Die englischen Übersetzungen von Boethius'** De Consolatione Philosophiae. Ph.D. diss., Albertus-Universität zu Königsberg, 1908. Königsberg: Hartungsche Buchdruckerei, 1908.

   Fehlauer gives a summary of data on the **Metra** and the criticism on the problem of their authorship. He does not present an original opinion on the question.

7. ----------. **Die englischen Übersetzungen von Boethius'** De Consdatione Philosophiae. Berlin: Emil Felber, 1909.

   This is the published book form of the dissertation listed above (Fehlauer 1908).

8. Ford, Susan Chappell. "Poetry in Boethius' **Consolation of Philosophy.**" Ph.D. diss., Columbia University, 1967.

   Because the **Meters of Boethius** are so central an issue to this chapter, I include this thorough study which is primarily on the Latin **Metra** because the background information is essential for an understanding of the Anglo-Saxon translation.

9. Fox, Samuel. **Alfred's Anglo-Saxon Version of the** Meters of Boethius: **With an English Translation and Notes.** London: n.p., 1835.

   This is the first edition of the alliterative **Meters** which prints them independent of Alfred's prose translation.

10.   ----------. **Alfred's Anglo-Saxon Version of Boethius** De Consolatione Philosophiae **With a Literal English Translation, Notes, and Glossary.** London, 1864. Reprint. New York: AMS, 1970.

This is another early edition of Alfred's **Consolatio** translation containing the **Meters.**

11.   Godden, Malcolm. "King Alfred's Boethius." In **Boethius: His Life, Thought and Influence,** edited by Margaret Gibson, 419-24. Oxford: Basil Blackwell, 1981.

The article summarizes the scholarship on Alfred's **Consolatio** translation; it includes a paragraph on the history of the **Metra** and the scholarship pertaining to them.

12.   Grein, Christian C.W.M. **Bibliothek der angelsächsischen Poesie.** 2 vols. Göttingen: n.p., 1858.

This is a collection containing the alliterative **Meters of Boethius.**

13.   ----------. "Zur Textkritik der angelsächsischen Dichter." **Germania,** 10 (1865): 416-29.

This article contains a list of typographical errors and suggested improvements for the author's earlier **Sprachschatz der angelsächsischen Dichter.** Included is information pertaining to the **Meters.**

14.   Hartmann, K.A. Martin. "Ist König Alfred der Verfasser der alliterierenden Übertragung der **Metra des Boethius?" Anglia: Zeitschrift für englische Philologie** 5 (1882): 411-50.

The author gives a thorough review of scholarship found in editions and literary histories on the **Meters of Boethius**. The article contains counter arguments to Thomas Wright's opinion that Alfred did not write the alliterative **Meters**. It states that Alfred and none other produced the **Meters**.

15.   Kern, J.H. "A Few Notes on the **Metra of Boethius** in Old English." **Neuphilologus** 8 (1923): 295-300.

Before offering notes on textual problems, Kern states that it is impossible to ascribe the proem of the **Meters** to Alfred.

16.   Krämer, Ernest, ed. **Die altenglischen** Metra des Boethius. Bonner Beiträge zur Anglistik, no. 8. Bonn: P. Hanstein's Verlag, 1902.

The introduction to the edition first treats manuscript information and then deals extensively with the question of the authorship of the **Meters**. Krämer concludes that Alfred was the writer of both the prose and verse renderings of the text and of both proems as well.

17.   Krapp, George Philip, ed. **The Paris Psalter and the Meters of Boethius.** New York: Columbia University Press, 1932.

This collection contains the alliterative **Meters of Boethius**.

18.   Leicht, Alfred. "Ist König Ælfred der Verfasser der alliterierenden **Metra des Boethius**?" **Anglia: Zeitschrift für englische Philologie** 6 (1883): 126-70.

Based on the world views expressed in the prose
and verse **Meters**, the same author, Leicht says,
could not have produced both. Thus, Alfred wrote
the prose version, but not the verse.

19.   ----------. "Zur angelsächsischen Bearbeitung des
Boethius." **Anglia: Zeitschrift für
englische Philologie** 7 (1884): 178-202.

This article accomplishes two things: 1) it asserts
that the prologue to the prose translation of the
Consolatio, like that of the **Meters**, is not the
personal work of Alfred, and 2) it compares the
prose translation with its Boethian source.

20.   Metcalf, Allan A. "The Poetic Language of the
Old English **Meters of Boethius**." Ph.D. diss.,
University of California at Berkeley, 1966.

Metcalf makes a detailed study of the vocabulary
used in the only Old English poetry which
corresponds to an Old English prose text. The
article divides the words into various categories
and draws conclusions from the entries on the
lists.

21.   ----------. "On the Authorship and Originality of
the **Meters of Boethius**."
Neuphilologische Mitteilungen 71 (1970):
185-7.

Metcalf here maintains that too much originality
in the **Meters** would have led to inconsistency in
the Old English **Consolatio** translation as a
whole (prose and verse together).

22.   ----------. **Poetic Diction in the Old
English** Meters of Boethius. Indiana University,

Series Practica, no. 50. The Hague: Moulton, 1973.

This is a thorough study of the poetic vocabulary used in the **Meters of Boethius**. It compares it with the vocabulary of the prose version and with that of Old English poetry in general. This is the published edition of the dissertation listed above (Metcalf 1966).

23.   Myrvaagnes, Naomi Suconick. "A Stylistic Study of the Old English **Meters of Boethius**." Ph.D. diss., New York University, 1970.

The effect of the prose rendering of the **Consolatio** by Alfred, the source of the **Meters**, is not just apparent in the content of the poems. It is also noticeable in the syntax of the **Meters**.

24.   Patch, Howard Rollin. **The Tradition of Boethius: A Study of His Importance in Medieval Culture.** New York: Oxford University Press, 1935.

This book is useful for the general information it gives on Alfred and his work as a translator.

25.   Rawlinson, Christopher. **King Ælfred's** Consolation of Philosophy. Oxford: n.p., 1698.

This is the earliest edition of Alfred's **Consolatio** translation and it contains the **Meters**.

26.   Sedgefield, Walter John, ed. **King Alfred's Old English Version of Boethius** De Consolatione Philosophiae. 1899. Reprint.

Darmstadt: Wissenschaftliche Buchstellschaft, 1968.

This edition of the Old English text also contains the Old English alliterative **Meters.**

27.   Sisam, Kenneth. "The Authorship of the Verse Translation of Boethius's **Metra.**" In **Studies in the History of Old English Literature,** 293-7. Oxford: Clarendon Press, 1953.

Sisam argues that Alfred did, in fact, write the prose Proem.

28.   Stewart, Hugh Fraser. **Boethius: An Essay.** London: 1891. Reprint. New York: Burt Franklin, 1974.

Stewart's comments on the alliterative **Meters** are confined to a single footnote, but his general information on Alfred is useful background for a study of the **Meters.**

29.   van de Vyver, A. "Les Traductions du **De Consolatione philosophiae** de Boèce en littérature comparée." **Humanisme et Renaissance** 6 (1939): 247-73.

The article is useful for its perspective: it places Alfred and his translations at the beginning of the European **Consolatio** tradition.

30.   Wright, Thomas. **Biographia Britanica Literaria I.** London: n.p., 1842.

This work contains the first critical suggestion that Alfred did not write the alliterative **Meters of Boethius.**

31.   Zimmermann, Otto. **Über den Verfasser der altenglischen** Metren des Boethius. Ph.D. diss., Universität Greifswald, 1882. Greifswald: Julius Abel, 1882.

Zimmermann attacks Thomas Wright's opinion that Alfred did not render the Boethius **Meters** into alliterative verse, on the basis of historical, stylistic, and contextual evidence.

CHAPTER III

THE MEDIEVAL GERMAN TRADITION

Notker Labeo's **Consolatio** Translation

The subject of this section is the **Consolatio** translation by Notker III (c.950-1022). This translator is designated as Notker III because two other illustrious men bearing the name Notker preceded him at his monastery in Switzerland. Notker III was given the epithet Labeo (thick lipped) because of a physical characteristic he is said to have had, and he is also referred to as "Notker the German" because of his contributions to the study of vernacular German during its early stages of development. He lived and worked at the monastery of St. Gall, where he had been placed by his uncle, Ekkehart I, also of St. Gall. Notker died there of the plague which soldiers of Henry II brought back from campaigns in Italy. Apart from information found in the works he left, much of our knowledge of Notker derives from the writings of his student, Ekkehart IV, whose view of the master is one of affection and admiration.

Several studies provide good introductions to the life and times of Notker. Paul Hoffmann's book, **Der Mittelalterliche Mensch: Gesehen aus Welt und Umwelt Notkers des Deutschen** (Hoffmann 1922), is perhaps the most thorough general study. James Midgley Clark's book, **The Abbey of St. Gall as a Center of Literature and Art** (Clark 1926), should also be consulted, despite a less-than-favorable review it received from E.K.Rand (Rand 1927). Rand's criticism was directed at Clark's lack of originality in approach and the lack of illustrations of the works of art discussed. Gustav Ehrismann's article, "Notker III (Labeo) von St. Gallen," in his handbook (Ehrismann 1932) gives a very fine summary of information on the life and works of its subject author. Among many other interesting insights, Ehrismann points out that Notker attempted to preserve some of the metrical quality of Boethius' meters, introducing rhymed lines into his otherwise prose translation. "Notker Labeo," an article in the **Verfasserlexikon** (Karg-Gasterstädt 1955), also offers information in succinct form. Stephan Sonderegger's book (Sonderegger 1970) contains a section on Notker's life and times, which is excellent as background information. These works, the two books and the three articles, also provide background to the complex problems relating to the study of Notker's **Consolatio** translation. Georg Braungart, in an article, writes:

> Bei Notkers Übersetzung des Boethius-Textes handelt es sich . . . nicht um eine Arbeit auf poetischen Eigenwert . . . , sondern um eine Hilfe für den Schüler . . . . Sie soll Sprache und Gehalt eines wichtigen Textes im **artes**-Unterricht besser verstehen helfen und damit zuletzt auch zu den biblischen Texten hinführen. (Braungart 1987, 14)

Thus, he shows that Notker's translation is very much a school text produced to benefit students of Latin at the monastic school at St. Gall.

A bibliography on Notker was prepared by Coleman (Coleman 1968), but it is incomplete and it lacks annotations.

Three other general works must also be mentioned at the beginning of this chapter on Notker's **Consolatio** translation. Hugh Fraser Stewart's **Essay** (Stewart 1891) is a study encompassing most areas of Boethian studies, and he includes a brief section on Notker's translation. Stewart's most original contribution is in providing strong evidence that both Notker and Chaucer used the same tradition of Latin commentaries, sharing the same erroneous information. Howard Patch's book (Patch 1935), **The Tradition of Boethius: A Study of His Importance in Medieval Culture**, too, contains a section on Notker's translation, though no new information is presented. A. Van de Vyver's article, "Les Traductions du **De consolatione philosophiae** de Boèce en littérature comparée" (van de Vyver 1939), places Notker's

Consolatio translation in the broader perspective of the European
vernacular tradition of Boethius' last work, including it in a listing of all
the then-known European translations. A recent article by Nigel Palmer
(Palmer 1981) considers the German Consolatio tradition, but its
primary emphasis is on the medieval translations exclusive of Notker's
work.

The sizable body of works Notker is known to have produced is
the immediate context for any scholarly study of his Consolatio
rendering.

> These include, on his own showing in a letter to Hugo II.,
> bishop of Sitten, Cato's De Moribus, Virgil's Bucolics, the
> Andrias of Terence, Marcianus Capella, Aristotle's
> Categories and De Interpretatione, treatises on rhetoric and
> arithmetic, a psalter, part of the book of Job, Boethius' tract on
> the Trinity, and the Consolation of Philosophy. (Stewart
> 1891, 192)

Notker produced his Consolatio translation as a study aid and textbook
for students of Latin. Primarily, his interest appears to have been in
teaching Latin vocabulary, because he greatly simplifies the syntax of the
original text and he often uses Latin terminology in his renderings of
difficult concepts.

The critical studies on Notker's Consolatio translation will be
grouped below into six different areas of research: 1) studies pertaining to
the manuscripts, 2) studies concerning linguistic problems (including
studies of grammar, syntax, and sound changes), 3) various sorts of
vocabulary studies, 4) genre problems, 5) the problem of Notker's use of
commentaries, and 6) Notker's reception of the Consolatio (Notker's
Christianizing of Boethius' work). These topics will be dealt with in the
order presented here, and only articles and works directly related to the
translation will be treated.

Apart from one fragmentary text, Notker's complete
Consolatio translation is contained in a single manuscript, MS St.
Gallen 825, from the tenth or eleventh century. It has been edited for
publication four times. First, E.G. Graff's edition, containing the Old
High German text without the accompanying Latin, appeared (Graff

1837). The next edition was included in Heinrich Hattemer's series of Old
High German texts (Hattemer 1844-1849). A more promising third
editing appeared in 1883, the work of Paul Piper (Piper 1883), but a
reviewer of that same year, Johann Kelle (Kelle 1883), presents a long list
of misreadings and errors found in its transcription. His negative
criticism indicated that another editing would eventually be needed. This
new work was accomplished by E.H. Sehrt and Taylor Starck (Sehrt and
Starck 1933-4). But even this last editing was given a less-than-favorable
review (Behaghel 1933/4), in which exception was taken to several
emendations made in the edition. The reviewer suggests that Sehrt and
Starck had taken too many liberties in altering readings in the manuscript.
This review was followed immediately by a reply from the editors, who
responded point-for-point to the negative criticisms (Sehrt and Starck
1934). Sehrt and Starck twice defended their edition in 1936. In one
article, Sehrt, writing alone, indicates their reasons for using **zuo**
consistently as a preposition (Sehrt 1936), and in the other, they present
together an extended note, adding to and changing some information from
the introduction to their edition, explaining the use of certain prepositions
in Notker's translation (Sehrt and Starck 1936). The Sehrt and Starck
edition contains the Old High German text just as it appears in the
manuscript, as a gloss upon the Latin. It is a very important piece of
scholarship, but in spite of the editors' explanations, some of the
problems noted in the review suggest that it, too, should be superseded by
a further re-editing of the manuscript. This re-editing project has been
undertaken by Petrus Tax. Thus far, two volumes of his text have
appeared. Volume one contains Notker's translation of the first two
books of the **Consolatio** (Tax 1986); volume two contains Notker's
translation of the third book of Boethius' work (Tax 1988). For short
excerpts or samplings from Notker's text, see the passages published in
Wilhelm Braune's **Althochdeutsches Lesebuch** (Braune 1969).
These offer a fair preview of Notker's translation.

In producing all of his writings, one of Notker's major concerns
was the German language. Using a system of accent marks, he
transcribed and preserved the phonetic subtleties of Old High German, and
this work is found most thoroughly developed in the **Consolatio**
translation. Furthermore, he is renowned for having formulated his
"Anlaut-Gesetz," which states the guidelines for such sound changes as **d**
to **t** or **b** to **p**. As will be seen, Notker's **Consolatio** translation is

indeed an invaluable document for philologists, but it is also much more: the translation is an important historical and literary document.

Because of its importance as an Old High German text, Notker's **Consolatio** translation has been the subject of several linguistic studies. Hermann Wunderlich, for example, produced a dissertation on Notker's syntax (Wunderlich 1883); this book is quite comprehensive in scope, including a study of the relationship of the translation to the Latin original and observations on sound changes. P. Sonnenburg published a general survey of the linguistic problems discovered in Notker's translation, and it includes a comparison between Notker's work and a similar translation of another Latin work by Ruodpert (Sonnenburg 1887). A thorough study of the sounds and evidence of sound changes seen in Notker's translation is presented in Franz Traeger's book (Traeger 1906). W.F. Twaddell's article attempts to explain a problematic point of grammar (Twaddell 1932); he proposes a model to explain why Notker uses a seemingly incorrect construction in verb position in his **Consolatio** translation.

Arthur Baur's study of Notker's use of the adjective focuses on a specific linguistic problem in the translation (Baur 1940). Similarly, Doris Handschuh's dissertation focuses on conjunctions in Notker's rendering (Handschuh 1964), and Ernst Bolli's book (Bolli 1975) deals with Notker's syntax. Some of the items listed above of course treat issues not limited entirely to Notker's **Consolatio** translation. For example, Twaddell concludes his article by saying the following about Notker's use of incorrect syntax around certain verbs:

> This instance furnishes an illustration of what may happen in the last stages of an important linguistic movement. A new set of categories is set up, and almost completely established; then an unusual and distinctly non-popular construction is placed in a wrong category; an analogy operates to produce a result alike anomalous before the change and after it. (Twaddell 1932, 406)

Although this was written about Notker's **Consolatio** translation, the linguistic observations are intended to have much broader implications for the study of Old High German.

For further information on the language of Notker's **Consolatio** translation, consult works by Alfred Karl Dolch (Dolch 1968), Franz Fraeger (Fraeger 1906), Dieter Furrer (Furrer 1971), M.H.

Jellinek (Jellinek 1932), and Oscar Wolfermann (Wolfermann 1886).
They each treat very specific points of grammar or linguistic problems.

Related to the topics of grammar and sound changes are the
studies of Notker's vocabulary. Preliminary information is to be found in
Johann Kelle's influential article, "Die philosophischen Kunstausdrücke in
Notker's Werken" (Kelle 1888). Although the article does not limit itself
to the **Consolatio** translation, its importance for subsequent scholarship
makes it a good starting point for students of that work. Similarly,
Kelle's book, "Die rhetorischen Kunstausdrücke in Notker's Werken"
(Kelle 1899), should also be consulted. A glossary to the first book of
Notker's translation was published by Nils Lindahl (Lindahl 1916), which
was followed by Alfred Karl Dolch's complete glossary to Book I (Dolch
1952, Teil I und II) and his study of the entire translation itself (Dolch
1952, Teil III). Edward Sehrt produced a tri-lingual (Latin, Old High
German, Modern German) dictionary to Notker's writings (Sehrt 1962).
These are all worthy tools for research on Notker's Old High German text.

Edward H. Sehrt and Wolfram K. Legner provided a general study
of Notker's vocabulary (Sehrt and Legner 1955), and Harold Kirshner
produced a study specific to Notker's scientific terminology (Kirshner
1963), focusing on Notker's translation of concepts of natural phenomena.
In a sizable article, K. Ostberg (Ostberg 1959) studies Notker's
distinctions in translating the Latin **animal/animans**, pointing out that
he was the first German writer to use **tier** to refer to the generic category
animal. Concerned with the relationship between Notker's vocabulary
and the corresponding Latin concepts is Evelyn Coleman's study of 1964
(Coleman 1964). Emil Luginbühl's article (Luginbühl 1970) must also
be mentioned in this context; it studies the translation of broader concepts
from the Latin into Notker's vocabulary, but the focus remains on
Notker's language and the development of German as a vehicle for
philosophical ideas. Generally, one can say that all of these vocabulary
studies, like the linguistic studies mentioned above, are aimed at adding to
our knowledge of the German language rather than at increasing the body
of critical information on Notker and his **Consolatio** translation.

Two works by Jerold C. Frakes raise the study of Notker's
translation from a linguistic to a conceptual level. First, in his
dissertation (Frakes 1982), he discusses the concept of **fortuna** in
Boethius' **Consolatio** and then as it appears in Alfred's and Notker's
translations. Later, in an article, he discusses the neo-Platonic
cosmological order as it is described by all three writers. He discovers:

Die dualistische Metaphysik der **Consolatio** wurde also in der Bearbeitung ihrer ersten Übersetzer zum pragmatisch-christlichen System des Gradualismus bei Alfred, der stark von der angelsächsischen **Bekehrungsmentalität** beeinflußt wurde, und zum unfreiwilligen Gerüst des Augustinismus des 11. Jahrhunderts bei Notker. (Frakes 1984, 74)

In these articles by Frakes, criticism has shifted from philology to the level of ideas. Another critic who approaches Notker's translation from a conceptual angle is Herbert Bolender. In an article, he studies the system of epistemology presented by Boethius toward the end of the **Consolatio**, finding that Notker adds a notion of **revelation** to Boethius' notion of **reason** as the highest human function. He writes:

Mit der Differenzierung der vierten Erkenntnisart in **humanus intellectus** und **diuinus intellectus** überbrückt er die Kluft zwischen menschlichem und göttlichem Erkennen, wie sie die **Consolatio** annimmt. (Bolender 1980, 337)

He concludes, however, that the monk of St. Gall had made this change unconsciously.

When we come to the tradition of Old High German glosses on the **Consolatio**, the critical insights pertain more directly to Notker's text; they address the problem of genre, an aspect rarely approached in the criticism on other translations in the European **Consolatio** tradition. Indeed, it is this generic aspect of Notker's **Consolatio** translation which defines its uniqueness in the tradition as a whole. The texts of the Old High German glosses were assembled in a five-volume study by Elias Steinmeyer and Eduard Sievers (Steinmeyer and Sievers 1879-1922), a series which has proved essential to all subsequent genre studies of Notker's translation. Werner Bach states the problem in his dissertation:

Einsam aufragend steht am Ausgang der althochdeutschen Literaturperiode Notker Labeo von St. Gallen, ihr klassischer Höhepunkt. Um ihn herum, vor ihm wie nach hinten, erblicken wir nur flaches Ödland. Wir bemerken keine Entwicklung, die zu ihm hinanführte, aus der er zu verstehen wäre, und erblicken, von Williram abgesehen, keine Entwicklung von ihm aus weiter, aus der wir seine Bedeutung für die damalige Zeit klarer erkennen

könnten. Daß Notker keine--wenigstens keine St. Galler--
Nachfolge gefunden hat, wird durch die Cluniazenser Reform
hinreichend erklärt. Problematisch bleibt die Tatsache, daß nach
150 Jahren des Schweigens auf dem Gebiete der
Übersetzungsprosa plötzlich eine Reihe meisterhaft gekonnter
Werke vor unseren Augen entstehen. Woher hat ihr Verfasser
dieses überragende Können? (Bach 1934, 2)

He concludes by pointing out that Notker's work was the high point of a
tradition of Old High German glosses, and that the purpose of these
glosses was instruction in Latin texts. Two later articles add further
entries to the list of Old High German glosses on the **Consolatio**. The
first, an article by Taylor Starck (Starck 1948), adds a glossed
Consolatio from Naples to Bach's list of manuscripts. In the other,
Rainer Reiche (Reiche 1970) adds a glossed manuscript from Vienna.
Consideration of the glosses is essential to an understanding of Notker's
translation because it places it in a literary tradition which had failed to
catch the attention of many critics--the tradition of German glosses on the
Consolatio, or of German glosses in general. Notker's translation was,
after all, prepared as a gloss upon the Latin text.

Studies on Notker's use of commentaries is another major area of
research. Pierre Courcelle's book, La Consolation de philosophie **dans
la tradition littéraire: antécédents et postérité de Boèce**
(Courcelle 1967), is basic, and essential, to any study of the
commentaries on the **Consolatio**.

G. Schepss, in his article (Schepss 1881), was the first critic to
mention similarities between Notker's comments and a commentary found
in the Maihinger manuscript of the British Museum. Important to all
subsequent criticism is an article by Johann Kelle (Kelle 1896): it
identifies one of the Latin manuscripts used by Notker in preparing his
own work, and it suggests that his indebtedness to the commentary found
in the Maihinger manuscript is indirect, deriving from a work ancestral to
both Notker and that commentary.

A dissertation by August Naaber (Naaber 1911) proves the point
made by Kelle (Kelle 1896) that Notker's commentary and the Maihinger
commentary have a common ancestor. In a book-by-book study produced
by Hans Naumann (Naumann 1913), Notker's dependence upon
commentaries is again treated, but credit is given to his original
comments on Boethius's text. A related problem, that of the Prologue in

MS St. Gall 825, is treated by K. Ostberg in an article (Ostberg 1962/1963); the sources of this additional prologue are discussed. Finally, Alfred K. Dolch discusses in an article (Dolch 1968) certain erroneous material added to Notker's translation, and this material, he suggests, may have originated in a commentary. In an effort to present as edited texts the various commentaries which might have been available to Notker as he prepared his **Consolatio** translation, Grant C. Roti, in his dissertation (Roti 1979), edits that portion of the Anonymous St. Gall Commentary which comments on Book I of Boethius' work.

Another problem which is vaguely related to the topic of commentaries derives from a reference to Catullus in Notker's **Consolatio** translation. If our historical information is correct, Notker should have known but few factual details about the life of Catullus. But references he makes contradict this notion. The problem was first pointed out by Anselm in a note (Amselm 1888), but no suggestion as to the source of the information was presented. Ernst Schwentner, too, mentions this problem (Schwentner 1955), complaining that no explanation had appeared since Anselm wrote. Unfortunately, Schwentner offers no explanation either.

A final, relatively late development in the criticism of Notker's **Consolatio** translation pertains to the medieval translators who "Christianize" the text. Ingeborg Schröbler's "Interpretatio Christiana in Notker's Bearbeitung von Boethius' **Trost der Philosophie**" presents a thorough study of Notker's Christianizing of the **Consolatio** (Schröbler 1951). Notker's translation proves to be a very Christian text, even though the degree of Christian influence in the original Latin text by Boethius is generally considered to be negligible. Schröbler's article was incorporated into her later, more general study (Schröbler 1953). An article by Benedikt Vollmann (Vollmann 1967) discusses Notker's understanding of the "simplicitas divinae providentiae," another important Christian concept in Notker's world view. Such studies provide insight into Notker's reading of the Boethian text.

In spite of the fact that Notker's **Consolatio** translation is among the most ancient of the European vernacular tradition, second in antiquity only to Alfred's, the problems critics still encounter are complex and their implications are relevant in a variety of areas of scholarship. The work, for example, on the genre and reception of Notker's translation is among the most thought-provoking scholarship on the European **Consolatio** tradition. It shows that Notker's translation, in addition to being an important linguistic artifact, deserves study for a variety of literary and historical reasons.

List of Relevant Titles

1. Anselm, G. "Eine Erwähnung Catulls bei Notker." **Rheinisches Museum für Philologie** 43 (1888): 309.

   This is the first critical notice given to a Catullus reference in Notker's **Consolatio** translation; Catullus was, of course, a Latin poet whose work, supposedly, would have been unknown to Notker.

2. Bach, Werner. **Die althochdeutschen Boethiusglossen und Notkers Übersetzung der** Consolatio. Ph.D. diss., Martin-Luther-Universität Halle-Wittenberg 1934. Würzburg: Buchdruckerei Richard Mayr, 1934.

   Bach shows that Notker's work is the high point of a tradition of Old High German glosses on the **Consolatio** rather than an isolated literary event. The article sheds light on the generic aspect of Notker's translation.

3. Baur, Arthur. **Das Adjektiv in Notkers Boethius unter besonderer Berücksichtigung seines Verhältnisses zur lateinischen Vorlage.** Zurich: Ernest Lang, 1940.

   This is a thorough study of the adjective in Notker's works, based primarily on the **Consolatio** translation. Baur's major contribution is in the area of syntax.

4. Behaghel, Dietrich. **Literaturblatt für germanische und romanische Philologie** 54 (1933/1934): n.pp.

   Behaghel attacks certain textual emendations made by Sehrt and Starck in their edition of Notker's works.

5. Bolender, Herbert. "Notkers **Consolatio**-Rezeption als widerspruchsfreie Praktik: eine Hypothese." **Beiträge zur Geschichte der deutschen Sprache und Literatur** 102 (1980): 325-38.

   Bolender shows that Notker modifies Boethius' system of epistemology to include **revelation** along with **reason** as the highest function in the process of **knowing**.

6. Bolli, Ernst. **Die verbale Klammer bei Notker: Untersuchung zur Wortstellung in der Boethius-Übersetzung.** Das Althochdeutsche von St. Gallen, no 4. Berlin: Walter de Gruyter, 1975.

   Bolli presents a detailed study of the syntax in Notker's **Consolatio** translation.

7. Braune, Wilhelm. **Althochdeutsches Lesebuch**, edited by E.A. Ebbinghaus. Tübingen: Max Niemeyer Verlag, 1969.

   This anthology contains a short sample of the text of Notker's **Consolatio** translation.

8. Braungart, Georg. "Notker der Deutsche als Bearbeiter eines lateinischen Schultextes: Boethius **De Consolatione Philosophiae.**"

Zeitschrift für deutsche Philologie 106
(1987): 2-15.

Braungart proves that Notker's **Consolatio**
translation was produced as a schoolbook for Latin
students at the monastic school at St. Gall.

9.   Clark, James Midgley. **The Abbey of St.
      Gall as a Centre of Literature and Art.**
      Cambridge: University Press, 1926.

      Clark gives a description of St. Gall, its historical
      development, and the art produced there.

10.   Coleman, Evelyn S. "Die Lehnbildungen in
      Notkers Übersetzung." In **Festschrift für
      Taylor Starck**, edited by Werner Betz, Evelyn
      S. Coleman, and Kenneth Northcott, 106-29. The
      Hague: Moulton and Co., 1964.

      This article studies Notker's **Consolatio**
      translation, as well as two other works by him, to
      determine the influence of Latin upon his Old
      High German vocabulary. It contains a complete
      checklist of borrowings.

11.   ----------. "Bibliographie zu Notker III von St.
      Gallen," In **Germanic Studies in Honor of
      Edward Henry Sehrt**, edited by Frothjov
      Andersen Raven, Wolfram K. Legner, and James
      Cecil King, 61-76. Miami Linguistic Series, no.
      1. Coral Gables, Fla.: University of Miami Press,
      1968.

      Coleman gives an alphabetical listing (without
      annotations) of books and articles pertaining to the
      life and times of Notker III.

12. Courcelle, Pierre. La Consolation de Philosophie dans la tradition littéraire: antécédents et postérité de Boece. Paris: Études Augustiniennes, 1967.

    This is a comprehensive study of the tradition of Consolatio commentaries.

13. Dolch, Alfred Karl. **Notker-Studien Teil I und II: lateinisch-althochdeutsches Glossar und althochdeutsch-lateinisches Wörterverzeichnis zu Notkers Boethius** De Consolatione Philosophiae **Buch I.** Ottendorfer Memorial Series of Germanic Monographs, no. 16. Leipzig: Buchdruckerei Robert Noske, 1952.

    This book is useful as a dictionary to Notker's Consolatio translation.

14. ----------. **Notker-Studien Teil III: Stil- und Quellen- probleme zu Notkers Boethius und Martianus.** Ottendorfer Memorial Series of Germanic Monographes, no. 16. Leipzig: Buchdruckerei Robert Noske, 1952.

    Linguistic problems and problems of literary affinity with commentaries and other glosses are the subject of this book.

15. ----------. "Quellenprobleme zu Notkers Boethius." In **Germanic Studies in Honor of Edward Henry Sehrt,** edited by Frithjov Andersen Raven, Wolfram K. Legner and James Cecil King, 77-82. Miami Linguistic Series, no. 1. Coral Gables, Fla.: University of Miami Press, 1968.

    Dolch briefly discusses two facts mentioned in Notker's Consolatio translation. One is an

astronomical occurrence; the other concerns lists
of Greek and Roman philosophers and the
misinformation they communicate. The problem
is to find the correct sources for these facts.

16.   Ehrismann, Gustav. "Notker III (Labeo) von St.
        Gallen." In **Handbuch des deutschen
        Unterrichts in höheren Schulen**. Vol. 6, pt.
        1, **Die Althochdeutsche Literatur**, 416-58.
        Munich: C.-H. Beck'sche Verlagsbuchhandlung,
        1932.

        Ehrismann gives a lengthy discussion of Notker's
        life and works; the article is a good general
        introduction to Notker and his translation.

17.   Fraeger, Franz. **Studien zur Sprache von
        Notkers** Boethius. Programm des königlichen
        humanistischen Gymnasium in Landshut für das
        Studienjahr 1905/1906. Landshut: Joseph
        Thomann'sche Buch und Kunstdruckerei, 1906.

        This is a linguistic study of Notker's translation of
        the **Consolatio**.

18.   Frakes, Jerold Coleman. "**Fortuna** in the
        Consolatio: Boethius, Alfred and Notker."
        Ph.D. diss., University of Minnesota, 1982.

        This dissertation consists in a semantic
        investigation of **Fortuna** in Boethius'
        Consolatio and in Alfred's and Notker's
        translations of the work. It seeks definitions for
        the term in the context of the cosmological order
        given in each work.

19.   ----------. "Die Rezeption der Neuplatonischen
        Metaphysik des Boethius durch Alfred und
        Notker." **Beiträge zur Geschichte der**

deutschen Sprache und Literatur 106
(1984): 51-74.

Frakes studies the neo-Platonic dualism of
Boethius' work as it is received by Alfred and
Notker in their translations.

20.   Furrer, Dieter. **Modusprobleme bei Notker:
die modalen Werte in den Nebensätzen
der** Consolatio-Übersetzung. Das
Althochdeutsche von St. Gallen: Texte und
Untersuchungen zur sprachlichen Überlieferung St.
Gallens vom 8. bis zum 12. Jahrhundert, no. 2.
Berlin: Walter de Gruyter, 1971.

Furrer is concerned with certain verb forms used
by Notker in his **Consolatio** translation and
their relation to corresponding verb forms in the
Latin text.

21.   Graff, E.G. **Althochdeutsche Übersetzung
und Erläuterung der von Boethius
verfassten fünf Bücher** De Consolatione
Philosophiae. N.p.: n.p., 1837.

This is an early edition of the translation, giving
the Old High German without the Latin.

22.   Handschuh, Doris. **Konjunktion in Notkers
Boethius-Übersetzung.** Ph.D. diss.,
Universität Zürich, 1964. Zurich: Juris-Verlag,
1964.

Handschuh considers the particles which introduce
clauses without inverting the verb, exclusive, of
course, of adverbs. Her study attempts to shed
light on the development of conjunctions in
German and on the merit of Notker as a translator.

23.   Hattemer, Heinrich H. **Denkmale des Mittelalters.** St. Gallens altteutsche Sprachschätze. Vol. 3, 7-255. St. Gallen: Druck und Verlag von Scheitlin und Zollikofer, 1844-1849.

       This is the second printed editing of Notker's **Consolatio** translation.

24.   Hoffmann, Paul Th. **Der Mittelalterliche Mensch: Gesehen aus Welt und Umwelt Notkers des Deutschen.** Gotha: Verlag Friederich Andreas Perthes, 1922.

       This is a study of the life and times of Notker III --and, more generally, a study of life at eleventh-century St. Gall.

25.   Jellinek, M.H. "Althochdeutsch PHAFFO--Gothic PAPA." **Zeitschrift für deutsches Altertum und deutsche Literatur** 69 (1932): 143-4.

       Jellinek, in a brief note in this article, defends Notker's rendering of the two terms mentioned in the title.

26.   Karg-Gasterstädt, Elizabeth. "Notker Labeo." In **Die deutsche Literatur des Mittelalters: Verfasserlexikon,** edited by Wolfgang Stammler and Karl Langosch. Vol. 5, 775-90. Berlin: n.p., 1955.

       The article contains general information on the life and works of Notker Labeo. It is a good general introduction to a study of his literary and historical importance.

27. Kelle, Johann. Review of **Die Schriften Notkers und seiner Schule**, ed. by Paul Piper. **Zeitschrift für Deutsches Altertum** 9 (1883), 313-29.

This is a thorough, and none too favorable, review of Piper's edition of **Notker's Works** (Vol. I, The Philosophical Works). It contains a long list of errors and suggested corrections of misreadings, all of which indicate the necessity of another edition.

28. ----------. "Die philosophischen Kunstausdrücke in Notkers Werken." **Abhandlung der königlichen bayerischen Akademie der Wissenschaften** 18 (1888): 1-58.

This article is not specific to Notker's **Consolatio** translation, but constitutes a seminal contribution to Notker scholarship.

29. ----------. "Über die Grundlage, auf der Notkers Erklärung von Boethius **De Consolatione Philosophiae** beruht." **Sitzungsberichte der königlichen bayerischen Akademie der Wissenschaften**, nv. (1896), 349-56.

Kelle identifies one of the manuscripts from St. Gall used by Notker in his translation. Three manuscripts were available to him, but the tenth-century Cod. Nr. 884, 4 was used. Kelle suggests that both Notker's **Consolatio** and the Maihinger manuscript have a common commentary in their ancestry [see (Naaber 1911) and (Schepss 1881)].

30. ----------. **Die rhetorischen Kunstausdrücke in Notkers Werken.** Munich: Verlag der königlichen Akademie, 1899.

The book is not specific to Notker's **Consolatio**
translation, but it constitutes a contribution to
Notker scholarship.

31.   Kirshner, Harold. "The Nature Vocabulary of
       Notker Labeo: a Study in Early German Scientific
       Terminology." Ph.D. diss., New York University,
       1963.

       Kirshner deals with Notker's translation of Latin
       nature terminology in his **Consolatio**
       translation.

32.   Lindahl, Niels. "Vollständiges Glossar zu Notkers
       Boethius **De Consolatione I.**" Ph.D. diss.,
       Uppsala, 1916.

       As the title indicates, this is a glossary to the first
       book of Notker's **Consolatio** translation. It is
       useful as a dictionary to the text.

33.   Luginbühl, Emil. **Studien zu Notkers**
       Übersetzungskunst. Das Althochdeutsche von
       St. Gallen, no. 1. Berlin: Walter de Gruyter, 1970.

       This book consists in a study of Notker's
       translation of terms relating to the "world of faith"
       and the "natural world and its order." The study is
       on Notker's translation of these terms.

34.   Naaber, August. **Die Quellen von Notkers:**
       Boethius De Consolatione Philosophiae. Ph.D.
       diss., Königliche Westfälische-Wilhelms-
       Universität zu Münster in Westfalen, 1911. Borna-
       Leipzig: Buchdruckerei Robert Noske, 1911.

       Naaber studies the relationship of Notker's
       Consolatio translation (specifically, his added
       comments) to the "Maihinger Scholion und

Kommentar," indicating that both have a common
ancestor [see (Kelle 1896) and (Schepss 1881)].

35.   Naumann, Hans. **Notkers Boethius:
      Untersuchung Über Quellen und Stil.**
      Quellen und Forschung zur Sprach- und
      Culturgeschichte der Germanischen Völker, no.
      121. Strassburg: Karl J. Trübner, 1913.

      Naumann gives a book-by-book study of Notker's
      dependence upon the commentaries designated as R
      and K. He points out Notker's additions and gives
      a thorough analysis of Notker's style.

36.   Ostberg, K. "Interpretations and Translations of
      Animal/Animans in the Writings of Notker
      Labeo." **Beiträge zur Geschichte der
      deutschen Sprache und Literatur:
      Tübingen** 81 (1959): 16-42.

      Ostberg gives an analysis of some linguistic
      developments in the works of Notker the
      translator--for example, the development of the
      generic term **tier** for animal. The article contains
      a section devoted specifically to the use of
      animal/animans in Notker's **Consolatio**
      translation.

37.   ----------. "The 'Prologi' of Notker's **Boethius**
      Reconsidered." **German Life and Letters** 16
      (1962/1963): 256-65.

      The author discusses the sources of the Prologue
      which precedes Notker's **Consolatio** translation
      in MS St. Gall (the only complete text of the
      translation).

38.   Palmer, Nigel F. "Latin and Vernacular in the
      Northern European Tradition of the **De**

Consolatione Philosophiae". In **Boethius: His Life, Thought and Influence,** edited by Margaret Gibson, 362-409. Oxford: Basil Blackwell, 1981.

This is an up-to-date summary of facts known about the **Consolatio** translation by Notker.

39.   Patch, Howard Rollin. **The Tradition of Boethius: A Study of His Importance in Medieval Culture.** New York: Oxford University Press, 1935.

This book contains a brief, general statement about Notker's **Consolatio** translation.

40.   Piper, Paul, ed. **Die Schriften Notkers und seiner Schule.** Germanischer Bücherschatz, no. 8-?. Freiburg und Tübingen: Akademische Verlagsbuchhandlung von J.C.B. Mohr, 1883.

This is the second printed edition of Notker's **Consolatio** translation.

41.   Rand, E.K. Review of **The Abbey of St. Gall as a Centre of Literature and Art,** by James Midgley Clark. **Speculum** 2 (1927): 354-56.

Rand gives a not-too-favorable review, arguing that the book's organization could be improved and that the chapters on the various art forms produced at St. Gall suffer from a lack of illustrations and a lack of originality in approach.

42.   Reiche, Rainer. "Unbekannte Boethiusglossen der Wiener Handschrift 271." **Zeitschrift für deutsches Altertum und deutsche Literatur** 99 (1970): 90-5.

Reiche describes a manuscript of the **Consolatio** (MS Vienna 271) containing Old High German glosses.

43.   Roti, Grant C. "Anonymous in Boetii Consolationem Philosophiae Commentarius ex Sangallensis Codice." Ph.D. diss., State University of New York at Albany, 1979.

Roti's dissertation presents a translation of that part of the Anonymous St. Gall Commentary which treats Book I of the **Consolatio**.

44.   Schepss, G. **Handschriftliche Studien zu Boethius** De Consolatione Philosophiae. Programm der Königlichen Studien-Anstalt Würzburg. Würzburg: CK der Thein'schen Druckerei, 1881.

The author recognizes similarities between Notker's translation of the **Consolatio** and a **Scholion** of the B-MS of the Fürstlich-Ottingen-Wallersteinische Library at Maihingen [see (Kelle 1896) and (Naaber 1911)].

45.   Schröbler, Ingeborg. "Interpretatio Christiana in Notkers Bearbeitung von Boethius' **Trost der Philosophie**." **Zeitschrift für deutsches Altertum und deutsche Literatur** 83 (1951): 40-57.

Schröbler indicates how Notker read the **Consolatio** as a Christian text. She points out his assumptions about the work and examines the comments which he added to the translation. This article was later incorporated as the first chapter of Schröbler's study of 1953.

46. ----------. **Notker III von St. Gallen als Übersetzer und Kommentator von Boethius'** De Consolatione Philosophiae. Hermaea Germanistische Forschung, no. 2 (neue folge). Tübingen: Max Niemeyer Verlag, 1953.

    This is a lengthy and thorough study of Notker's reading of the **Consolatio**; it indicates how he simplified and Christianized the text.

47. Schwentner, Ernst. "Catull, Boethius, Notker." **Germanisch-Romanische Monatsschrift** 36 (1955): 77-8.

    Schwentner points out a mysterious reference to Catullus in Notker's **Consolatio** translation. This problematic point had been indicated by Anselm in an article of 1888, but no further study has resulted.

48. Sehrt, Edward H. "Ze--Zuo in Notker." **JEGP: Journal of English and Germanic Philology** 35 (1936): 331-6.

    Sehrt defends Sehrt and Starck's decision to use **zuo** as a preposition in their edition of Notker's works. The original discussion of their reasons is to be found in the introduction to their edition (Sehrt and Starck 1933-4).

49. ----------. **Notker-Glossar: Ein althochdeutsch-lateinisch-neuhochdeutsches Wörterbuch zu Notkers des Deutschen Schriften.** Tübingen: Max Niemeyer Verlag, 1962.

    This book is a very useful tool in the study of Notker's **Consolatio** translation.

50.   Sehrt, Edward H., and Wolfram K. Legner, eds.
        Notker-Wortschatz. Halle: VEB Max
        Niemeyer Verlag, 1955.

        This is a study of vocabulary used in the works of
        Notker.

51.   Sehrt, Edward H. and Taylor Starck, eds. **Notkers
        des Deutschen Werke.** Althochdeutsche
        Textbibliothek, nos 32, 33, & 34. 1933-1934.
        Reprint. Halle: Max Niemeyer Verlag, 1966.

        This is the fourth of the printed editions of
        Notker's **Consolatio** translation [see: (Tax 1986;
        Tax 1988)].

52.   ----------. "Zum Text von Notkers Schriften."
        **Zeitschrift für deutsches Altertum und
        deutsche Literatur** 71 (1934): 259-64.

        This is a response to a negative review of the
        authors' edition of Notker's works. It responds
        point-for-point to Behaghel's negative criticism
        (Behaghel 1933/34) in order to justify the methods
        used by the editors.

53.   ----------. "Notker's Accentuation of the
        Prepositions **AN, IN, MIT.**" **Modern
        Language Notes** 51 (1936): 81-6.

        This is an extended note, adding to and changing
        some information from the introduction to the
        author's edition of Notker's **Consolatio**
        translation.

54.   Sonderegger, Stephen. **Althochdeutsch in St.
        Gallen.** St. Gall: Verlag Ostschweiz, 1970.

This book contains a section on Notker Labeo which is an excellent introduction to his life and times.

55.   Sonnenburg, P. **Bemerkungen zu Notkers Bearbeitung des Boethius.** Programm des königlichen Gymnasiums zu Bonn, 1886/1887. Bonn: Universitäts-Buchdruckerei von Carl George, 1887.

Sonnenburg gives a series of unconnected observations on points of grammar, word choice, and other matters. There is also a comparison with a Latin text translated by Ruodpert.

56.   Starck, Taylor. "Unpublished Old High German Glosses to Boethius and Prudentius." In **Medieval Studies in Honor of Jeremiah Denis Matthias Ford**, 301-17. Cambridge, Mass.: Harvard University Press, 1948.

Starck discusses a **Consolatio** manuscript with Old High German glosses found at Naples. It was made at St. Gall, and it belongs to the tradition of glossed manuscripts described by Werner Bach (Bach 1934).

57.   Steinmeyer, Elias and Edward Sievers. **Die althochdeutschen Glossen.** 5 vols. Berlin: Wiedmann, 1879-1922.

As the title indicates, these volumes contain material on the Old High German **Consolatio** glosses.

58.   Stewart, Hugh Fraser. **Boethius: An Essay.** London: 1891. Reprint. New York: Burt Franklin, 1974.

The short section on Notker's **Consolatio** translation contained in this book is a summary of general information. For this chapter, Stewart's main contribution is found in the section which he devotes to Chaucer; he shows that both Chaucer and Notker have similar textual errors, indicating that they probably translated from the same tradition of Latin manuscripts.

59. Tax, Petrus W., ed. **Boethius,** De Consolatione Philosophiae: **Buch I/II.** Altdeutsch Textbibliothek, no. 94. Tübingen: Max Niemeyer Verlag, 1986.

This is the first volume of the most recent editing of Notker's **Consolatio translation.**

60. ----------, ed. **Boethius,** De Consolatione Philosophiae: **Buch III.** Altdeutsch Textbibliothek, no. 100. Tübingen: Max Niemeyer Verlag, 1988.

This is the second in Tax's multi-volume re-editing of Notker's **Consolatio** translation.

61. Traeger, Franz. **Studien zur Sprache von Notkers** Boethius. Programm des königlichen humanistischen Gymnasium in Landshut für das Studienjahr 1905/1906. Landshut: Jos. Thomann'sche Buch- und Kunstbucherei, 1906.

This is a thorough study of the sounds and sound changes in the language of Notker's **Consolatio** translation.

62. Twaddell, W.F. "A Main Clause With 'Final' Verb in Notker's Boethius." **JEGP: Journal of English and Germanic Philology** 31 (1932): 403-6.

Twaddell clarifies an odd point of grammar in the
Consolatio translation. The existence of a
"second position" verb had established itself by
Notker's time, but he chose a wrong model,
causing certain of his usages to appear anomalous
among the writings of his times.

63.   Vollmann, Benedikt. "Simplicitas divinae
providentiae: zur Entwicklung des Begriffs in der
antiken Philosophie und seiner Eindeutschung in
Notkers **Consolatio-Übersetzung.**"
**Literaturwissenschaftliches Jahrbuch der
Görres-Gesellschaft** 8 (1967): 5-29.

Notker's translation of such terminology, as
suggested in the title of this article, is discussed as
a reception problem.

64.   van de Vyver, A. "Les Traductions du **De
Consolatione philosophiae** de Boèce en
littérature comparée." **Humanisme et
Renaissance** 6 (1939): 247-73.

Van de Vyver places Notker's translation into the
broader context of all the European **Consolatio**
translations.

65.   Wolfermann, Oskar. **Die Flexionslehre in
Notkers althochdeutscher Übersetzung
von Boethius:** De Consolatione Philosophiae,
**ein Beitrag zur althochdeutschen
Grammatik.** Altenburg: Oskar Bonde, 1886.

This book consists in a study of a linguistic
problem in Notker's **Consolatio** translation.

66.   Wunderlich, Hermann. **Beiträge zur Syntax
des Notker'schen Boethius.** Ph.D. diss.,

Friederich-Wilhelm-Universität zu Berlin, 1883.
Berlin: Buchdruckerei von Gustav Schade, 1883.

This is a textual study which concentrates on the syntax of the Boethius translation by Notker. It gives some consideration to sound changes, relationship to the Latin text, and other important issues, but it is primarily an attempt to add to the knowledge of the development of German syntax.

Other Medieval
German **Consolatio** Translations

Notker wrote his **Consolatio** translation in the late tenth
century, and from that time until the early fifteenth century, no other
vernacular German translation of the work appears to have been produced.
A good general source of information for students of this later tradition is
Nigel F. Palmer's article, "Latin and Vernacular in the Northern European
Tradition of the **De Consolatione Philosophiae**." He points out
that for the **Consolatio**:

> The earliest continental translation, that of Notker III of St. Gall,
> formed part of a programme to make the principal school texts
> available in German. (Palmer 1981, 363)

To this he adds:

> If we turn to the later Middle Ages, we find that the
> **Consolatio** is still treated as a "school text"--by which, in this
> period, we must understand a book studied in grammar schools
> and universities as well as monastery schools--and there still
> seems to be a need for vernacular versions as an aid to the
> understanding of the Latin. (Palmer 1981, 363)

Thus, the Old High German **Consolatio** tradition is an element in the
larger tradition of medieval scholasticism.
    Palmer's article provides a very complete list of fifteenth-century
German translations, summarizing material on previously discovered
manuscripts and discussing other manuscripts which had never before
attracted critical notice. He lists seven different translations, two in verse,
three in prose, and two others which have been attested to but are now
apparently lost. The two verse translations are of primary interest to
Palmer. The first survives only in transcriptions of the **Münster
Fragments** which were lost in a fire in 1945. The other, Palmer's own

99

discovery, "is a partial version of books III, IV and V contained in a fifteenth-century Erfurt manuscript of the **Consolatio** in the Bodleian Library, Oxford, MS Hamilton 46" (Palmer 1981, 364). The three prose versions are 1) a Low German rendering of Book I from about 1464, 2) a translation by Konrad Humery from about 1462/63, and 3) two lost translations, one by Peter von Kastl (from about 1401) said to have been printed at Nürnberg in 1473 and another (from about 1477) ascribed to Niklas von Wyle. No further information is available on the Niklas von Wyle translation. Palmer discusses none of the prose versions, but his article is the best source for information on the verse renderings, all of which are relatively obscure.

Little critical interest has been shown in these later German **Consolatio** translations. However, the transcriptions of the lost **Münster Fragments** are printed in A. Bömer's article, "Fragmente einer gereimten deutschen Boethiusübersetzung" (Bömer 1908). As pointed out above, it is only through these transcriptions that we have any knowledge of this translation. A dissertation on Konrad Humery's translation was published by Michael Mommert (Mommert 1965). It contains many quotations from the text. According to Mommert's description, Humery was a German Humanist, and his translation has many of the characteristics of a Renaissance work. More general information on Konrad Humery can be found in Wieland Schmidt's article in the **Verfasserlexikon** (Schmidt 1936). An article by Fidel Rädle and F.J. Worstbrock on Boethius, also in the **Verfasserlexikon** (Rädle and Worstbrock 1978), gives good summary information on the life of Boethius, Notker's **Consolatio** translation, and several of the later vernacular versions.

Perhaps the most interesting problem in the criticism on these later translations concerns the lost work attributed to Peter von Kastl. It was first mentioned by Bernard Pez [Bernardus Pezius] (1723) in the **Thesaurus Anecdotorum Novissimus** of 1721-1729; the specific reference is found in Tome IV, paragraph iv, pages 23-25. Pez writes:

> Ex pluribus unum notamus de Boetio, cuius Libros V. **de Consolatione Philosophiae de Latino in Teutonicum anno Domini MCCCI. a Magistro Petro, Presbytero Professo Monasterii in Castello Ord. S. Bened. in Reichenbach** constituto translatum fuisse auctor est Andreas

col. 598. Haec translatio non videtur alia quam quae anno 1472, unacum Commentariis, D. Thomae attributis, Norimbergae in maximo folio prodiit, estque studiis meritissimi Viri Johannis Buchelsii, Serenissimo Electori Palation Rheni a Confiliis et Bibliotheca. (Pez 1723, xxiv)

Editors and critics henceforth accepted the existence of the translation mentioned by Pez almost without question, but problems have been noted. For example, Stewart, in his **Essay,** says:

> In the year 1410 Peter, Presbyter in Kastl, a Benedictine monk, is said to have written a translation of the **De Consolatione.** Pezius, I know not on what grounds, suspects this to be the one which was printed, together with the Latin text and St. Thomas Aquinas's Commentary, by Coburger at Nuremberg in 1473. (Stewart 1891, 237-38)

In spite of discrepancies in information, however, the translation is referred to in many studies such as the general surveys by Ehrismann (Ehrismann 1932) and Patch (Patch 1935), and critics have continued to make passing references to it. But referring both to the translation ascribed to Peter von Kastl and the one attributed to Niklas von Wyle, Palmer says: they "are recorded but do not seem to have come down to us" (Palmer 1981, 364). One of my own articles (Kaylor 1991) examines all the facts known about Peter von Kastl and his translation. An earnest search still needs to be made for Peter work; it could eventually appear in some European library, possibly in the Vatican Library.

Brief mention may be made here of articles pertaining to the study of Low German translations. Again, a general survey of the subject is given in Palmer's article (Palmer 1981). Gédéon Huet's article of 1895 (Huet 1895), "La Première édition de la **Consolation** de Boèce en Néerlandais," not only gives information on the Low German edition but compares its illuminations and its commentary with a certain French manuscript of the **Consolatio.** A. van de Vyver lists the Low German translations in an article (van de Vyver 1939); C.G.N. de Vooys published an article, "De Middelnederlandse Boethius-vertaling van Jacob Vilt" (de Vooys 1941), in which he discusses one of them; and J.M. Hoek's dissertation (Hoek 1943) studies all the **Consolatio** translations in Middle Low German.

The most remarkable fact about the German **Consolatio** tradition is the hiatus between Notker's work of the eleventh century and the translations which appeared in the fifteenth century. The fragments and complete manuscripts of the later tradition represent a broad spectrum of translations, in verse or in prose, typical of medieval or early Renaissance approaches. Partly because of the variety in these translations, they represent an important part of the European **Consolatio** tradition.

List of Relevant Titles

1. Bömer, A. "Fragmente einer gereimten deutschen Boethiusübersetzung." **Zeitschrift für deutsches Altertum und deutsche Literatur** 50 (1908): 149-58.

    Bömer describes several fragments of a verse translation of the **Consolatio** found in the university library at Münster. They are in fifteenth-century German. The article includes a transcription of the fragments.

2. Ehrismann, Gustav. "Notker III (Labeo) von St. Gallen." In **Handbuch des deutschen Unterrichts in höheren Schulen.** Vol. 6, pt. 1, **Die althochdeutsche Literatur,** 416-58. Munich: C.-H. Beck'sche Verlagsbuchhandlung, 1932.

    Ehrismann's article is a good introduction to the study of Notker's works and influence.

3. Hoek, Jacobus Martinus. **De Middelnederlandse vertalingen van Boethius'** De Consolatione Philosophiae. Ph.D.

diss., Amsterdam, 1943. Harderwijk: Drukkerij-Uitgverij "Flevo," 1943.

This is a study of the medieval **Consolatio** translations of the Netherlands.

4. Huet, M. Gédéon. "La première édition de la Consolation de Boèce en néerlandais." In **Mélanges Julien Havet**, edited by Ernest Leroux, 501-69. Paris: n.p., 1895.

The article points out certain correspondences between a **Consolatio** edition from the Netherlands and a younger MS of the Bibliothèque Nationale. It studies the illuminations of both the edition and the manuscript and discusses the commentary found with the edition.

5. Kaylor, Noel Harold, Jr. "Peter von Kastl: Fifteenth-Century Translator of Boethius." **Fifteenth-Century Studies** 18 (1991): 133-142.

This article presents all the facts known about Peter von Kastl and his **Consolatio** translation.

6. Mommert, Michael. **Konrad Humery und seine Übersetzung der** Consolatio Philosophiae: **Studien zur deutschen Boethius-Tradition am Ausgang des Mittelalters**. Ph.D. diss., Westfälische Wilhelms-Universität, 1965. Münster: Westfälische Wilhelms-Universität, 1965.

This dissertation has as its subject the Middle High German **Consolatio** translation by the medieval Humanist Konrad Humery. The study treats historical, linguistic, and literary matters.

7.   Palmer, Nigel F. "Latin and Vernacular in the
      Northern European Tradition of the **De
      Consolatione Philosophiae.**" In **Boethius:
      His Life, Thought and Influence**, edited by
      Margaret Gibson, 362-409. Oxford: Basil
      Blackwell, 1981.

      This is primarily a survey, but much information
      appears for the first time, particularly a description
      of a Middle High German **Consolatio**
      translation in a manuscript designated as Oxford
      MS Hamilton 46.

8.   Patch, Howard Rollin. **The Tradition of
      Boethius: A Study of His Importance in
      Medieval Culture.** New York: Oxford
      University Press, 1935.

      The author presents a short summary of
      information on certain medieval German
      Consolatio translations other than that by
      Notker, such as the one attributed to Peter von
      Kastl.

9.   Pez (Pezius), Bernard. **Thesaurus
      Anecdotorum Novissimus.** Vol. 4, xxiv and
      273-636. Augsburg: Augustae Vindelicorum and
      Gracii, 1723.

      This is the first printed reference to the medieval
      Consolatio translation by Peter von Kastl.

10.   Rädle, Fidel and F.J. Worstbrock. "Boethius,
      Anicius Manlius Severinus." In **Die deutsche
      Literatur des Mittelalters:
      Verfasserlexikon**, edited by Kurt Ruh, et al.
      Vol. 1, 908-28. Berlin: Walter de Gruyter, 1978.

This article is included because it contains a list of twenty manuscripts of the **Consolatio** which contain medieval German glosses.

11. Schmidt, Wieland. "Konrad Humery." In **Die deutsche Literatur des Mittelalters: Verfasserlexikon,** edited by Wolfgang Stammler. Vol. 2, 537-41. Berlin: Walter de Gruyter, 1936.

   Schmidt presents the basic facts known on the life and work of Konrad Humery.

12. Stewart, Hugh Fraser. **Boethius: An Essay.** London: 1891. Reprint. New York: Burt Franklin, 1974.

   Stewart mentions only one medieval German **Consolatio** translation other than Notker's--that lost translation by Peter von Kastl.

13. de Vooys, C.G.N. "De Middelnederlanse Boethius-vertaling van Jacob Vilt." **Tijdschrift voor Nederlandsche Taal-en Letterkunde** 60 (1941): 1-25.

   The article describes a medieval **Consolatio** translation from the Netherlands.

14. van de Vyver, A. "Les Traductions du **De Consolatione philosophiae** de Boèce en litérature Comparée." **Humanisme et Renaissance** 6 (1939): 247-73.

   Van de Vyver lists all the known translations of the **Consolatio,** including those in medieval German.

CHAPTER IV

THE MEDIEVAL FRENCH TRADITION

Jean de Meun's Consolatio Translation

The tradition of medieval French translations of the
Consolatio is by far the richest and most complex of all: to date,
thirteen different works have been noted and described, and more than a
handful of these have appeared as printed editions. Of these thirteen, the
first eleven date from a two-hundred-year period, the thirteenth and
fourteenth centuries. So numerous are the manuscripts which survive that
the types of studies they have stimulated are more diverse than for any of
the other vernacular Consolatio traditions. The translations include
works that are signed, unsigned, anonymous, forged, literary, semi-
literate, conscientiously translated, heavily padded with interpolations, in
verse, prose, and verse-prose; they are translated into a variety of dialects.

Because so few facts concerning Jean's life are certain, this
chapter will begin with a brief selection of entries which attempt to
answer the question, who was Jean de Meun? Then, textual studies and
related problems will be discussed.

An article published by Quichert provides information
concerning a house which Jean occupied during his later years at Paris
(Quichert 1880). These facts come to us from documents which survive
from the early fourteenth century.

Jean's personal bibliography is the subject of an article by Paulin Paris. Paris writes:

> C'est au début de sa traduction du livre **De consolatione** de Boëce que Jean Clopinel [Jean de Meun] nous a donné ces précieuses indications. Après avoir achevé le **Roman de la Rose**, il traduisit le livre de Vegèce **De re militari**, le livre des Merveilles d'Irlande, celui d'Aelred De spirituelle amitié, les **Épîtres d'Abélard et d'Héloïse**, enfin la Consolation de philosophie [sic]. Si nous ajoutons à cette liste les deux ou trois poèmes dévots qu'il écrivit dans les dernières années de sa vie, nous aurons l'ensemble des oeuvres authentiques de Jean de Meun. Il en a probablement fait d'autres encore, mais les moyens nous manquent aujourd'hui de constater l'authenticité de celles qu'on lui a plus tard attribuées. (Paris 1881, 392)

Paris' study describes all works by Jean, with the notable exception of the **Roman de la Rose**, and gives quotations from them. However, the **Consolatio** translation which Paris discusses is not the prose work which was finally satisfactorily ascribed to Jean de Meun, a problem which will be discussed fully in the next section of this chapter. For readers today, the usefulness of Paris' article comes from its descriptions of Jean's other works and the light they shed upon his translation methods.

The few biographical facts known about Jean are summarized in an article written for the **Grande Encyclopédie** by Antoine Thomas.

> On sait peu de chose de sa biographie. Venu sans doute comme étudiant à l'université de Paris, il parait avoir passé la plus grande partie de sa vie dans cette ville, où il habitait en dernier lieu une maison de la rue Saint-Jacques . . . . (Thomas c.1900, 97)

Following this statement, the author discusses Jean's works, particularly the **Roman de la Rose**. All the material is presented in less than two columns.

Indeed, it is from the **Roman de la Rose** that most information about Jean's life has been deduced. For example, in her dissertation (Ralph 1940), Dorothy Marie Ralph draws conclusions about Jean's importance as a thinker from her reading of that text. Gaston Paris

once called Jean de Meun "le Voltaire du moyen âge"; using this
observation as a statement of thesis, Ralph proceeds to compare the life,
times, and works of these two writers who respectively symbolize for her
the thirteenth and eighteenth centuries in France. Very few new facts are
added in this work, however.

A very peculiar tradition is the subject of Albert B. Friedman's
study (Friedman 1950), "Jean de Meun an Englishman?" The author
traces erroneous entries in early English literary histories which led readers
to believe that the author of the **Roman de la Rose** was in fact an
Englishman living in Paris. The source of this error is found to be a
confusing bit of grammar in the earliest English reference to Jean and the
eventual false identification of him with an obscure English author.

Norman Cohn draws information from evidence found in the
Roman de la Rose to show that Jean's world-view is that of a
thirteenth-century academic under the influence of the newly rediscovered
Aristotle (Cohn 1961). He analyzes Jean's major concerns in three
categories (the nature of the cosmos, new attitudes toward sex, and
democratic and egalitarian social doctrine), finding him to be a progressive
and penetrating thinker, very much in the mainstream of the philosophical
currents of his day.

René Louis' "Esquisse d'une biographie de Jean de Meun" (Louis
1975), treats the usual data gleaned from the **Roman de la Rose**, the
later translations, and the **Testament** (apparently Jean's last work). His
discussion includes one of the few controversies surrounding Jean's life: a
certain Jean de Meun, archdeacon of Beauce, left a will which has been
published, but critics have generally discounted the possibility that this
Jean and the poet could be the same. Louis argues that they are the same,
adding to his account the new facts which the will offers.

The handful of articles discussed above present our total
knowledge of the life of Jean de Meun. As might be expected, this
information falls into two rather distinct biographical realms: Jean's
thought and philosophy, on the one hand, and his life and times, on the
other. This information is not enough to give a clear picture of the poet,
but it does provide a basic temporal and philosophical frame of reference
for researchers concerned with the **Consolatio** translation.

When we come to Jean de Meun's translation itself, the problems
become more complex, requiring in some cases a certain amount of
detective work. Following one paragraph concerning the general studies

of the translation, this section is divided into three parts. First, those articles are discussed which attempt to discern which translation Jean actually wrote. Second, studies are treated which represent work preliminary to the publication of an edition of Jean's text. Third, textual studies are treated.

Several general studies are useful as introductions to Jean's **Consolatio** translation. First, there is Stewart's **Essay** (Stewart 1891), in which his section on the French tradition includes a statement on Jean's translation. When Stewart was writing, the fact that Jean had prepared a prose translation had not yet been established, but Stewart favors what proved to be the correct work because, as he indicates, it influenced Chaucer as he produced his **Boece.** An article by Charles-Victor Langlois (C.-V. Langlois 1928) places Jean's translation in the context of all medieval French **Consolatio** translations. His description is brief, but it mentions most of the facts known at the time. Howard Patch devotes a section of his book, **The Tradition of Boethius: A Study of His Importance in Medieval Culture** (Patch 1935), to the French **Consolatio** tradition, giving some details on Jean's translation. Antoine Thomas and Mario Roques expanded on the work of Charles-Victor Langlois, giving first-hand descriptions of the major manuscripts of the then-known French translations (Thomas and Roques 1938). Theirs is by far the best of the general articles on the French tradition. Roberto Crespo's article in Italian offers a comprehensive study of Jean de Meun's translation (Crespo 1969).

Jean de Meun wrote a preface to his **Consolatio** translation and a dedication to Philip VI, who commissioned the work. Roberto Crespo showed that much of the preface was translated directly from William of Aragon's commentary (Crespo 1973). The preface and the dedication, however, are attached to two very different translations, one in prose and the other in prose and verse. Since it is unlikely that Jean wrote both of the translations, deciding which work could justifiably be ascribed to the poet of the **Roman de la Rose** became an early concern for critics. Glynnis Cropp has also examined this prologue (Cropp 1982, **Romania**), discovering that its sources include four pre-existing prologues. She also finds that the translator who produced the later, somewhat longer prologue, which is found attached to the **Livre de Boece de Consolation** (Dwyer 7), was probably the person responsible for producing the glosses in the glossed version of that translation.

The problem of the ambiguous works was first recognized by Léopold Delisle. He published a notice of forty-seven manuscripts found in the Bibliothèque Nationale which contain **Consolatio** translations, and among these he discerns eight translations, including manuscripts of the two translations in question. Working primarily on intuition, he assigned the prose work to Jean de Meun:

> Des quarante-sept manuscrits de la **Consolation philosophique** que possède la Bibliothèque nationale, le seul qui me semble pouvoir être rapporté à la fin du XIIIe siècle ou au commencement du XIVe est un fragment de trois colonnes et demie, qui se trouve au fol. 48 du ms. latin 8654 B et qui est intitulé: "Ici sunt plusieurs notables de la translacion du liver Boëce de **Consolacion**, que mestre Jehan de Meun translata en françois. . . ."
> La date du ms. latin 8654 B ne permet guère de suspecter l'exactitude de la rubrique qu'on vient de lire. Il faut en conclure que la traduction de la **Consolation** commençant par les mots "Halas! Je qui jadis fis jolives chançonnetes . . . ." est bien l'oeuvre de Jean de Meung. (Delisle 1873, 5-6)

There follows, then, a brief description of this translation and of the translation containing the pirated dedication by Jean de Meun.

The response to Delisle's work was almost immediate. In 1873, Paul Meyer reviewed the article, in which Delisle numbered the prose translation as "I" and the verse-prose translation as "II." Meyer writes, "Pour moi je crois que la seconde seule (dont on a une infinité de mss.) est de Jean de Meun" (Meyer 1873), and so, without further comment or scholarly justification, he dismisses Delisle's ascription and claims that the verse-prose translation is the work of the poet of the **Rose**. Paul Meyer's respected opinion was readily accepted by critics of the **Consolatio** translations for decades. As has already been pointed out, Paulin Paris, following Meyer, assigned the verse-prose translation to Jean de Meun in his article (Paris 1881), and his ascription was unquestioning.

The next development in this matter occurs in Stewart's **Essay** (Stewart 1891). The author is aware of the problem of the two different translations bearing the identical dedication to Philip IV, and he avoids any decision of his own on the matter, but he presents fresh information concerning Chaucer's possible use of a French translation in the preparation of his Middle English **Boece**. He prints parallel passages from the prose translation (from BN MS fr. 1097), Chaucer's translation, and the verse-prose translation, showing that there is reason to believe that Chaucer had access to the work in prose but not to the one in verse-prose.

Stewart is not interested, however, in making a definitive statement concerning Chaucer's use of a manuscript (similar, he says, to BN MS fr. 1097), so he concludes his remarks with, "Nothing short of a thoroughgoing and systematic comparison of [the **Boece** and the prose translation] could make an opinion on the subject worth having, and so I do not propose to offer one" (Stewart 1891, 206). Although nothing definitive is accomplished here, something of importance is hinted at: Chaucer would probably have used the translation by Jean de Meun, had he used a French translation at all. This argument is seldom cited directly, but it does have some validity. Chaucer's initial interest in Boethius was probably stimulated by his reading of the **Roman de la Rose**, so his reading of the **Consolatio** translation by the same author would be a logical consequence of that interest.

The passage from the **Roman de la Rose** which critics point to as the signal to Chaucer to make a translation reads:

> Ce puet l'en bien des clers enquerre
> Qui **Boece de Confort** lisent,
> Et les sentences qui la gisent;
> **Dont grans biens as gens laiz feroit**
> **Qui bien le lor translateroit.** (ll. 5052-6)
> (Skeat 1894-7, x)

It is possible that these lines influenced Chaucer's decision to translate the **Consolatio**, but the problem will be discussed more fully in the chapter on Chaucer. Convincing proof that the prose translation represented by BN MS fr. 1097 was the genuine Jean de Meun translation came only in 1913. Ernest Langlois, after having completed his edition of the **Roman de la Rose** in 1912 (E. Langlois 1912), subjected the two different **Consolatio** translations to a very thorough linguistic analysis (primarily, a study of the dialects of the translators), which indicated that the verse-prose work could not be from the pen of Jean de Meun, but that the prose work very well could be (E. Langlois 1913). To this argument he added others which reinforce his findings: Jean de Meun's earlier translations are also into prose, and the prose **Consolatio** translation is more precise in spirit than the verse-prose work (this reverses the opinion held by Meyer, returning to the position maintained by Delisle). Scholarship on the Jean de Meun **Consolatio** translation had finally gained a firm footing.

Nevertheless, a final argument favoring the prose translation as the work of Jean de Meun appeared (Cline 1936). James Cline noticed that F.N. Robinson, in his edition of Chaucer, had not accepted Ernest Langlois' attribution to Jean of the prose translation. Using information from the dedication and citing medieval translation methods, he deduced that the prose work was by Jean. In the dedication, Jean promises to hold from the original "plainement la sentence." Cline argues that this statement had been generally misunderstood to mean that Jean was promising a "free translation." "Free translation" does not properly convey Jean's phrase. It refers, rather, to an "open" or literal translation which does no violence to the original idiom. Cline bases his argument on earlier English translations of the Bible which had made similar promises. Taken in the sense in which Cline argues, the dedication to Philip IV more accurately describes the prose translation. The article is interesting primarily for the light it casts upon late medieval translation theory, a field in which relatively little information exists. The definitive arguments in favor of the prose translation as Jean's work, however, are generally held to be those maintained in the article by Ernest Langlois (E. Langlois 1913). A. van de Vyver, in an article that offers a checklist of all the then-known European **Consolatio** translations (van de Vyver 1939), concurs with this finding.

Also, in an article on the medieval **Consolatio** tradition (Dedeck-Héry 1936), Venceslas Louis Dedeck-Héry published a full transcription of the manuscript fragment which first led Léopold Delisle to assign the prose translation to Jean de Meun (BN MS lat. 8654 B). The study shows that this fragment is not a faithful copying out of a complete manuscript of Jean's translation; the fragment shows influence from dialects of the northwest of France. This premier article introduces the work of a critic who eventually would establish a text and publish an edition of Jean de Meun's translation.

By 1940, Dedeck-Héry was able to group the then-known manuscripts of Jean de Meun's prose translation into two groups or families, indicating well-argued affiliations among them (Dedeck-Héry 1940). His "a" group proved to be truer to a proto-text than group "b," and it was a manuscript from group "a" which, as shall be seen, Chaucer probably used in preparing his **Boece**. For further information on the manuscripts of Jean de Meun's translation, see articles by Richard Dwyer (Dwyer 1976), Keith Atkinson (Atkinson 1978), and Glynnis Cropp (Cropp 1979, "Quelques manuscrits").

Dedeck-Héry died in 1946. He had dedicated much of his professional life to work on Jean de Meun's translation. His edition, which lay all but completed at the time of his death, was published in 1952 (Dedeck-Héry 1952). It remains the critical edition of the Jean de Meun text.

This third section of the chapter focuses on two areas of criticism: 1) studies of the text of Jean de Meun's translation and 2) studies of the relationship of the text to Chaucer's translation. In the first category, there are few articles. A.J. Denomy's study of the vocabulary used in Jean's translation (Denomy 1954) presents a list of all words which appeared in the French language for the first time in this work. Maude Temple provided information about a glossed manuscript of Jean's translation (Temple 1917) which she claims to be basic to the school of Neo-Victorine thinkers of the early fifteenth century.

Until Stewart's **Essay** appeared in 1891, the idea that Chaucer might have used a French translation in writing his **Boece** had been dismissed. But Stewart showed that the French text consulted in earlier evaluations of the problem was not the work of Jean de Meun. He proceeded to show through a few parallel passages that Chaucer probably had access to the prose translation, which is typified by BN MS fr. 1097. Mark Liddell presented more parallel passages and came to the conclusion that Chaucer did, in fact, use the French translation mentioned by Stewart (Liddell 1895). Also in 1895, Mark Liddell had promised a parallel edition of Chaucer and the French translation which he indicated Chaucer had used. He was working on both before definite proof had been presented that the prose translation was the work of Jean and before the critical edition of Jean's work had been published. Liddell's volume never appeared.

Later, two critics working independently arrived at a more
positive conclusion that Chaucer had made use of Jean's **Consolatio**
translation. Bernard Jefferson, in his book on Chaucer's **Boece** (Jefferson
1917), gives further evidence in the form of parallel passages that Chaucer
had used Jean's work as an aid in preparing his own. He had, of course,
the advantage of proof that he was dealing with the genuine Jean de Meun
translation. In the same year, John Livingston Lowes argued that the
vocabulary and syntax of Jean's work are very similar to Chaucer's (Lowes
1917). He based his study on excerpts which had first appeared in
Langlois' article. Lowes' work is much more extensive and conclusive
than the work of either Stewart or Liddell, but it, too, suffers from lack of
a complete French text of Jean's work.

Dedeck-Héry returned to the manuscripts of Jean's and Chaucer's
translations and produced a comprehensive catalogue of all the parallels
between the works (Dedeck-Héry 1937). He was able to conclude that
Chaucer had, in all probability, used Jean de Meun's text as an aid in
preparing his own translation. Somewhat later (Dedeck-Héry 1944), he
concluded that the closest analogue to Chaucer's **Boece** among the
manuscripts of Jean de Meun's translation is Besançon, MS 434, one of
the manuscripts from group "a" of his earlier study. He felt that **the**
manuscript used by Chaucer had not yet been found, but he expressed
hope that such a manuscript, perhaps containing the text of Jean's
translation as well as the commentary which Chaucer consulted, might
one day be found.

The Besançon MS 434 was first mentioned in a summary of
previously unnoticed manuscripts of medieval French **Consolatio**
translations compiled by Louise Stone (Stone 1937) a few years before
Dedeck-Héry began his work. Robert Lucas published a list of all the
known manuscripts of the Jean de Meun translation (Lucas 1970), and
many of these had not been consulted by Dedeck-Héry when he compiled
his edition of the work. The following year, Richard Dwyer published
information about yet another manuscript in the tradition (Dwyer 1971).
Eventually, the discovery of more manuscripts may necessitate a revision
of the original critical edition.

As seen above, the criticism on Jean de Meun's **Consolatio**
translation represents something of a comedy of scholarly errors. The
major problems in the early criticism have been satisfactorily solved, but
many subtle problems remain. Information has been accumulating for

nearly a century, and we are still far from any clear picture of Jean de Meun himself or a thorough evaluation of his translation and its significance. Nevertheless, much groundwork has been laid, and in many instances, fact finally has replaced speculation.

List of Relevant Titles

1. Atkinson, J. Keith. "Some Further Confirmations and Attributions of Manuscripts of the Mediaeval French Boethius." **Medium Aevum** 47 (1978) 22-9.

    Atkinson adds more manuscripts to the list published by Dwyer in 1976 (see Dwyer 1976).

2. Cline, James M. "Chaucer and Jean de Meun: **De Consolatione Philosophiae**." **Journal of English Literary History** 3 (1936): 170-81.

    Using medieval translation practices to formulate a theory, Cline studies Jean de Meun's dedication to Philip IV to help prove that the prose translation is by the author of the **Roman de la Rose**. The article is particularly interesting for the light it casts upon medieval translation techniques.

3. Cohn, Norman. **The World View of a Thirteenth-Century Parisian Intellectual: Jean de Meun and the** Roman de la Rose. Newcastle upon Tyne: University of Durham, 1961.

    Cohn examines Jean de Meun's philosophical ideas in the context of the thirteenth-century university tradition.

4. Crespo, Roberto. "Jean de Meun traduttore della **Consolatio Philosophiae** de Boezio." **Atti della Academia della Scienza de Torino:**

Classe de Scienze morali, Storiche e
Filologiche 103 (1969): 71-170.

Crespo gives a comprehensive study of Jean de
Meun's Consolatio translation, summarizing
the facts for an Italian audience.

5.   ----------. "Il prologo alla traduzione della
        Consolatio Philosophiae di Jean de Meun e
        il Commento di Guglielmo d'Aragona." In
        Romanitas et Christianitas: Studia Iano
        Henrico Waszink AD Kal. Nov. A.
        1973, 13 lustra complenti oblata, edited
        by Boer, et al., 55-70. Amsterdam: North-Holland
        Publishing, 1973.

        Crespo attempts to prove that much of Jean de
        Meun's preface to his Consolatio translation
        was translated from the commentary by William
        of Aragon.

6.   Cropp, Glynnis M. "Quelques manuscrits
        méconnus de la traduction en prose de la
        Consolatio Philosophiae par Jean de Meun."
        Scriptorium 33 (1979): 260-6.

        Four additions are made to the list of manuscripts
        of Jean de Meun's prose Consolatio translation.

7.   ----------. "Le Prologue de Jean de Meun et Le
        Livre de Boece de Consolacion."
        Romania 103 (1982): 278-98.

        In this article, Cropp examines the prologue found
        at the beginning of the Jean de Meun prose
        Consolatio translation and the somewhat longer
        prologue found at the beginning of the verse-prose
        translation. The verse-prose translation also bears
        Jean's name, but it has been shown not to be his

work. She finds that the Jean de Meun prologue is an amalgam of four pre-existing prologues; the translator who produced the "continuation of the prologue" is less faithful to the Latin sources than Jean, but that translator is probably also the commentator who is responsible for the glosses in the glossed version of the **Livre de Boece de Consolation.**

8.   Dedeck-Héry, Venceslas Louis. "Un Fragment inédit de la traduction de la **Consolation** de Boèce par Jean de Meun." **Romanic Review** 27 (1936): 110-24.

This article contains a thorough study of the fragmentary **Consolatio** translation (BN MS latin 8654) which originally helped Delisle identify the prose translation bearing the dedication to Philip IV as the work of Jean de Meun.

9.   ----------. "Jean de Meun et Chaucer, traducteurs de la **Consolation** de Boèce." **PMLA** 52 (1937): 967-91.

Using a series of parallel texts, the author shows that Chaucer consulted the Jean de Meun prose translation of the **Consolatio** in preparing his own **Boece.**

10.   ----------. "The Manuscripts of the Translation of Boethius' **Consolatio** by Jean de Meung." **Speculum** 15 (1940): 432-43.

Dedeck-Héry divides the seventeen manuscripts of Jean de Meun's prose translation into two groups, drawing affiliations for the nine manuscripts of group "a" and the eight of group "b." Group "a," and particularly the manuscripts designated as P-1, are the basis of Dedeck-Héry's edition of the translation.

11. ----------. "Le **Boèce** de Chaucer et les manuscrits français de la **Consolation** de Jean de Meun." **PMLA** 59 (1944): 18-25.

Among the manuscripts of Jean de Meun's translation of the **Consolatio**, Dedeck-Héry indicates one, "B" (Besançon 434), which most nearly corresponds to Chaucer's work. But he indicates that **the** manuscript which Chaucer consulted remains to be found.

12. ----------, ed. "Boethius' **De Consolatione** by Jean de Meun." **Mediaeval Studies** 14 (1952): 165-275.

This is the critical edition of the Jean de Meun **Consolatio** translation.

13. Delisle, Léopold. "Anciennes traductions françaises de la **Consolation** de Boëce conservées à la Bibliothèque Nationale." **Bibliothèque de l'école des Chartes** 34 (1873): 5-32.

This article contains the first attribution of the all-prose translation of the **Consolatio** (including the important BN MS fr. 1097) to Jean de Meun. The author bases the ascription upon a rubric found in BN MS Latin 8654B.

14. Denomy, Alex J. "The Vocabulary of Jean de Meun's Translation of Boethius' **De Consolatione Philosophiae**." **Mediaeval Studies** 16 (1954): 19-34.

Denomy lists the words which first entered the
French language through Jean de Meun's
Consolatio translation.

15.   Dwyer, Richard A. "Manuscripts of the Medieval
       French Boethius." **Notes and Queries** 216
       (1971): 124-5.

       Among the several additions to the list of
       manuscripts of medieval French **Consolatio**
       translations prepared by Lucas in his article (Lucas
       1970), Dwyer adds one to the list of prose
       translations by Jean de Meun.

16.   ----------. **Boethian Fictions: Narratives in
       the Medieval French Versions of the**
       Consolatio Philosophiae. Mediaeval Academy of
       America, no. 83. Cambridge, Mass.: Mediaeval
       Academy of America, 1976.

       Dwyer examines the narrative interpolations which
       were made into the text of the **Consolatio** by its
       medieval French translators. Jean de Meun does
       not add such extended narratives, but this study is
       included here because it sheds light upon the
       translation methodology of Jean's period.

17.   Friedman, Albert B. "Jean de Meun an
       Englishman?" **Modern Language Notes** 65
       (1950): 319-25.

       Friedman traces the sixteenth, seventeenth, and
       eighteenth-century mistaken notion that Jean de
       Meun was an Englishman (referred to as John
       Moon).

18.   Jefferson, Bernard L. **Chaucer and the**
       Consolation of Philosophy **of Boethius**. 1917.
       Reprint. New York: Haskell House, 1965.

This work is included here because the author held the opinion that Chaucer used the Jean de Meun translation in preparing his **Boèce**, and the evidence presented in his book is convincing.

19. Langlois, Charles-Victor. "La **Consolation** de Boèce, d'après Jean de Meun et plusieurs autres." In **La Vie en France au moyen âge**. Vol. 4, **La Vie spirituelle**, 269-326. Paris: Librairie Hachette, 1928.

This is an update of the list of **Consolatio** translations given in 1873 by Delisle. Since Delisle wrote, the controversy concerning the authorship of the prose translation bearing Jean de Meun's dedication to Philip IV had been settled, ascribing that translation to Jean de Meun. The article takes this new information into account.

20. Langlois, Ernest, ed. Le Roman de la Rose **par Guillaume de Lorris et Jean de Meun**. 5 vols. Société des Textes Français. Paris: Firmin Didot, 1912.

Langlois' work on this edition led to the proof that the prose translation with the dedication to Philip IV was by Jean de Meun.

21. ----------. "La Traduction de Boèce par Jean de Meun." **Romania** 42 (1913): 331-69.

Langlois establishes proof that the prose translation bearing the dedication to Philip IV is the Jean de Meun translation.

22. Liddell, Mark. "Chaucer's Translation of Boece's 'Boke of Comfort' (Announcement of Chaucer's Use of the French Translation in His Own

Translation of Boethius)." **Academy** 1 (1895): 227.

This is the first systematic effort [after Stewart's hint in his **Essay** (see Stewart 1891, 203-6)] to show, through parallel passages from the Latin text, Chaucer's **Boèce**, and Jean de Meun's translation, that Chaucer was definitely influenced by Jean de Meun's work.

23.   Louis, Réné. "Esquisse d'une biographie de Jean de Meun, Continuateur du **Roman de la Rose** de Guillaume de Lorris." In **Études lingériennes d'histoire et d'archéologie médiévale**, 257-65. Paris: Publications de la Société, 1975.

Louis draws together all the scattered facts we know about the life of Jean de Meun. His sources include Jean's works and a few historical documents.

24.   Lowes, John Livingston. "Chaucer's **Boethius** and Jean de Meun." **Romanic Review** 8 (1917): 383-400.

Lowes uses material from Jean de Meun's prose translation which appeared in Ernest Langlois' article of 1913. He gives more extensive and more conclusive evidence of Chaucer's use of Jean de Meun's translation in preparing his own.

25.   Lucas, Robert H. "Mediaeval French Translations of the Latin Classics to 1500." **Speculum** 45 (1970): 225-53.

Included in this article is a list of the then-known manuscripts of Jean de Meun's prose translation.

26.   Meyer, Paul. Review of "Anciennes traductions
       françaises de la **Consolation** du Boëce
       conservées à la Bibliothèque Nationale"
       [**Bibliothèque de l'École des Chartes**, vol.
       34], by Léopold Delisle. **Romania** 2 (1873):
       271-3.

       This review of Delisle's article (Delisle 1873)
       attributes the verse-prose translation (with a
       dedication to Philip IV) to Jean de Meun. This
       ascription lacks, however, any scholarly
       justification and was finally proved wrong.

27.   Paris, Paulin. "Jean de Meun, traducteur et poète."
       In **Histoire littéraire de la France** 28
       (1881): 391-439.

       Paris describes Jean's works, apart from the
       Roman de la Rose. The author chooses to
       discuss, however, the verse-prose **Consolatio**
       rather than the prose work which was eventually
       ascribed to Jean.

28.   Patch, Howard Rollin. **The Tradition of
       Boethius: A Study of His Importance in
       Medieval Culture.** New York: Oxford
       University Press, 1935.

       Howard Patch casts his vote with Delisle (Delisle
       1873), ascribing the prose **Consolatio**
       translation (with its dedication to Philip IV) to
       Jean de Meun.

29.   Quichert, J. "Jean de Meung et sa maison à Paris."
       Bibliothèque de l'École des Chartes nv.
       (1880): 46-52.

Quichert gives information from medieval documents concerning a house occupied by Jean de Meun during his later years in Paris.

30.   Ralph, Dorothy Marie. "Jean de Meun, the Voltaire of the Middle Ages." Ph.D. diss., University of Illinois (Urbana), 1940.

Ralph draws several parallels between the times and philosophies of Jean de Meun and Voltaire. He gives an interesting perspective on Jean de Meun as a medieval thinker.

31.   Skeat, Walter W., ed. **The Complete Works of Geoffrey Chaucer.** Oxford University Press, 1894-7. Reprint. London: Oxford University Press, 1933.

This edition is included here because a quotation from it is used in this chapter.

32.   Stewart, Hugh Fraser. **Boethius: An Essay.** London: 1891. Reprint. New York: Burt Franklin, 1974.

The book contains a chapter summarizing the early translations of the **Consolatio.** Stewart points out that, though the verse-prose translation which Paul Meyer (Meyer 1873) assigned to Jean de Meun does appear in several extant manuscripts, the prose translation assigned to Jean by Delisle (Delisle 1873) influenced Chaucer's translation. With this chapter, Stewart effectively re-opened the question of the influence of Jean upon Chaucer.

33.   Stone, Louise W. "Old French Translations of the **De Consolatione Philosophiae** of Boethius:

Some Unnoticed Manuscripts". **Medium Aevum** 6 (1937): 21-30.

Among the many medieval French manuscripts of the various **Consolatio** translations listed in this article, there also appear several previously unlisted manuscripts of the Jean de Meun translation. The manuscript which became the basis of the critical edition prepared by Dedeck-Héry (Dedeck-Héry 1952) is mentioned on this list.

34. Temple, Maude Elizabeth. "The Glossed **Boèce de Consolation** of Jean de Meung: Medieval Prolegomena to French Classic Rationalism." **PMLA** [Proceedings for the Thirty-Fourth Annual Meeting of 1916] 32 (1917): xxviii.

This is a note about the importance to the early fifteenth-century school of Neo-Victorine thinkers of a glossed manuscript of Jean de Meun's **Consolatio** translation.

35. Thomas, Antoine. "Jean de Meun ou de Meung." In **Encyclopédie des sciences, des lettres et des arts (La Grande Encyclopédie)**, sv. Paris: H. Lamirault, c.1900.

This is a brief article summarizing the few facts we know about the life of Jean de Meun.

36. Thomas, Antoine, and Mario Roques. "Traductions françaises de la **Consolation Philosophiae** de Boèce." In **Histoire littéraire de la France** 37 (1938): 419-506 and 542-47.

Thomas and Roques, following Delisle (Delisle 1873) and others, accept the prose **Consolatio** translation with the dedication to Philip IV as the work of Jean de Meun.

37. van de Vyver, A. "Les Traductions du **De Consolatione philosophiae** de Boèce en littérature comparée." **Humanisme et Renaissance** 6 (1939): 247-73.

This article contains a catalogue of all the then-known medieval European **Consolatio** translations. Most of the currently-recognized medieval French translations are included.

Other Medieval
French **Consolatio** Translations

One of the major obstacles to furthering scholarship on the tradition of medieval French **Consolatio** translations has been the problem of inventory, both in the number of manuscripts and in the number of translations. At first, forty-seven manuscripts in French in the Bibliothèque Nationale were divided into eight different translations. But new manuscripts continue to be noted in libraries around the world, and new problems continue to appear.

Each critic of the tradition has assessed the various translations for different purposes and in different ways, and each has classified them in systems using different rubrics. For this reason, there is some difficulty in coordinating information from the various sources. I will begin this chapter by indicating the correspondence between these listings, in order to avoid any possible confusion of references made in the criticism and in the remainder of this chapter.

Richard Dwyer has presented a list on which the several French translations are assigned numbers which generally reflect the chronology in which they were prepared, with lower numbers being given to earlier works (Dwyer 1976):

1. Prose version by an anonymous Burgundian (early thirteenth century)
2. Prose version by an anonymous Wallonian (late thirteenth century)
3. Prose version by Bonaventura da Demena (late thirteenth century)
4. Prose version by Pierre de Paris (ca. 1305-9)
5. Prose version by Jean de Meun (ca. 1300)
6. Mixed prose and verse version (early fourteenth century)
7. Revised mixed version (Anonymous verse-prose translation) (mid-fourteenth century)

8. Verse version by the Anonymous of Meun
    (mid-fourteenth century)
9. Verse version by Renaut de Louhans (ca. 1336-7)
10. Verse revision of Renaut by an anonymous
    Benedictine monk (ca. 1380)
11. Verse abbreviation of Renaut (fourteenth century)
12. Second mixed version (early fifteenth century?)
13. Mixed version printed by Colard Mansion:
    Bruges, 1477, and reprinted by Antoine Verard:
    Paris, 1494

Because it is so recent and so complete, this is probably the best listing
for critical work on the tradition, but the categories developed by Glynnis
Cropp for the "revised mixed version," also called the "anonymous verse-
prose translation," of the mid-fourteenth century (Dwyer 7) reflect work
done toward a critical edition of that translation and they should be adapted
(Cropp 1979, **Notes and Queries**). In one of her articles, Cropp adds
manuscripts which were not included on Dwyer's list, dividing them into
two traditions: I) Manuscripts without glosses, and II) Manuscripts with
glosses. All of these various manuscripts are fully described by Cropp in
a later publication (Cropp 1982/1983). In a review of Dwyer's book,
Keith Atkinson (Atkinson 1978) complains, for valid reasons, that Dwyer
should not have created a new system of numbering for the manuscripts;
he finds the Thomas and Roques system to be superior to Dwyer's (see
Thomas and Roques 1938).

    The history of systematizing the translations begins with
Léopold Delisle (Delisle 1873). The acquisition by the Bibliothèque
Nationale of a new manuscript containing the **Consolatio** prompted
Delisle to review all such manuscripts held by the library. He discerned
eight translations:

I.	Jean de Meun's prose translation	(Dwyer 5)
II.	The verse-prose translation falsely attributed to Jean de Meun	(Dwyer 7)
III.	An anonymous verse-prose translation	(Dwyer 6)
IV.	A translation usually designated as the anonymous of Meun	(Dwyer 8)

This inventory yields four verse, two verse-prose, and two prose translations. The author's purpose in systematizing his information is simple:

> Sans donc examiner les autres questions qui se rattachent à ce point de notre histoire littéraire, et sans même essayer un classement chronologique, j'ai cru qu'il serait utile d'indiquer exactement les différents textes français de la **Consolation**, et d'en citer des passages d'après lesquels on pourra constater l'identité des exemplaires conservés dans les autres bibliothèques. (Delisle 1873, 5)

Delisle thus provides a checklist for others who might be interested in working with the translation tradition. As pointed out in the first section of this chapter, Delisle identified the prose translation of Jean de Meun, so it appears correctly labeled on his listing. His article also made another important contribution: it proved that the translation beginning with "Celui qui bien bat les boissons," translation VIII (Dwyer 10), could not have been the work of Charles d'Orléans. Delisle's conscientious article was, however, a solid beginning for studies of these translations. For a description of a manuscript which corresponds closely to the translation designated as Dwyer 10, see an article, "An Unnoticed Manuscript of a Medieval French Verse Translation of the **Consolatio** of Boethius," by Glynnis Cropp (Cropp 1984).

A problem did occur, however, when Paul Meyer reviewed Delisle's article (Meyer 1873). Expressing an opinion, but basing it on no detailed study, Meyer reduced Delisle's list from eight to six translations. He said that Delisle's III (Dwyer 6) and II (Dwyer 10) seemed to be too similar to count as separate translations. Such is also the case, he found, with VI (Dwyer 11) and VIII (Dwyer 10). Meyer's dismissal of two translations was based on an oversight: the critics were not dealing with several discrete and isolated translations; they had before them a tradition of translations, an intricately woven fabric of works, many of which were influenced by, or based on, earlier translations. Ernest Langlois managed to add a seventh translation, the one by Pierre de Paris, to the six accepted by Meyer before the turn of the Centruy (E. Langlois 1889). Paul Meyer's revision was eventually abandoned, and an appreciation of the complexity of the medieval French tradition grew.

The negative effects of Meyer's revisions are seen in a study of the whole European Boethian tradition, which was produced by Hugh Fraser Stewart (Stewart 1891). He proposes no system of classification for the French translations, but he discusses them under the following headings: "The Provençal Poem, Boëce"; "Anonymous Writer (thirteenth century) and Jehan de Meun (1297-1305)," which concerns the revised mixed version (Dwyer 7) and the translation (Dwyer 5) which later proved to be the work of Jean de Meun; "Pierre de Paris (thirteenth or early fourteenth century)" (Dwyer 4); "Anonymous Poet (138- ?)" (Dwyer 10); "Jehan de Cis (fourteenth century)" (Dwyer 8), which later was shown to have been falsely attributed to Jean de Cis; and "Frère Renaut de Louhans" (Dwyer 9). Because of Meyer's revision, Stewart did not examine the two translations which were dismissed from Delisle's list. Had he done so, he might have discovered many interesting facts about the interrelationships between the prose translation (Dwyer 5) and Chaucer's **Boece**. His work is basically descriptive, but it must be praised for the original contributions which his thorough research and personal review of the translations yield. At that time, criticism of the tradition had not yet reached a level of comparative study.

An updated list of medieval French **Consolatio** translations was published by Charles-Victor Langlois (C.-V. Langlois 1928). His work adds few new facts, but it does bring together information never before printed in a general study, and it reflects an expanding view of the tradition. His discussion and descriptions include not only the translations available at his time but also medieval French paraphrases of the **Consolatio**. His study is not limited to translations found in only one library, so it is more complete than Delisle's work (Delisle 1873).

C.-V. Langlois		Delisle	Dwyer
I.	A paraphrase by Simund de Freine	-	-
II.	An anonymous Burgundian translation	-	1
III.	A Wallonian Prose translation	-	2

IVa.	Paraphrases of the **Consolatio** (in the **Roman de la Rose**)	-	-
IVb.	The prose translation by Jean de Meun	I	5
V.	The translation by Pierre de Paris	-	4
VIa.	An anonymous verse-prose translation	III	6
VIb.	The anonymous verse-prose translation once falsely attributed to Jean de Meun	II	7
VII.	A translation by an anonymous writer of Meun	IV	8
VIII.	The translation by Bonaventura da Demena	V	3
IX.	The translation by Renault de Louhans	VII	9
Xa.	The translation opening with "Celui qui bien bat les boissons"	VIII	10
Xb.	A verse abbreviation of Renaut's translation	VI	11

On this list, Jean de Meun is properly assigned the prose translation which had finally been ascribed to him by Ernest Langlois (E. Langlois 1913). Also agreeing with the article of 1913, Charles-Victor Langlois notes the relationship between translations VIa (Dwyer 6) and VIb (Dwyer 7). The second work, VIb, is a reworking of VIa, but "les deux versions ne sont donc pas deux éditions successives d'un même traducteur" (C.-V. Langlois 1928, 283). The second translator arbitrarily made changes in the text of VIa, "but not always for the better." Not only did the translator of VIb pirate the prologue and preface from Jean de Meun's work, he also plagiarized from the text of VIa. Finally, C.-V. Langlois agrees with Meyer in classifying translation Xb (Dwyer 11) as an abridgement of Xa (Dwyer 10).

This list indicates a developing understanding of the complexity of the medieval French **Consolatio** tradition in two ways. First, it includes information about the paraphrases (Jean de Meun's paraphrases in the **Roman de la Rose** certainly had importance both for the French tradition and for the European tradition as a whole); and second, it begins to add information about the complex affinities among the translations.

As an example of the complexity of relationships within this tradition, Keith Atkinson and Glynnis Cropp have studied three translations [(Thomas and Roques V, VI, and IX) or (Dwyer 6, 7, and 9)], establishing the affinities between them (Atkinson and Cropp 1985). Translation V (Dwyer 6) is found to be the oldest of the three and parental to the other two.

A work by Howard Patch discusses the entire European tradition of Boethius (Patch 1935). Although the book is an essential tool in Boethian studies, giving information on legends and facts about the life of the author of the **Consolatio,** his influence in the history of ideas, and the influence of Boethius' last work upon literature, the chapter on the translations is too general to be truly helpful. From the French tradition, Patch describes the Provençal version and the translation by Renaut de Louhans. Only short mention is made of some of the other translations. The bibliographical material given on pages 153-55, however, is valuable, and it is current to 1935. The book remains, however, one of the best general introductions to basic problems students encounter in Boethian research.

Charles-Victor Langlois was aware that his listing produced only a preliminary, utilitarian announcement of the existence of the various translations, and that it would be replaced by a more detailed analysis of the material. He prefaces his short study with: "Toutes ces traductions seront étudiées d'ensemble, synoptiquement, au t. XXXII, en préparation, de l'Histoire littéraire de la France" (C.-V. Langlois 1928, 424).

The study mentioned above, begun by Antoine Thomas and finished by Mario Roques, first appeared in volume thirty-seven rather than volume thirty-two; it is the first which attempts to be comprehensive, seeking to include the whole medieval French tradition (Thomas and Roques 1938). The authors thoroughly examine manuscripts of all the translations, and their descriptions include original insights as well as facts gleaned from earlier secondary sources. There is, however, no attempt to be exhaustive in describing the various works. In his opening paragraph, Thomas explains: "Nous nous proposons de faire connaître ici les traductions françaises qui en ont été faites depuis le début du treizième jusqu'au milieu du quatorzième siècle" (Thomas and Roques 1938, 419). Later he continues:

Dans le cadre que nous impose le plan de l'**Histoire**
littéraire, il nous est impossible, comme on pense, de
consacrer une étude approfondie à toutes les traductions que nous
avons passées en revue. Nous ne pouvons guère offrir au lecteur
qu'un échantillon de chacune d'elles, pour lui permettre de juger
du procédé et du mérite de chaque traducteur. Nous avons choisi
à cet effet le mètre 5 (l'âge d'or) du livre II . . . . (Thomas and
Roques 1938, 424)

The article begins with a summary statement on the medieval
commentaries on Boethius' **Consolatio** and on the earlier translations or
paraphrases (by Alfred the Great, Notker Labeo, the Old Provençal
Boëce, and the work by Simund de Freine). The descriptions include
information on the major manuscripts, historical data on the known
translators, and linguistic studies of the texts. Thomas and Roques
discuss nine translations in some detail, and allude briefly to two others:

Thomas and Roques	Dwyer
I.	1
II.	2
III.	5
IV.	4
V.	6
VI.	7
VII.	8
VIII.	3
IX.	9
A translation left unnumbered, but briefly mentioned in the article	10
A translation mentioned only in an addendum to the article	11

One of the most important qualities of this work derives from the fact that
the authors have acquainted themselves so well with the original
manuscripts. Also, for the first time in a general study, there is an
appreciation of the importance of the commentaries. Though they are but

briefly mentioned at the beginning of the article, the commentaries are henceforth known to be of general interest to readers researching the tradition. In this context, it is necessary to mention the comprehensive study by Pierre Courcelle which is useful to any student of the commentaries on the **Consolatio** (Courcelle 1967).

A short list of translations was published by A. van de Vyver (van de Vyver 1939), "Les Traductions du **De Consolatione Philosophiae** de Boèce en littérature comparée." The author first summarizes the works of Boethius, indicating their importance in transmitting the knowledge of Classical Antiquity to the Middle Ages, then noting the importance of their translation in a European context: "Pour l'histoire de l'humanisme, il importe d'établir, avec plus de précision qu'on ne l'a fait, la part que, par les traductions, chaque langue moderne a prise à la transmission de cet héritage antique" (van de Vyver 1939, 247). The article mentions and briefly describes all the then-known translations. Part I lists the translations which exist only in manuscript form; Part II lists the incunabula. Finally, in a general discussion, it touches on the importance of the comparative studies for the **Consolatio** tradition. Van de Vyver had access to Thomas and Roques' article of the preceding year, so the translations are assigned the numbers from that system, but they are discussed in a different order. Van de Vyver's study is very useful for quick reference to the particular translations. The information is surprisingly detailed, considering the brevity of the entries.

More recently, there appeared a study of the medieval French **Consolatio** tradition by Richard Dwyer. The author examines the many narrative digressions incorporated into the translations. He finds that they reflect a general, "inorganic" aspect of medieval aesthetics:

> When a translator intrudes into a hymn of universal love a rape story, he may impede our comprehension of universal love. But when he extends examples in a poem on death's universal sway to include more persons than Roman ex-consuls, he advances our understanding of the frightfulness of that sway. Between these extremes occur some interesting effects of medieval literary eclecticism. (Dwyer 1976, 87)

The author has pinpointed an important aspect of the medieval French **Consolatio** tradition and suggests a classification of the digressions. It is in Appendix II of this book that Dwyer's listing of translations and manuscripts, the listing which has been referred to throughout this chapter, is to be found.

In the following discussion of studies on the translations in the medieval French tradition, I will not attempt to present the development of all the factual data which scholars have discovered. Summaries of this sort exist in the general studies which were mentioned in the previous section of this chapter. The article by Thomas and Roques (Thomas and Roques 1938) is particularly useful for such information, and it usually identifies the source in which the translations are first mentioned. I will treat the works, where possible, in the order in which they appear on Dwyer's list (Dwyer 1976). Two items which do not appear on his list will be dealt with chronologically, before discussing the translations.

The Old Provençal **Boëce** dates from the tenth century, and it is preserved as a fragment in a single eleventh-century manuscript in the Public Library of Orléans, MS 374. It was first published by Raynouard (Raynouard 1813-1817), but this version was superseded by an edition by Paul Meyer which remains the critical edition of the text (Meyer 1877). Only about thirty-two stanzas survive from this re-working of the **Consolatio,** but they constitute the oldest extant poetic work in Provençal. Franz Hüdgens published the text along with its translation into modern German (Hüdgens 1884). This study also compares the Provençal version with the Latin original. The notes accompanying the text are extensive and reliable.

A study of the Old Provençal text was published by Nicola Zingarelli (Zingarelli 1920), and it is accompanied by a thorough study of its content. As for the linguistic aspects of the work, Vladimir Rabotine, in his "Le **Boëce** provençal: étude linguistique," not only reprints the text but also discusses both its phonetic and morphological points of interest (Rabotine 1930). A summary study was produced by Christoph Schwarze (Schwarze 1963); it is useful as a compendium of facts rather than for new information. Guy Mermier has prepared a translation of the work into Modern English (Mermier 1989). The article which contains this translation also offers a preface and notes on the text.

Simund de Freine wrote his **Roman de Philosophie** in the late twelfth century. The work is an adaptation of the **Consolatio** in about sixteen hundred and fifty lines of Anglo-Saxon verse. In addition, Amaury Duval wrote a short notice on the author and the work.

> Ce poète, d'origine normande, naquit en Angleterre vers la fin du
> XIIe siècle; il fut chanoine de Hereford dans le pays de Galles. Il
> est bien connu comme poète latin; mais on ignorait qu'il s'était
> aussi distingué comme poète français: ce n'est que depuis
> quelques années que M. l'abbé de la Rue nous a fait connaître un
> assez long poème français, dont il est incontestablement auteur.
> (Duval 1835, 822)

I judge from this statement, and from the lack of any further reference,
that the report from M. l'abbé de la Rue was a personal one, addressed to
M. Duval, making Duval's the first printed notice of the work. The
article praises Simund's work for its clarity and brilliant images. Duval
offers some short passages from the **Roman** in support of these
statements.

The summary of a lecture on Simund de Freine and his works,
delivered by John E. Matzke, was printed in the proceedings of the
conference. Matzke discusses the two French poems which have been
ascribed to Simund: The **Roman de Philosophie** and a **Vie de
Saint Georges**.

> The **Roman de Philosophie** is known to exist in three
> manuscripts--in London, British Museum 20 B. XIV., in Oxford,
> Bodleian Library, Douce 210, and in Cheltenham, Sir Thomas
> Philipps Library, 8836. (Matzke 1902, xc.)

The fact that the manuscript information appears here is important
because Matzke had just completed an edition of both poems by Simund
for the Société des Anciens Textes Français. The **Roman de
Philosophie** appeared in 1909 (Matzke 1909) and the edition has been
highly praised. Gustav Gröber stated that Simund de Freine used the
commentary by Guillaume de Conches in preparing his text (Gröber
1902). A thematic study by Françoise Joukovsky-Micha should be
mentioned here because it includes Simund's work: "La Notion de 'vaine
gloire' de Simund de Freine à Martin le Franc" [(Joukovsky-Micha 1968,
Part I) and (Joukovsky-Micha 1968, Part II)]. Beyond this and brief
mention in the general studies, textual studies are lacking on this work.

The oldest of the true translations of the Latin **Consolatio** is a prose version by an anonymous Burgundian (Dwyer 1). It seems to be a translation worthy of study. Thomas and Roques say:

> Dans toute l'oeuvre de traducteur . . . le texte latin est rendu fidèlement, sans omission, mais il est interrompu à chaque instant, soit par de courtes gloses explicatives, soit par de longs commentaires, Les gloses ne sont généralement pas annoncées. (Thomas and Roques 1938, 425-6)

An edition of this translation mentioned in an article by Keith Atkinson (see Atkinson 1978, 28-9, "Some Further Confirmations") has been completed by Margaret Bolton-Hall (Bolton-Hall 1988).

Two editions of the prose version by an anonymous Wallonian (Dwyer 2) appeared in 1976. One, by Rolf Schroth, was published (Schroth 1976); the other, a dissertation by Keith Atkinson, remains unfortunately unpublished (Atkinson 1976). Atkinson has also prepared full critical editions, complete with variants, of two other medieval French **Consolatio** translations [(Thomas and Roques V and VII) or (Dwyer 6 and 8)]. Currently, they exist in manuscript form, but they should be published soon.

The published edition of Dwyer 2, prepared by Schroth, was reviewed by Kurt Baldinger, who adds one correction for all the critics who have mentioned the translation:

> Der Übersetzer der Hs. Troyes 898 ist nicht Wallone, d.h. schreibt nicht eine Wallonische Skripta, wie auch Schroth noch zu Unrecht behauptet, sondern eine nordost-pikardische Skripta und stammt vermutlich aus dem pikardischen Sprachgebiet Flanderns (flandr. im FEW). (Baldinger 1978, 185)

This statement is presented, however, without substantiating evidence. Keith Atkinson, in an article (Atkinson 1981), presents linguistic evidence which makes Baldinger's finding fairly conclusive. Atkinson goes even further than Baldinger by proving that the translator of MS Troyes 898 was from Hainaut in the region of Mons.

Very little has been published on the translation by Bonaventura da Demena (Dwyer 3). Richard Dwyer, in an article on the translator (Dwyer 1974, **French Studies**), places him in Sicily under the Angevin occupation. He suggests that the work's numerous digressions were included to provide delight and instruction to his audience. Furthermore, he suggests that the translation of Boethius may have provided consolation to the Sicilians under foreign rule at the time. There is, as yet, no edition of the work, nor is there any promise of one.

A description of MS Vat. 4788 (Dwyer 4), published by Ernest Langlois, contains excerpts from the text of this **Consolatio** translation by one Pierre de Paris (E. Langlois 1889). The passages quoted illustrate Pierre's method of translation. Antoine Thomas made a more thorough study of the text, providing two extended extracts which exemplify the style of the translation (Thomas 1917). He also gives historical information about Pierre de Paris. The translation is complicated by many elaborations which seem to be purely the invention of the author. Thomas and Roques wrote:

> Pierre de Paris s'est appliqué à élucider toutes les allusions mythologiques, historiques, littéraires, cosmologiques, géographiques, etc., qu'il a rencontrées dans la **Consolatio**. A-t-il eu à sa disposition quelque manuscrit de Boèce avec gloses interlinéaires ou marginales, comme nous en possédons tant? A-t-il connu le commentaire de Guillaume de Conches, qui pouvait, jusqu'à un certain point, tenir lieu d'un manuscrit glosé? Il semble que non. Autrement, il serait bien coupable, car, il faut l'avouer, on est souvent stupéfait de l'inintelligence avec laquelle il rend en français le texte de son auteur, et plus stupéfait encore de l'ignorance et de la suffisance dont il fait preuve dans les passages correspondants du commentaire, ou il aggrave les maladresses ou les contresens de sa traduction en racontant "l'histoire" pour satisfaire la curiosité du lecteur. (Thomas and Roques 1938, 446)

An edition of this translation is still lacking, and more thorough investigations into the commentary associated with it are needed.

The translation by Jean de Meun (Dwyer 5) has already been discussed in the first part of this chapter. For the mixed prose and verse version of the early fourteenth century (Dwyer 6), one study, which was published by Laurenz Fäh, exists on certain specific linguistic aspects of the medieval French text (Fäh 1915). It is a dissertation which presents a thorough investigation of the sounds, grammar, and syntax of the translation, using MS 365 of the Stadtbibliothek of Berne as a base text. Since it is the earliest French **Consolatio** translation in which an attempt is made to put Boethius' prose into prose and his verse into verse, and since its influence has been noted in subsequent translations, an edition should generate further scholarship on the French **Consolatio** tradition.

The revised prose and verse version (Dwyer 7) has also been discussed in the context of the Jean de Meun translation because this work is preceded by the pirated Jean de Meun preface and dedication to Philip IV. Its historical context and its stylistic and structural peculiarities have been fully described in an article by Glynnis Cropp (Cropp 1987). In another article (Cropp 1991), she discusses revisions made in three late manuscripts; concerning the magnitude of these revisions, she concludes:

> Interesting as some of these new variants are, they hardly deserve to be recorded in an edition based on a limited number of manuscripts. They do, however, give further proof of the resilience of a translation sufficiently malleable to sustain additions, changes and subtractions and, retaining a recognizable identity, to remain faithful to its own traditions from the mid-fourteenth century to the end of the fifteenth century. (Cropp 1991, 30)

Cropp has also discussed the prologue to the Jean de Meun translation and the longer one at the beginning of the verse-prose translation (Cropp 1982, **Romania**); she finds that the person responsible for the glosses in the glossed version of that translation is also probably responsible for the lengthened version of Jean's prologue. In an early article (Cropp 1981), she discusses some late glosses which were added to the translations; these dealt with two contemporary (that is, early fifteenth-century) assassinations. In another article (Cropp 1986), Cropp established that the glosses were derived almost exclusively from the commentary by Guillaume de Conches, and that the selection of materials for the glosses was not particularly systematic. An edition of the revised prose and verse translation (Dwyer 7) has been promised by Cropp (see Cropp 1979, 296, **Notes and Queries**); the production of such an edition is a major scholarly project, requiring years of work because of the many manuscripts which must be collated and transcribed. In preparation for this work, she has examined and classified all the known manuscripts. Their descriptions appear in her article, "Les Manuscrits du 'Livre de Boece De Consolacion'" (Cropp 1982/1983).

Just as Paul Meyer's revision of Léopold Delisle's inventory of 1873 created confusion in the criticism of the Jean de Meun translation, so did his ascription of the translation contained in MS 576 (Dwyer 8) of the Bibliothèque Nationale to one Jehan de Cis. Renaut de Louhans mentions having seen a translation by Jehan de Cis in the preface to his own translation (Dwyer 9), and Paul Meyer assigned that authorship to MS 576. Antoine Thomas shows that this ascription is probably incorrect, suggesting that Jehan de Cis be assigned the prose translation (Dwyer 5), which was eventually proved to be the work of Jean de Meun (Thomas 1892). Meyer was the victim of two false assumptions: 1) that the MSS of the Bibliothèque Nationale represented all the medieval French **Consolatio** translations and 2) that the reference in Renaut's text was accurate. At this time, any translation by Jean de Cis is a lost work. The text of MS 576 is the subject of a study by Keith Atkinson in which a passage (Book III, meter xii) is provisionally offered as an edited sample of the text (Atkinson 1980). Elsewhere, Atkinson gives the translation lengthy discussion, describing it as not simply a translation but as a translation-commentary (Atkinson 1987).

The translation by Renaut de Louhans was one of the first to attract critical attention. In the 1870s, two articles by M. August Vayssière appeared, giving biographical information about the author [(Vayssière 1872/1873 and 1875) and (Vayssière 1876/1877)]: they praise Renaut as one of Poligny's finest citizens. In 1877, an entry entitled "Des estats du siecle" appeared in the **Recueil général et complet des Fabliaux** (Raynaud and de Montaiglon 1877). The entry contains part of the story of an "inconstant scholar," which Giulio Bertoni was later able to identify as an excerpt from Renaut's **Consolatio** translation. He says:

> il lui a échappé que la pièce dont il est question est tirée de la traduction en vers de la **Consolatio** de Boèce par Renaut de Louhans (1336), ce que Montaiglon et Raynaud n'ont pas plus remarqué. Il est évident que, si cette remarque avait été faite, la petite pièce ne figurerait pas dans le **Recueil général des Fabliaux**, d'autant plus que le ms. de Genève [which was the

source of the text for the **Recueil**] nous donne un texte
corrompu et incomplet. (Bertoni 1910, **Zeitschrift**, 368-9)

Astrik Gabriel traced the Latin sources for the anecdote which Renaut
incorporated into his translation, and he published the conclusion to the
tale, which the text in the **Recueil** had omitted (Gabriel 1958).

Franz Nagel submitted his doctoral research on the translation
(Dwyer 9) by Renaud de Louhans (Nagel 1890) and published it one year
later (Nagel 1891). His work is a formal and philological description of
the text. An unsigned review of the book is not favorable; the reviewer
feels that Nagel should have studied better manuscripts of the other
medieval French **Consolatio** translations which he affiliates with
Renaut's work (Review 1891). An edition of this translation is being
prepared by Béatrice Atherton as a Ph.D. dissertation for the University of
Queensland (Australia), and the project is well under way.

Giulio Bertoni published a notice on two manuscripts of
Renaut's translation found in the Bibliothèque cantonale of Fribourg
(Suisse) (Bertoni 1910, **Notice**). The study is basically a description of
the two manuscripts, but several interesting critical points are also made.
Renaut is shown to have used the early fourteenth-century anonymous
verse-prose translation (Dwyer 6) in preparing his own translation. That
anonymous translator had been plagiarized by the translator who produced
the mid-fourteenth-century revised verse-prose translation (Dwyer 7).
Renaut's work is perhaps most interesting for its digressions, and one
source for the interpolated material is the Pseudo-Aquinas commentary
(which, according to Bertoni's proof, was not written by Aquinas).
Unfortunately, no edition exists of this translation.

Apart from material appearing in the general studies, little
scholarship has been produced on the two translations which were based
on Renaut's work: the verse revision of Renaut by an anonymous
Benedictine monk (Dwyer 10, which Delisle earlier had shown not to be
the work of Charles d'Orléans), and the verse abbreviation of Renaut
(Dwyer 11). Richard Dwyer published a description of another medieval
French **Consolatio** translation which he refers to as the second verse-
prose version (Dwyer 12); after describing the manuscript, he says:

> The translation is . . . related to at least five of the known
> versions: de Meung's prose, the meters of Renaut de Louhans and
> Thomas' VII [Dwyer 8], and the epilogue of the version once

attributed to Charles d'Orléans. To say that this version is highly derivative, however, is only to open a discussion that cannot be satisfactorily concluded until some one hundred twenty MSS, scattered from Baltimore to Fribourg, have been carefully collated. Yet those affiliations, once traced, could lead to noteworthy insights into the continuous late-medieval attempts to rework the prose and verse of this evergreen consolation against the empty felicity of the world. (Dwyer 1965).

This problem of inventory, which Dwyer mentions, continues to plague scholarship on the medieval French Consolatio tradition. But it is by such work as Dwyer's that the problem becomes less severe.

Gustave Brunet published a description of the Consolatio translation which was printed in Bruges in 1477 by Colard Mansion (Dwyer 13). He suggests that Mansion may himself have been the translator of the work (Brunet 1967).

These, then, are the studies which have been made on the various translations in the medieval French Consolatio tradition. In conjunction with material in the general studies, they constitute the investigation of the thirteen varied works which have been noted to date. For some translators, philological studies are lacking; for others, editions. For almost all, detailed analyses of the affiliations with other translations and the commentaries still need to be made.

As has been pointed out frequently throughout this chapter, the identification of manuscripts has been a major problem. The earliest inventories of the manuscripts are in the catalogues of the holdings of various libraries. For example, the Catalogue général des manuscrits français de la Bibliothèque Nationale (Leroux 1931) lists fifty-four manuscripts containing various medieval French Consolatio translations. From such lists, investigators have worked toward a full inventory of all manuscripts containing such translations. Louise Stone published information about some unnoticed manuscripts (Stone 1937). Richard Dwyer described three manuscripts from the National Library of Wales (Dwyer 1966). Glynnis Cropp noted a manuscript found in the Public Library of Auckland, New Zealand (Cropp 1969). Robert Lucas attempted to compile a complete list of all medieval French manuscripts containing Consolatio translations (Lucas 1970), which was revised by Richard Dwyer the following year (Dwyer 1971).

B.S. Donaghey noted still another manuscript (Donaghey 1973). More information was then published by Richard Dwyer (Dwyer 1974, **Medium Aevum**), who two years later produced the list which gives the classification system used in this chapter (Dwyer 1976). Still further notices on manuscripts which have appeared since 1976 include: an article by Keith Atkinson (Atkinson 1978, "Some Further Confirmations"), Glynnis Cropp's checklist (Cropp 1979, **Notes and Queries**), my own addition to Cropp's checklist (Kaylor 1981), Glynnis Cropp's notice of unnoted manuscripts of the Jean de Meun translation (Cropp 1982, **Notes and Queries**), and Cropp's description of the manuscripts of the "Libre de Boece de Consolation" (Cropp 1982/1983). In all probability, the number of noted manuscripts will continue to grow, and our knowledge of the tradition will continue to be revised.

Before concluding this chapter, mention must be made of two other studies which do not fit comfortably in the sections above, but which are relevant to this chapter. First, Barnet Kottler's article (Kottler 1955) points out that, by the fourteenth century, the Latin manuscripts of the **Consolatio** had developed their own vulgate tradition, due to scribal error and incorporated interpolations which have subsequently formed traditions of their own. Very little work has been done on the Latin manuscripts which the various translators used to produce their translations. Second, interesting speculation about the audiences of the translations and about why that so many translators decided to work with the **Consolatio** is found throughout the articles by Richard Dwyer. Of particular interest in this context is his article entitled, "Appreciation of Handmade Literature" (Dwyer 1974, **Chaucer Review**). As more information accumulates about the translators and their translations, the criticism should begin to diversify and treat areas other than the philological.

List of Relevant Titles

1.   Atkinson, Keith. "A Critical Edition of the Medieval French Prose Translation of **De Consolatione Philosophiae** of Boethius Contained in the MS 898 of the Bibliothèque municipale, Troyes." Ph.D. diss., University of Queensland, Australia, 1976.

This is an unpublished dissertation. Another edition of the translation was published the same year (see Schroth 1976).

2.   ----------. Review of **Boethian Fictions: Narratives in the Medieval French Versions of the** Consolatio Philosophiae, by Richard A. Dwyer. **Medium Aevum** 47 (1978): 141-4.

Atkinson's review is generally favorable, but he does complain that Dwyer created a new numbering system for the translations. He feels the Thomas-Roque system should have been revised and retained.

3.   ----------. "Some Further Confirmations and Attributions of Manuscripts of the Mediaeval French Boethius." **Medium Aevum** 47 (1978): 22-9.

Atkinson adds several manuscripts of various medieval French **Consolatio** translations to Dwyer's list of 1976.

4.   ----------, ed. "An Early Fourteenth-Century French Boethian Orpheus." **Parergon: Bulletin of the Australian and New Zealand Association for Medieval and Renaissance Studies** 26 (1980) (special issue: entire issue).

This study contains edited portions of the text of the Anonymous of Meun, which Atkinson prefers to call the Anonymous Picard (Dwyer 8).

5.   ----------. "Le Dialecte du **Boèce** de Troyes 898 à propos d'une édition récente." **Romania** 102 (1981): 250-9.

In this article, Atkinson offers further information to corroborate Baldinger's assessment (Baldinger 1978) that the dialect of this translation (Dwyer 2) is not Wallonian but that of medieval Hainaut.

6. ----------. "A Fourteenth-Century Picard Translation-Commentary of the **Consolatio Philosophiae**. In **The Medieval Boethius: Studies in the Vernacular Translations of** De Consolatione Philosophiae, edited by Alastair J. Minnis, 32-62. Woodbridge, Suffolk: D.S. Brewer, 1987.

Atkinson discusses the translation contained in BN MS 576 (Dwyer 8, elsewhere called the Anonymous of Meun translation). He places the work before 1315, and he finds its most salient feature to be its interpretative additions. His article contains a detailed study of the prologue, and his appendix shows, using the Labours of Hercules image, the translator's use of William of Aragon's commentary. The work is seen to be not simply a translation but a vernacular translation-commentary.

7. Atkinson, Keith and Glynnis M. Cropp. "Trois traductions de la **Consolatio Philosophiae** de Boèce." **Romania** 106 (1985): 198-232.

Atkinson and Cropp study translations designated by Thomas and Roques as V (Dwyer 6), VI (Dwyer 7), and IX (Dwyer 9), discovering that V is the oldest of the three and parental to both VI and IX. Both VI and IX have been modified by materials added from commentaries in order to suit the needs of fourteenth- and fifteenth-century lay audiences.

8. Baldinger, Kurt. Review of **Eine altfranzösische Übersetzung der** Consolatio **Philosophiae des Boethius (Handschrift Troyes No.** 898), by Rolf Schroth. **Zeitschrift für romanische Philologie** 94 (1978): 181-5.

    The review suggests some improvements and changes in interpretation. Baldinger maintains that the translator was not Wallonian but north-eastern Picard (see Atkinson 1980 and 1981).

9. Bertoni, Giulio. "Des estats du siecle.' **Zeitschrift für romanische Philologie** 34 (1910): 368-9.

    This short note identifies the "Des estats du siecle," printed in the **Recueil général et complet des Fabliaux** (Raynaud 1877), as one of the digressions in the translation of the **Consolatio** by Renaut de Louhans.

10. ----------. **Notice sur deux manuscrits d'une traduction française de la** Consolation de Boëce **conservés à la Bibliothèque cantonale de Fribourg (Suisse)**. Fribourg, Switzerland: Imprimerie Saint-Paul, 1910.

    Bertoni treats two manuscripts of the **Consolatio** translation by Renaut de Louhans from the Bibliothèque cantonale de Fribourg; he concentrates on the digressions, some of which are excerpted.

11. Bolton-Hall, Margaret. "A Critical Edition of the Translation of Boethius' **Consolation of Philosophy** Contained in the Manuscript: Vienna Nat. Lib. Lat. 2642." Ph.D. diss., University of Queensland, 1988.

This is the critical edition of the early thirteenth-century Burgundian **Consolatio** translation (Dwyer 1).

12. Brunet, Gustave. **La France littéraire au XVème siècle ou catalogue raisonné des ouvrages en tous genres imprimés en langue française jusqu'à l'an 1500.** Geneva: Slatkin Reprints, 1967.

This book contains a notice and description of a **Consolatio** translation printed by Colard Mansion in 1477 (possibly the editor's own translation).

13. Courcelle, Pierre. La Consolation de philosophie **dans la tradition littéraire: antécédents et postérité de Boèce.** Paris: Études Augustiniennes, 1967.

This is a study of the commentaries on the **Consolatio.** The general information presented here is necessary for any understanding of the medieval French translations of Boethius and their relationship to the commentaries.

14. Cropp, Glynnis M. "La Traduction française de la **Consolatio Philosophiae** de Boèce: encore un manuscrit." **Romania** 90 (1969): 258-70.

In this article Cropp adds yet another entry to the list of manuscripts of the French **Consolatio** translations. This one was found in the Public Library of Auckland, New Zealand.

15. ----------. "A Checklist of the Medieval French Anonymous Verse-Prose Translations of the **Consolatio** of Boethius." **Notes and Queries** 224 (1979): 294-6.

This is a preliminary attempt to compile a list of all manuscripts of the verse-prose **Consolatio** translation.

16. ----------. "Two Historical glosses in **Le Livre de Boece de la Consolacion." New Zealand Journal of French Studies** 2 (1981): 5-20.

    This article contains information on two late glosses added to the translation (Dwyer 7); they pertain to two early fifteenth-century assassinations.

17. ----------. "Additional Manuscripts of the Medieval French Anonymous Verse-Prose Translation of the **Consolatio** of Boethius." **Notes and Queries** 227 (1982): 292-4.

    Cropp adds manuscripts noted since her previous article of 1979.

18. ----------. "Le Prologue de Jean de Meun et **Le Livre de Boece de Consolacion." Romania** 103 (1982): 278-98.

    In this article, Cropp examines the prologue found at the beginning of the Jean de Meun prose **Consolatio** translation and the somewhat longer prologue found at the beginning of the verse-prose translation. The verse-prose translation also bears Jean's name, but it has been shown not to be his work. She finds that the Jean de Meun prologue is an amalgam of four pre-existing prologues; the translator who produced the "continuation of the prologue" is less faithful to the Latin sources than Jean, but that translator is probably also the commentator who is responsible for the glosses in the glossed version of the **Livre de Boece de Consolation.**

19. ----------. "Les Manuscrits du **Livre de Boece de Consolacion.**" **Revue d'Histoire des Textes** 12/13 (1982/1983): 263-352.

In this article, Cropp gives a description of all the known manuscripts of the Medieval French Anonymous Verse-Prose Translation of the **Consolatio.**

20. ----------. "An Unnoticed Manuscript of a Medieval French Verse Translation of the **Consolatio** of Boethius." **Notes and Queries** 229 [n.s. 31] (1984): 156-8.

In this article, Cropp describes a manuscript which, with only two major discrepancies, corresponds "closely" with MS BN fr. 577 (Dwyer 10).

21. ----------. "Les Gloses du **Livre de Boece de Consolacion.**" **Le Moyen Age** 42 (1986): 367-81.

Cropp studies the glossed versions of the **Livre de Boece de Consolacion,** finding that the glosses are drawn almost exclusively, although in no particularly systematic fashion, from the commentary of Guillaume de Conches. This glossed version of the translation (Dwyer 7), as evidenced by the number of existing manuscripts, enjoyed great success in the fifteenth century.

22. ----------. "**Le Livre de Boece de Consolacion:** From Translation to Glossed Text." In **The Medieval Boethius: Studies in the Vernacular Translations of** De Consolatione Philosophiae, edited by Alastair J. Minnis, 63-88. Woodbridge, Suffolk: D.S. Brewer, 1987.

The article consists in two major sections.
Section one discusses the historical context in
which the translation (Dwyer 7) developed from an
unglossed to a glossed text. Section two gives a
full discussion to three aspects of the work: the
prologue, the prose and verse styles, and the
glosses.

23.   ----------. **"Le Livre de Boece de
         Consolacion:** Revision of the Translation in
         Some Later Manuscripts." **Parergon** n.s. 9
         (1991): 17-20.

In this article, Cropp discusses revisions in three
manuscripts of the **Livre de Boece de
Consolacion;** the article adds to work she has
done on the development of the translation from
an unglossed to a glossed text (Cropp 1987).

24.   Delisle, Léopold. "Anciennes traductions
         françaises de la **Consolatio** de Boèce conservées
         à la Bibliothèque Nationale." **Bibliothèque de
         l'école des Chartes** 34 (1873): 5-32.

This article contains the first systematic study of
the medieval French manuscripts of the
Consolatio. It attempts no chronological
presentation nor literary analysis but it divides the
then-known forty-seven manuscripts in the
Bibliothèque Nationale into two prose, two verse-
prose, and four verse translations. The work
provides a solid basis for all later studies.

25.   Donaghey, Brian S. "Another English Manuscript
         of an Old French Translation of Boethius."
         Medium Aevum 42 (1973): 38-41.

This is a notice and description of an unnoted manuscript of the **Consolatio** translation once falsely ascribed to Charles d'Orléans (Dwyer 10).

26. Duval, M. Amaury. "Simon de Fresne." In **Histoire littéraire de la France.** Vol. 18, 822-4. Paris: Firmin Didot, 1835.

This is the first published description of the French poem by the Anglo-Norman poet Simon de Fresne. The article notes that the poem, in 1600 verses, is an imitation rather than a translation of the **Consolatio.** Simon is shown to have flourished c.1220.

27. Dwyer, Richard A. "Another Boèce." **Romance Philology** 19 (1965): 268-70.

Dwyer describes the unique manuscript (N.L.W. MS 5038D) of a **Consolatio** translation found in the National Library of Wales (Dwyer 12).

28. ----------. "Old French Translations of Boethius' **Consolatio Philosophiae** in the National Library of Wales." **National Library of Wales Journal** 14 (1966): 486-8.

Three manuscripts (N.L.W. MSS 5031, 5038, 5039) found in the National Library of Wales are described. Two are copies of the verse-prose **Consolatio** translation with the pirated dedication to Philip IV (Dwyer 7). The third (Dwyer 12) is an independent work which combines many elements from earlier translations.

29. ----------. "Manuscripts of the Medieval French Boethius." **Notes and Queries** 216 (1971): 124-5.

Dwyer offers additions and corrections to the list
of manuscripts of medieval French **Consolatio**
translations presented by Lucas in his article of
1970.

30.   ----------. "The Appreciation of Handmade
Literature." **Chaucer Review** 8 (1974): 221-40.

Dwyer discusses the many permutations made in
the several medieval French **Consolatio**
translations. He attempts to account for them by
indicating a particularly medieval attitude toward
literature.

31.   ----------. "Bonaventura da Demena, Sicilian
Translator of Boethius." **French Studies** 28
(1974): 129-33.

Dwyer suggests that Bonaventura da Demena may
have produced his French **Consolatio** translation
in Sicily; he also provides some historical
information which sheds light on the translation.

32.   ----------. "The Old French Boethius: Addendum."
Medium Aevum 43 (1974): 265-6.

This is an update and revision of information in
B.S. Donaghey's article of 1973.

33.   ----------. **Boethian Fictions: Narratives in
the Medieval French Versions of the**
Consolatio Philosophiae. Mediaeval Academy of
America, no. 83. Cambridge, Mass.: Mediaeval
Academy of America, 1976.

Dwyer examines the narrative interpolations into
the text of the **Consolatio** by its medieval
French translators. It is discovered that these

interpolations are added to make the texts more
interesting and "more medieval."

34. Fäh, Laurenz. **Die Sprache der
altfranzösischen Boëtius-Übersetzung,
enthalten in dem Ms. 365 der
Stadtbibliothek Bern.** Freiburg (Schweiz):
Buchdruckerei Gebrüder Fragnière, 1915.

Fäh describes the manuscript mentioned in the
title and provides a thorough linguistic,
grammatical, and syntactic study of the text.

35. Gabriel, Astrik L. "The Source of the Anecdote of
the Inconstant Scholar." **Classica et
Mediaevalia** 19 (1958): 152-76.

Gabriel discusses an anecdote, published as "Des
estats du siecle," which also appears as an
interpolation into the text of the **Consolatio**
translations of both Renaut de Louhans and an
anonymous Benedictine. He discusses the origin
of the anecdote and sheds light on the translator's
methods.

36. Gröber, Gustav. "Erbauliche und theologische
Prosa." In **Grundriss der romanischen
Philologie.** Vol. 2, 1025-6. Strassburg:
Trübner, 1902.

This is a short notice stating that Simund de
Freine used the commentary by Guillaume de
Conches and that the translation by Renaud de
Louhans seems to be a reworking of MS BN
1096.

37. Hündgen, Franz, ed. **Das altprovenzalische
Boëthiuslied unter Beifügung einer
Übersetzung, eines Glossars, erklärender**

Anmerkungen sowie grammatischer und metrischer Untersuchung. Oppeln: Eugen Frank's Buchhandlung, 1884.

This is a study of the Provençal paraphrase of the **Consolatio,** complete with a very valuable translation into modern German.

38.   Joukovsky-Micha, Françoise. "La Notion de 'vaine gloire' de Simund de Freine à Martin le Franc (Part 1)." **Romania** 89 (1968): 1-30.

This is a thematic study which is included here because it discusses the work of Simund de Freine.

39.   ----------. "La Notion de 'vaine gloire' de Simund de Freine à Martin le Franc (Part II)." **Romania** 89 (1968): 210-39.

This is the conclusion to the article listed above (Joukovsky-Micha 1968).

40.   Kaylor, Noel Harold, Jr. "An addition to the Checklist of Manuscripts of the French Anonymous Verse-Prose Translation of the **Consolation** of Boethius." **Notes and Queries** 226 (1981): 196-7.

In this brief note, I add one previously unnoted manuscript to Glynnis Cropp's list of verse-prose **Consolatio** translations containing the pirated Jean de Meun preface (see Cropp 1979).

41.   Kottler, Barnet. "The Vulgate Tradition of the **Consolatio Philosophiae** in the Fourteenth Century." **Mediaeval Studies** 17 (1955): 209-14.

Kottler posits that, by the fourteenth century, there was a vulgate tradition of the Latin **Consolatio** which is at variance with the standard critical editions we use today. Jean de Meun would have used such a faulty manuscript in preparing his own text.

42. Langlois, Charles-Victor. "La **Consolation** de Boèce, d'après Jean de Meun et plusieurs autres." In **La Vie en France au moyen âge**. Vol. 4, **La Vie spirituelle**, 269-326. Paris: Librairie Hachette, 1928.

Basically, this is an update of the bibliographical information presented by Delisle on the various medieval French **Consolatio** translations. Delisle discusses eight translations. To these, Langlois adds information about two paraphrases and three newly discovered translations.

43. Langlois, Ernest. "Les Manuscrits de Rome: Vat. 4788." **Notices et extraits des manuscrits de la Bibliothèque Nationale et autres bibliothèques** 33 (1889): 261-65.

Langlois adds a seventh translation to the six French translations accepted by Paul Meyer [his reduction from the eight identified by Delisle (see Delisle 1873)], one contained in MS Vat. 4788 by Pierre de Paris. He gives a brief description of the translation and some extracts from the text.

44. ----------. "La Traduction de Boèce par Jean de Meun." **Romania** 42 (1913): 331-69.

In this article, which definitively assigns the prose translation bearing the dedication to Philip IV to Jean de Meun, Langlois also discusses the problems of two verse-prose translations (Dwyer 6

and 7). He identifies Dwyer 6 as earlier and more
fluent than Dwyer 7, and he shows that 7 relied
heavily upon 6.

45.   Leroux, Ernest. **Catalogue général des
       manuscrits français de la Bibliothèque
       Nationale.** Vol. 1, 301-2. Paris: Librairie Ernest
       Leroux, 1931.

       Leroux gives an update of the list of manuscripts
       of medieval French translations of the
       Consolatio in the Bibliothèque Nationale; it
       contains additional manuscripts not listed by
       Delisle.

46.   Lucas, Robert H. "Mediaeval French Translations
       of the Latin Classics to 1500." **Speculum** 45
       (1970): 225-53.

       The article includes a list of the manuscripts of all
       the then-known medieval French **Consolatio**
       translations.

47.   Matzke, John E. "The Anglo-Norman Poet
       Simund de Freine." **Transactions and
       Proceedings of the American
       Philological Association** 33 (1902): xc.

       This note gives a summary of Matzke's paper on
       the facts known about the life and works of
       Simund de Freine.

48.   ----------, ed. "Le Roman de Philosophie." In **Les
       Oeuvres de Simund de Freine,** 1-60. Société
       des Anciens Textes Français Paris: Firmin Didot,
       1909.

This is the critical edition of Simund de Freine's paraphrase of the **Consolatio, Le Roman de Philosophie.**

49. Mermier, Guy. "**Boeci:** An English Translation of the Old Provencal [sic] Fragment with a Preface and Notes." In **Contemporary Readings of Medieval Literature,** edited by Guy Mermier, 21-35. Ann Arbor: University of Michigan Press, 1989.

As the title suggests, this article contains an English translation of the Old Provençal text.

50. Meyer, Paul. Review of "Anciennes traductions françaises de la **Consolation** du Boëce conservées à la Bibliothèque Nationale" [**Bibliothèque de l'École des Chartes,** vol. 34], by Léopold Delisle. **Romania** 2 (1873): 271-3.

This review of Delisle's work (Delisle 1873) attempts to attribute the verse-prose translation (with the dedication to Philip IV) to Jean de Meun. In so doing, it creates many scholarly problems. It lacks the elegance of Delisle's attribution, and it lacks its scholarly basis. It also reduces Delisle's eight different translations to six.

51. ----------, ed. **Recueil d'anciens textes bas-latin, provençaux et français, accompagné de deux glossaires.** Paris: F. Vieweg, 1877.

This is a critical edition of the fragmentary Provençal **Boëce.**

52. Nagel, Franz. **Die altfranzösische Übersetzung der** Consolatio Philosophiae **des**

Boëthius von Renaut von Louhans. Ph.D.
diss., Friederichs-Universität Halle-Wittenberg,
1890. Halle: Ehrhardt Karras, 1890.

This is a study of the Old French translation of the
Consolatio by Renaut de Louhans. After a brief
description of the work, a detailed philosophical
study of the text is presented. This study is based
on a manuscript from the Bibliothèque des
königlichen Domgymnasiums zu Magdeburg.

53.   ----------. "Die altfranzösische Übersetzung der
Consolatio philosophiae des Boëthius von
Renaud von Louhans." **Zeitschrift für
romanische Philologie**, 15 (1891): 1-23.

This is the published version of Nagel's
dissertation which appeared the preceding year.

54.   Patch, Howard Rollin. **The Tradition of
Boethius: A Study of His Importance in
Medieval Culture.** New York: Oxford
University Press, 1935.

This is an introductory volume in which chapter
III ("Translations of the **Consolatio**") is devoted
to the Old French translations.

55.   Rabotine, Vladimir. **Le Boèce provençal:
étude linguistique.** Ph.D. diss., Strasbourg,
1930. Strasbourg: Librairie Universitaire d'Alsace,
1930.

Rabotine presents a complete linguistic study of
the Old Provençal **Boèce** and promises a critical
edition.

56.   Raynaud, Gaston and Anatole de Montaiglon.
"Des estats du siecle." In **Recueil général et**

complet des Fabliaux des XIIIè et XIVè siècles. Vol. 2, 264-8. 1877. Reprint. New York: Burt Franklin, 1964.

A selection entitled "Des estats du siecle" was published in this collection of Fabliaux of the thirteenth and fourteenth centuries. It is a transcription of a short Old French tale. It was later identified as a passage from a translation of the Consolatio (see Bertoni 1910, Zeitschrift).

57. Raynouard. [An edition of the Old Provençal Boëce.] N.p.: n.p., 1813-1817.

This is the first published edition of the Old Provençal Boëce.

58. Review of Die altfranzösische Übersetzung der Consolatio Philosophiae des Boethius von Renaut von Louhans, by Franz Nagel. Romania 20 (1891), 329-30.

This review points out the inadequacy of using one single manuscript in a philological study of a translation containing many manuscripts; it also complains that the digressions in the translation were not fully researched in the Boethian commentaries.

59. Schroth, Rolf. Eine altfranzösische Übersetzung der Consolatio Philosophiae des Boethius (Handschrift Troyes Nr. 898): Edition und Kommentar. Europäische Hochschulschriften, Reihe 8: Französische Sprache und Literatur. Vol. 36. Frankfurt: Peter Lang, 1976.

This is an edition of the **Consolatio** translation
found in this manuscript: Troyes 898.

60.   Schwarze, Christoph. **Der altprovenzalische**
       Boeci. Forschungen zur romanischen Philologie,
       no. 12. Münster, Westfalen: Aschendorffsche
       Verlagsbuchhandlung, 1963.

       This book represents a major study of the Old
       Provençal **Boëce.**

61.   Stewart, Hugh Fraser. **Boethius: An Essay.**
       London: 1891. Reprint. New York: Burt Franklin,
       1974.

       The book contains a summary chapter in which
       descriptions of various medieval French
       Consolatio translations are given. Stewart
       gives a good perspective on the critical problems
       which had plagued the study of the translations up
       to his time. He offers few solutions, however.

62.   Stone, Louise W. "Old French Translations of the
       De Consolatione Philosophiae of Boethius:
       Some Unnoticed Manuscripts." **Medium
       Aevum** 6 (1937): 21-30.

       The article adds many manuscripts, both English
       and continental, to the list of medieval French
       Consolatio translations.

63.   Thomas, M. Antoine. "Jean de Sy et Jean de Cis."
       Romania 21 (1892): 612-15.

       The author points out that Jean de Sy was a
       translator of the Bible (under the patronage of
       King Jean le Bon). His observations on Jean de
       Cis have since been proved incorrect.

64. ----------. **Notice sur le manuscrit latin 4788 du Vatican**. Paris: Imprimerie Nationale, 1917.

   Thomas describes the manuscript containing the **Consolatio** translation by Pierre de Paris (MS Vat. Latin 4788). Of particular interest are two extended extracts from the text itself.

65. Thomas, M. Antoine and Mario Roques. "Traductions françaises de la **Consolation Philosophiae** de Boèce." In **Histoire littéraire de la France** 37 (1938): 419-506 and 542-7.

   This article attempts a comprehensive survey of the medieval French **Consolatio** translations. It gives many extracts from the various translations, and it attempts to clear up certain of the linguistic and historical problems in the scholarship. This is a key article in the study of the French translations.

66. Vayssière, M. August. "Renaud de Louens, poète franc-comtois du XIVe siècle (Part 1)." **Bulletin de la Société d'agriculture, sciences et arts de Poligny** 13 (1872/1873 and 1875): 345-56.

   This article summarizes the few facts known about Frère Renaut de Louhans. The major point made in this article is that Renaut is a poet in whom Poligny should take pride.

67. ----------. "Renaud de Louens, poète franc-comtois du XVIe siècle (Part 2)." **Bulletin de la société d'agriculture, sciences et arts de Poigny** 17 (1876/1877): n.pp.

This is the conclusion of the article by Vayssière
listed above.

68.   van de Vyver, A. "Les Traductions du **De
       Consolatione philosophiae** de Boèce en
       littérature comparée." **Humanisme et
       Renaissance** 6 (1939): 247-73.

       This article attempts to give a comprehensive
       inventory of all European **Consolatio**
       translations. A short descriptive summary of
       available information is given on each translation.

69.   Zingarelli, Nicola. "Il **Boezio** Provenzale e la
       Leggenda di Boezio." **Reciconti del reale
       Istituto Lombardo di Scienze e Lettere** 53
       (1920): 193-221.

       In this article, the author studies the Old Provençal
       Boëce and the legend which existed in the Middle
       Ages about the life of Boethius.

CHAPTER V

THE MIDDLE ENGLISH TRADITION

Chaucer's **Consolatio** Translation

Geoffrey Chaucer, born c.1340, is acknowledged to be the greatest English poet before Shakespeare, and he is called the "Father of English Poetry." In his professional life, he worked under three successive English kings in various positions of public service. He died in 1400 and was buried in Westminster Abbey, a final honor bestowed in recognition of accomplishments in his avocation, the creation of poetry.

Chaucer's literary reputation results primarily from the fame of his **Canterbury Tales,** the unfinished work of his later years. After nearly six centuries, the sometimes bawdy, sometimes profound tales continue to be enjoyed as great literature. Appendaged to the final tale, the "Parson's Tale," is a brief, prose retraction in which Chaucer repudiates his greatest poetic works:

> . . . the Book of Troilus; the Book also of Fame; the Book of the xxv Ladies; the Book of the Duchesse; the Book of Seint Valentynes Day of the Parlement of Briddes; the Tale of Caunterbury . . . . (Fisher 1977, 397)

The poet says that he preferred to be remembered for his "translacioun of Boece de Consolacion and othere bookes of legendes of seintes, and

163

omelies, and moralitee, and devocioun . . ." (Fisher 1977, 397). Chaucer sets his **Consolatio** translation off from the majority of his works, and he places it among his pious works. In spite of any possible insincerity in his retraction of the poetic works, it is obvious that he regarded Boethius' last work as a Christian document and its translation to his spiritual credit.

The general, introductory studies relevant to Chaucer's translation include Hugh Fraser Stewart's **Essay**. Stewart's opinion of the **Boece** is not one of unbridled praise.

> It possesses a double interest for us,--first, as an instance of fourteenth-century prose, and secondly, as an instance--the only known one--of Chaucer's method of literal translation. I say advisedly literal translation, for although Chaucer often fails to catch the spirit of the Latin, he keeps, as a rule, so closely to the letter as to render necessary the interpolation of a multitude of glosses to make the meaning of many passages at all intelligible. Indeed it is open to question whether the translator quite understood some of them himself. (Stewart 1891, 217-8)

Stewart's book contains a catalogue of Chaucer's mistranslations and misreadings; the author also observes that Chaucer and Notker share some unusual readings of the text. This fact indicates that both translators used the same tradition of Latin manuscripts. Tim Machan, however, disagrees with Stewart's assessment of the merit of Chaucer's translation. In his dissertation (Machan 1984, dissertation) and in the published book which succeeded it (Machan 1985), he studies the techniques of translation used in the **Boece**, finding that Chaucer is indeed skillful and successful, both as translator and philologist.

Friedrich Fehlauer's dissertation (Fehlauer 1908) places Chaucer's translation into a broader perspective--that of all English **Consolatio** translations through the fifteenth century, but otherwise it gives no new information. In its approach, Guy Bayley Dolson's dissertation (Dolson 1926, dissertation) is related to Fehlauer's; the lives and works of all English writers influenced by the **Consolatio** are briefly discussed, but again, no new information is presented on Chaucer's translation.

A. van de Vyver's article (van de Vyver 1939) places Chaucer's work in an even broader context than does Fehlauer's--that of all European

Consolatio translations. Like most of the other general studies, van de
Vyver's article is basically a list, adding no new information on either the
work or the author. Its value for scholarship lies in its scope.

Certain works which need only brief mention in this context
include: Fehlauer's published dissertation (Fehlauer 1909) and Ewald
Flügel's dissertation (Flügel 1892); a series of further articles by Dolson
[(Dolson 1921) (Dolson 1922, **Classical Weekly**) (Dolson 1922,
"Southey and Landor")]; the Introduction to a translation by Richard Green
(Green 1962); and a dissertation and an article by Walter Houghton
[(Houghton 1931, dissertation) (Houghton 1931, "S.E.M.")]. For
information on various authors generally influenced by the **Consolatio**,
see [(Coolidge 1963) (Dolson 1922, "Imprisoned English Authors")
(Donaghey 1967) (Robertson 1964) (Wimsatt 1972) (Herzig (1973)].

The classic study of Chaucer's Middle English vernacular
translation of the **Consolatio** is Bernard L. Jefferson's book (Jefferson
1917). It gives no historical account of the **Boece**, but rather a close
textual analysis. It treats systematically most areas of scholarship
pertaining to the translation: the problem of commentaries, affiliations
with translations in other linguistic traditions, and translation errors. An
article by Eleanor Prescott Hammond adds to Jefferson's list of
mistranslations (Hammond 1926). This particular information is
presented in one of the two brief notes which comprise her article.

John S.P. Tatlock's concordance to Chaucer's works is useful to
students of the **Boece** (Tatlock 1927): using it, students can trace
concepts throughout Boethius' work.

Finally, Howard Rollin Patch's book provides a comprehensive
view of the importance of Boethius in the Middle Ages and of such
translators of the **Consolatio** as Chaucer. Patch takes a more positive
view of the **Boece** than did Stewart:

> . . . we may note Chaucer's masterly rearrangement of material
> for lyric purposes. But short selections cannot represent the
> merits or the qualities of his translation, and may quite unfairly
> expose its defects. That he caught the spirit of the original is
> obvious, and that he was imbued with it appears in his
> subsequent quotation or echo of line after line in most of his
> works, usually in words that suggest his own **Boece**. He drew
> from nearly every part of the **Consolatio** in a way that shows
> his complete mastery of it; he introduced its material not only in

less significant moments in his plots but at important places
where the philosophical meaning becomes apparent. (Patch
1935, 70-1)

Indeed, this critic praises the merits of Chaucer's translation, but the most
unabashed appreciation of the **Boece** is found in W.P. Witcutt's article .
He maintains that Boethius' system, as Chaucer rendered it into English,
represents light for the darkness of our materialistic age.

The proper medium in which an English-speaking man should
read Boethius is the Chaucerian translation. The **De
Consolatione** will then appear not as something foreign and
remote, but as it is--something that belongs to **us**, something
that is ours. (Witcutt 1936/37)

Witcutt views the **Boece** as a very pious work, and his article reads more
like a sermon than a piece of scholarship, but it is an interesting
document of the reception of Chaucer's **Consolatio** translation.
Russell A. Peck has prepared a very comprehensive bibliography on
Chaucer's **Boece** and some of the other lesser known works by Chaucer
(Peck 1988); it is an extensive reference work which, for the **Boece**, goes
far beyond the scope of this annotated bibliography in listing sources.

Walter Skeat, in his edition of Chaucer's works (Skeat 1894-7),
points out that the poet's first encounter with Boethius probably came
through his reading of Jean de Meun.

We are chiefly concerned here with the **Consolation of
Philosophy**, a work which . . . first influenced Chaucer
indirectly, through the use of it made by Jean de Meun in the
poem entitled **Le Roman de la Rose**, as well as directly, at a
later period, through his own translation of it. Indeed, I have
little doubt that Chaucer's attention was drawn to it when,
somewhat early in life, he first perused with diligence that
remarkable poem; and that it was from the following passage
that he probably drew the inference that it might be well for him
to translate the whole work:--

Ce puet l'en bien des clers enquerre
Qui **Boece de Confort** lisent,

> Et les sentences qui la gisent,
> **Dont grans biens as gens laiz feroit**
> **Qui bien le lor translateroit.** (ll. 5052-6)
> (Skeat 1894-7, x)

Skeat's observation enjoys general acceptance among the critics of the **Boece**.

Lisi Cipriani, in an article (Cipriani 1907), "Studies in the Influence of the **Romance of the Rose** upon Chaucer," agrees with Skeat, pointing out that Chaucer's introduction to Boethius was via the **Roman de la Rose**. For this reason, critics should exercise caution in identifying Boethian influence in Chaucer's works: the influence might well have come from Jean's use of Boethius (as in the Boethian soliloquies in the **Troilus**, for example).

Having considered the critics who deal in a general way with Chaucer's **Boece**, we must now turn to the scholarship which focuses on specific problems. It falls into three categories. First, there are the studies of such preliminary matters as the date of Chaucer's **Boece** and the manuscripts and editions. Second, there are analyses of Chaucer's prose style. Third, there are investigations on Chaucer's sources, which divide conveniently into three relatively independent areas of scholarship: Latin manuscripts, Latin commentaries, and French translations which Chaucer may have consulted when preparing his translation. These categories of criticism will be treated in this section of the chapter in the order in which they are listed here.

The **Consolatio**, discovered relatively late by Chaucer, with its profound effect upon the poet's thinking, has been useful in dating his more problematic works. For example, John Koch, in his article (Koch 1922), uses the **Boece** as the fixed point for a relative dating of Chaucer's other works. By studying where Chaucer puts the content of the **Consolatio** to use, he was able to suggest the order in which the works were written. Building upon Koch's work and information gathered by such critics as Skeat and Cipriani who recognized Chaucer's debt to Jean de Meun (Cipriani 1907), Victor Langhans assigned the **Boece** to c.1380, before Chaucer had written his major works, but after he had produced the **Book of the Duchess** (1364) and the **Parliament of Fowls** (1374). In his article (Langhans 1929), the **Boece** proves important in dating the "Melibeus." Boethian material is so conspicuous by its absence that Chaucer must have written the tale before he made his translation.

Eleven manuscripts and manuscript fragments of Chaucer's **Boece** have been catalogued:

1) MS Camb. Ii.3.21
2) MS Camb. Ii.1.38
3) MS Addit. 10340
    [British Library]
4) MS Addit. 16165
    [British Library]
5) MS Harl. 2421
6) Bodl. 797
7) Auct. F.3.5
8) Hengwrt MS
    [Canterbury Tales] Hn
9) MS Salisbury, Sarum 113
10) Phillips Collection MS 9472
11) **Fragmenta Manuscripta** 150
    [University of Missouri-Columbia].

On the quality, completeness, and importance of each manuscript, the introductions to the various editions of the **Boece** offer the best information. The most recently discovered fragment is described in an article by George Pace and Linda Voigts (Pace and Voigts 1979). These authors suggest that such a fragment, used as the end pages of another manuscript, might represent the remains of a manuscript discarded by Caxton after making his edition. Tim Machan, in an article, studies the scribal glosses in these manuscripts, concluding that "although some glosses do imply a glossarial tradition in the **Boece** manuscripts, this tradition evidently was corrupted in such a way that it will be impossible to determine where in the textual tradition the first glossed manuscript . . . occurred and how its glosses were transmitted" (Machan 1987, 133). In another article (Machan 1988), this same critic discusses the special problems editors of medieval texts encounter. His specific example is Chaucer's **Boece**. Rita Copeland studies Chaucer's **Consolatio** translation in order to indicate the importance of rhetoric as a tool of interpretative translation (Copeland 1987); the article includes a summary of Chaucer's use of Jean de Meun's translation and of commentaries in coming to understand and translate the Latin text.

Chaucer, unlike many of the other medieval translators of the **Consolatio**, enjoyed some fame during his lifetime, and partly because neither the writer nor his work was ever forgotten or lost, there is no problem of authorship for the **Boece**. It was in print within one hundred years of its completion. The history of its printed editions begins with Caxton, about 1478 (Caxton c.1478): the **Boece** is thought to have been edited about the time Caxton was publishing Chaucer's other works. This first editing was reprinted in 1978 by Beverly Boyd (Boyd 1978). Richard Griffith, in his very favorable review of Boyd's work, points out the need for a facsimile edition of Caxton's text (Griffith 1980).

Caxton has been described as a literary critic of some ability, but N.F. Blake, in an article (Blake 1967), exposes this notion as a myth. Blake points out that many of the critical comments assigned to Caxton were simply borrowed, having been written by others. Even Caxton's eulogy to Chaucer was written by someone else. Another myth was exposed by Guy Bayley Dolson in an article (Dolson 1926, **American Journal of Philology**): he proved that Caxton did not translate the **Consolatio** himself, as some records indicate, but that Chaucer's translation had been falsely ascribed to him. Dolson traces the entire history of this error through the criticism.

The second editing of Chaucer's works (Thynne 1532) was accomplished by William Thynne. This **Boece**, however, is simply a re-publication of Caxton's work of half a century earlier, with little re-editing, if any at all.

The next two editings of the text, both made for the Chaucer Society, were printed alone, not as part of a collection of Chaucer's works. Richard Morris became the first modern editor of the translation (Morris 1886), producing a text based on Addit. MS 10340. His choice of a base manuscript was not the best, however; so F.J. Furnivall produced another text (Furnivall 1886), based on the famous MS Ii.3.21. The text represented by this second manuscript is supposedly closer to Chaucer's translation than the one consulted by Morris.

Walter Skeat published **The Complete Works of Geoffrey Chaucer** between 1894 and 1897 (Skeat 1894-7), which included the **Boece**. Skeat's introductions are very helpful, giving good summaries of scholarship relevant to various problems in the **Boece**. Also important for its introductions and notes is the Globe Edition of Chaucer's Works

(Liddell, Heath, McCormick and Pollard 1908). F.N. Robinson produced a one-volume edition of Chaucer's works which became a popular college text (Robinson 1957). A recent edition of Chaucer's works, edited by John H. Fisher (Fisher 1977), is very readable edition, glossing linguistic difficulties at the bottom of each page. Finally, Robinson's text has been reedited by Larry Benson (Benson 1987), and this edition, called **The Riverside Chaucer** (or "Robinson III"), includes such features as glosses at the bottom of pages and many pages of textual and explanatory notes. These are the editions of Chaucer's **Consolatio** translation.

Chaucer chose prose for only four of his works: the **Boece**, the "Melibeus," the "Parson's Tale," and the **Astrolabe**--the **Equitorie of the Planetis** is a fifth, if it is indeed Chaucer's work. When compared with his poetic works, their effect has generally proved disappointing. The four works have received no substantial acclaim for aesthetic quality, and few students today read the "Melibeus" or the "Parson's Tale" as part of the **Canterbury Tales** (primarily because Coghill did not translate them into Modern English), but their place at the beginning of an English prose tradition is significant. Johann Frieshammer published a thorough study of the linguistic aspects of Chaucer's prose (Frieshammer 1910) in which he finds the prose works to be touchstone pieces in the history of English literature.

Hugh Fraser Stewart's rather negative opinion of Chaucer as a translator of Latin, which he expressed in his **Essay**, has been quoted above, but in the same book (Stewart 1891), he also mentions some of the Boethian meters in which certain lines are rendered into verse. This would indicate that Chaucer the poet is still visible under the prose of his translation. Concerning certain portions of the **Consolatio** which Chaucer translated elsewhere into verse (the so-called Boethian lyrics), Stewart says:

> Let the reader take Troylus's soliloquy on Freewill and Predestination (book iv, st. 134-148) and read it side by side with the corresponding passages in **Boece** (M., pp 152-159), and he cannot fail to feel the superiority of the former to the latter. With what clearness and precision does the argument unfold itself, how close is the reasoning, how vigorous and yet graceful is the language!

It is to be regretted that Chaucer did not do for all the metra of the **Consolation** what he did for the fifth of the second book. A solitary gem like "The Former Age" makes us long for a whole set. (Stewart 1891, 228)

George Saintsbury voices a slightly different opinion in his book, **A History of English Prose Rhythm.** Unlike most of the earlier critics, he fails to lament the fact that Chaucer did not translate the meters of the **Consolatio** into English verse: "Translations of verse into verse are, very frequently, not worth the paper they are written on . . ." (Saintsbury 1912, 72). Nevertheless, he praises Chaucer's cadenced prose, attributing its effects, however, to Chaucer's "good ear" rather than to any conscious effort in consistently using rhythmic prose patterns.

George Philip Krapp writes, in his book-length study: "For the development of the technic of English writing in verse, Chaucer is important; for the development of the technic of English prose, he is almost negligible" (Krapp 1915, 10). Chaucer, he writes, followed the conventional custom of writing most of his greatest works in verse. Although he lived during a time when, through the work of Wycliff and his followers, English prose was becoming acceptable, Chaucer was no innovator in the use of prose.

According to Robert Root, "The prose style of the translation, cumbersome and at times confused, and for our modern taste much too rhetorical, is in striking contrast with the directness and simplicity, the clearness and grace of Chaucer's verse" (Root 1934, 10). Thus, he voices here the critical attitude held generally toward Chaucer's prose: in comparison to his magnificent verses, it disappoints the reader.

Margaret Schlauch, however, viewed Chaucer's prose style quite differently, drawing the conclusion that Chaucer was consciously using and adapting stylistic devices from both native and Latin sources. For example, she writes:

The frequency of cadence and other rhythmical devices is related to total subject matter and to the intended audience of a given text. The manner ranges from the artful patterned frequently lyrical rhythms of the Boethius and "Melibeus," with their echoed cadences and quasi-refrains, to the less adorned discourse of the "Parson's Tale," to the straightforward exposition of the

Astrolabe, with its free and original Prologue. (Schlauch 1950, 588-9)

As noted above, Chaucer's use of cadenced prose had been observed before, but Schlauch is the first critic to place so much positive value on it. Schlauch published another article (Schlauch 1966) in which she examined more thoroughly Chaucer's four prose works, gathering further evidence of his deliberate use of cadences. Her findings have not, so far, been accepted. Morton Donner, in an article, studies Chaucer's inventiveness in creating vocabulary to translate his various sources of the **Consolatio.** He concludes:

> In [the] **Boece,** his [Chaucer's] sense of responsibility to
> Boethius's meaning combines with his appreciation of the
> semantic properties of linguistic forms to produce a system of
> derivations and adaptations that will justly, as Dame Philosophy
> puts it, "unplyten . . sentence with wordes." (Donner 1984,
> 202)

Special praise is given to Chaucer's inventiveness in creating gerunds and participles.

Caroline D. Eckhart, in an article (Eckhart 1983), makes a very intelligent statement on why Chaucer may have chosen to do his **Consolatio** translation entirely in prose rather than in the mixture of prose and verse which is found in the Latin original. For Chaucer, verse is the language of ambiguity and prose is the language of exact meaning, "naked wordes." The **Boece** represents one of Chaucer's efforts to create an unambiguous text, so he chose prose as a vehicle for the whole work.

This brings us to the source studies on Chaucer's **Consolatio** translation. As stated, they can be divided into three areas of focus: 1) the problem of a Latin manuscript; 2) criticism concerned with Latin commentaries; and 3) Chaucer's use of a French translation in preparing his **Boece.** Edmund Tait Silk, in his dissertation (Silk 1930), identifies MS Camb. Ii.3.21 as belonging to the probable manuscript tradition which Chaucer consulted while producing his **Boece.** Exception to Silk's findings is taken in Barnet Kottler's dissertation (Kottler 1953): the Cambridge manuscript is very close to Chaucer's translation, but enough variant readings exist to warrant a continued search for **the** manuscript tradition used by Chaucer. Kottler adds this argument in an article (Kottler 1955), pointing out that the critical texts of the **Consolatio** used today are from about eighty-four manuscripts dating from the ninth, tenth, and eleventh centuries. By the fourteenth century, a vulgate tradition had developed for the Latin text, giving widely variant readings to the **Consolatio**. One of these later manuscripts would better represent the Latin source used by Chaucer. The article emphasizes the importance of studies of the later **Consolatio** manuscripts in order to understand the vernacular translations more completely.

Scholarship on the commentaries used by Chaucer begins with Mark Liddell's article (Liddell 1897). Liddell suggests that the commentary attributed to Thomas Aquinas, the so-called Pseudo-Aquinas, influenced Chaucer, both directly and indirectly, through its use in the French translation which Chaucer also consulted. Kate O. Petersen, however, shows Liddell to be in error. In her article (Petersen 1903), she maintains that most of the material from the Pseudo-Aquinas which Chaucer seems to have borrowed is also found in Trevet's commentary on the **Consolatio**. She makes a good case for Trevet's as the only commentary consulted by Chaucer in preparing his **Boece**. Edmund Taite Silk's dissertation (Silk 1930), mentioned above in connection with the problem of Latin manuscripts, describes MS Camb. Ii.3.21. Not only is this Latin text very close to Chaucer's translation, but it is also often written or bound up with Trevet's commentary. An examination of the complex problem of influence from the commentaries upon Chaucer's **Boece** is given in Alistair Minnis' article (Minnis 1981), which considers many possibilities of direct influence; the article also notes such indirect influences as those of commentaries upon subsequent commentaries. Mark J. Gleason, in an article, studies Chaucer's use of Trevet's commentary very thoroughly. He discovers that the glosses

> indicate that Chaucer was interested in writing a personal,
> scholarly, working translation of Boethius and that he employed
> Trevet's commentary as a vital source for understanding the
> philosophy and learning of Boethius. (Gleason 1987, 102)

Finally, Minnis, in an article (Minnis 1987), argues convincingly that Chaucer not only had access to Trevet's commentary but also to glosses from the commentary of Remigius of Auxerre: "Trevet was his

[Chaucer's] commentator **par excellence**, while the Remigian glosses constituted a minor source" (Minnis, 1987, 119).

   John Hollander's article (Hollander 1956) speculates, on the basis of vocabulary found in the **Boece**, that Chaucer's knowledge of music theory was more substantial than formerly believed. This information has little significance for studies of Chaucer and the **Consolatio** commentaries, but it indicates another area for investigation into Chaucer's sources: the field of music.

   Although no direct connection with Alfred the Great's **Consolatio** translation has been discovered, an indirect connection has long been known: Trevet had consulted Alfred's work while preparing his commentary, and Chaucer consulted Trevet. Peggy Faye Shirley's dissertation (Shirley 1977) compares Alfred's and Chaucer's translations. She also makes no direct connection between the works, but she concludes that the differences reflect the temperaments of the two translators and the demands of their times. Olga Fischer's article (Fischer 1979) compares the philosophical terms found in Alfred's and Chaucer's translations. Old English is seen to have been an adequate vehicle for the philosophical concepts contained in the **Consolatio**, whereas Chaucer, using Middle English, was much more dependent on loanwords.

   Chaucer's use of a French translation in preparing his **Boece** has been the subject of much critical debate. As early as 1886, Richard Morris, in his edition of Chaucer's **Consolatio** translation, stated very plainly:

> Chaucer did not English Boethius second-hand, through any early French version, as some have supposed, but made his translation with the Latin original before him. (Morris 1886, xiii)

Morris had been studying the wrong French manuscript, however. The text he used in making his comparison was not that prepared by Jean de Meun, and it, indeed, had not influenced Chaucer. Hugh Fraser Stewart, in his **Essay** (Stewart 1891), expressed some doubts about Morris' findings. He presented parallel passages from Chaucer's translation and from the French equivalents from MS BN fr. 1097, a manuscript later shown to belong to the tradition of Jean de Meun's translation. The similarities in phrasing were immediately apparent. But in spite of this evidence, Skeat still maintained that Chaucer translated the **Consolatio** independent of any French translator (Skeat 1894-7).

As a result of work on an edition of John Walton's **Consolatio** translation, an edition which failed to materialize, Mark Liddell discovered that Chaucer had, indeed, relied upon the Jean de Meun translation. He published his discovery in an article (Liddell 1895). Critics have not disputed this fact since the article's publication. Working on the edition of Walton's translation which did materialize, Mark Science discovered that the word in Chaucer's **Boece** which translates the Latin **degeneret** should be emended (Science 1923). He was led to this opinion by the word's French origin and by the fact that he was convinced of Chaucer's use of French sources in the preparation of his translation. Tim Machan, responding to this article and to information given in the introduction to Science's edition of John Walton's **Consolatio** translation (Machan 1984, **Notes and Queries**), finds that no emendation is necessary.

Ernest Langlois proved conclusively that the manuscript, MS BN fr. 1097, does represent the translation made by Jean de Meun (E. Langlois 1913), and using the extensive quotations made available in Langlois' article, John Livingston Lowes proved the correspondence between Chaucer's work and Jean's (Lowes 1917): the similarities of phrasing and word choice are very convincing. Working independently, Bernard Jefferson published in the same year parallel passages from Chaucer's **Boece** and MS BN fr. 1097 (Jefferson 1917), presenting arguments similar to Lowes'. Furthermore, James Cline showed in an article (Cline 1936) that Chaucer had modeled his method of translation on that used by Jean de Meun in his French prose translation of the **Consolatio**. Venceslas Dedeck-Héry, in an article (Dedeck-Héry 1936), adds his voice to those of critics who believe that Chaucer's **Consolatio** translation was influenced by Jean's. Criticism on both the French translation and Chaucer's had finally established the fact of Jean's influence upon Chaucer. Venceslas Dedeck-Héry devoted most of his academic career to Jean de Meun's translation of the **Consolatio**. His greatest accomplishment was his critical edition of the text (Dedeck-Héry 1952), published posthumously. The edition was the necessary instrument for any definitive comparative study of the French and English translations. Mentioning only the possibility of influence of commentaries upon both Chaucer and Jean, however, Dedeck-Héry listed instances in which both translators had added the same materials as glosses upon the Boethian text (Dedeck-Héry 1937). Nevertheless, in an article (Dedeck-Héry 1940), the similarities were shown to be considerable. Finally, the cautious Dedeck-Héry began an article with: "Que Chaucer, pour sa traduction de Boèce, se soit servi de celle de Jean de Meun est un fait établi" (Dedeck-Héry 1944, 18). He then moved on to a new level of inquiry by attempting to discover which particular manuscript Chaucer might have used. He divided the tradition into two groups, "a" and "b." Group "a" contains the famous MS BN fr. 1097. Another manuscript from that group, B (Besançon 434) shows the greatest affinity to Chaucer's **Boece**, but since that particular manuscript had entered the collection of King Charles V of France in 1372, Chaucer's manuscript can, at best, only have been analogous to it.

As indicated by this review of the criticism, the problem of sources for Chaucer's **Boece** is a complex one, and if the article by Minnis (Minnis 1981) is indicative of future research, what have been three relatively independent areas of inquiry may develop into one very intricate network of affiliations, combining investigations of the commentaries with investigations of the French **Consolatio** translation. As noted above, this is indeed the direction taken in some of Minnis' research (Minnis 1987).

Though well known, Chaucer's translation seemed inadequate even in its own time: within thirty years, the **Consolatio** was rendered into English verse by John Walton, working under the patronage of Lady Elizabeth Berkeley.

List of Relevant Titles

1.   Benson, Larry D., ed. **The Riverside Chaucer**. 3rd ed. Boston: Houghton Mifflin, 1987.

       This volume contains the most recent editing of Chaucer's **Boece**.

2.   Blake, N.F. "Caxton and Chaucer." **Leeds Studies in English**, n.s. 1 (1967): 19-36.

       Blake argues that Caxton was not a good critic of the literature he published. He points out that

Caxton's observations on Chaucer's works are "second-hand"; the edition of c.1479, for example, contains an evaluation of Chaucer which is highly derivative. Caxton also seems to have appropriated his eulogy to Chaucer from one Surigone rather than to have commissioned it.

3. Boyd, Beverly, ed. **Chaucer According to William Caxton: Minor Poems and Boece.** Lawrence, Kansas: Allen Press, 1978.

This is a re-printing (not a facsimile) of the text of the **Boece** as it was printed by Caxton.

4. Caxton, William. **Chaucer's** Boece. N.p.: n.p., c.1478.

This is the first published edition of Chaucer's **Consolatio** translation.

5. Cipriani, Lisi. "Studies in the Influence of the **Romance of the Rose** upon Chaucer." **PMLA** 22 [n.s., 25] (1907): 552-95.

Cipriani points out that Chaucer's first encounter with Boethius was indirect, through the writings of Jean de Meun. Furthermore, many Boethian influences upon Chaucer's work have parallels in the **Roman de la Rose.**

6. Cline, James M. "Chaucer and Jean de Meun: **De Consolatione Philosophiae.**" **Journal of English Literary History** 3 (1936): 170-81.

Chaucer used a method of open translation (expansion of Latin words into English phrases) as opposed to word-for-word translation in preparing his **Boece.** Thus, he can be said to have erred in the direction of unnecessary fullness. He was

following a method established by Jean de Meun
in his prose translation of the **Consolatio.**

7.   Coolidge, John S. "Boethius and 'That Last
      Infirmity of Noble Mind.'" **Philological
      Quarterly** 42 (1963): 176-82.

      Fame in Milton's **Lycidas** is referred to as "That
      Last Infirmity of Noble Mind." The reference has
      been attributed to Tacitus' **Histories**, vol. 4, v.
      This article indicates a more probable source to be
      the **Consolatio.** The context, according to
      Coolidge, is more appropriate.

8.   Copeland, Rita. "Rhetoric and Vernacular
      Translation in the Middle Ages." **Studies in the
      Age of Chaucer** 9 (1987): 41-75.

      Using Chaucer's **Boece** and Walton's
      Consolatio translation as subjects, Copeland
      studies medieval translation in terms of rhetoric
      and rhetoric's function as an interpretative tool.

9.   Dedeck-Héry, Venceslas Louis. "Un Fragment
      inédit de la traduction de la **Consolation** de
      Boèce par Jean De Meun." **Romanic Review**
      27 (1936): 110-24.

      Having transcribed all the manuscripts of the Jean
      de Meun prose **Consolatio** translation, Dedeck-
      Héry compares those texts to Chaucer's
      translation. He affirms, after much tentative
      consideration, that Chaucer did use Jean's
      translation and that his debt is considerable. The
      article strengthens Lowes' argument (Lowes 1936)
      by introducing more examples of passages which
      indicate indebtedness. It also appreciates the
      possibility of mutual influences from some
      independent source, such as Trevet's commentary.

10. ----------. "Jean de Meun et Chaucer, traducteurs de
la Consolation de Boèce." PMLA 52 (1937): 967-
91.

In this article, Dedeck-Héry compares certain
passages from the **Consolatio** translations made
by Jean and Chaucer.

11. ----------. "The Manuscripts of the Translation of
Boethius' **Consolatio** by Jean de Meung."
Speculum 15 (1940): 432-43.

The article contains material preliminary to any
search for the manuscript of Jean de Meun's
Consolatio translation used by Chaucer in
preparing his **Boece**.

12. ----------. "Le **Boèce** de Chaucer et les manuscrits
français de la **Consolatio** de Jean de Meun."
PMLA 59 (1944): 18-25.

Dedeck-Héry demonstrates here that Chaucer used a
manuscript of the Jean de Meun translation from a
group designated as "group a"--similar to the text
found in a fragmentary manuscript, F3 (fragment,
Bodl. Rawl. G.41).

13. ----------, ed. "Boethius' **De Consolatione** by
Jean de Meun." **Mediaeval Studies** 14 (1952):
165-275.

This is the critical edition of Jean de Meun's
Consolatio translation. Chaucer used this
translation in preparing his **Boece**.

14. Dolson, Guy Bayley. "I.T.--Translator of
Boethius." **American Journal of Philology**
42 (1921): 266.

Dolson suggests that "I.T." was John Thorpe rather than the John Thorie who had been suggested by Stewart and Rand in their Loeb Classical Library edition of Boethius.

15.   ----------. "Boethius' **Consolation of Philosophy** in English Literature During the Eighteenth Century." **Classical Weekly** 15 (1922): 124-6.

The Eighteenth Century has left four translations of Boethius' last work, and interest in the **Consolatio** during the century is verified by statements recorded by Dr. Johnson and members of the Literary Club with whom he associated.

16.   ----------. "Imprisoned English Authors and the **Consolation of Philosophy** of Boethius." **American Journal of Philology** 43 (1922): 168-9.

The article mentions several English writers (Thomas Moore, John Leslie, James I of Scotland) who found comfort in the **Consolatio** while in prison.

17.   ----------. "Southey and Landor and the **Consolation of Philosophy** of Boethius." **American Journal of Philology** 43 (1922): 356-8.

Dolson corrects an assertion that Landor's model for the **Imaginary Conversations** of 1824 was the work of Plato rather than that of Boethius. Both Southey and Landor are shown to have been influenced by the **Consolatio.**

18.   ----------. "The Consolation of Philosophy of
       Boethius in English Literature;" Ph.D. diss.,
       Cornell University, 1926.

       This work places Chaucer's Boece in the context
       of all occurrences of influence from the
       Consolatio on English literature. It gives no
       comparative analysis.

19.   ----------. "Did Caxton Translate the De
       Consolatione Philosophiae of Boethius?"
       American Journal of Philology 47 (1926):
       83-6.

       This article traces the history of the myth of a
       Caxton translation of the Consolatio. Caxton
       merely printed Chaucer's Boece.

20.   Donaghey, Brian S. "Alexander Pope's and Sir
       William Turmbull's Translations of Boethius."
       Leeds Studies in English n.s. 1 (1967): 71-
       82.

       Pope translated the opening and final lines of
       Book III, meter 9, of the Consolatio. In this
       article, Donaghey suggests the date 1703 for the
       translation. He also suggests that Pope's
       translation influenced Sir William Turmbull,
       about the same time, to make his own hasty
       translation.

21.   Donner, Morton. "Derived Words in Chaucer's
       Boece: the Translator as Wordsmith." Chaucer
       Review 18 (1984): 187-203.

       Donner here gives a study of Chaucer as creator of
       new vocabulary. The article praises him for his
       inventiveness, particularly in creating new gerunds

and participles to convey active meaning in his
Consolatio translation.

22.   Eckhardt, Caroline D. "The Medieval
        Prosimetrum Genre (from Boethius to
        Boece)." Genre 16 (1983): 21-38.

        Eckhart sees Chaucer's use of prose for his **Boece**
        as consistent with his general practice: he used
        verse when he wanted to be ambiguous and prose
        when he wanted to be direct.

23.   Fehlauer, Friedrich. **Die englischen**
        Übersetzungen von Boethius' De
        Consolatione Philosophiae. Ph.D. diss., Albertus-
        Universität zu Königsberg, 1908. Königsberg:
        Hartungsche Buchdruckerei, 1908.

        Fehlauer presents a summary of the scholarship on
        the **Boece**; he places it in the context of all
        English translations through the fifteenth century.

24.   ----------. **Die englischen Übersetzungen**
        von Boethius' De Consolatione Philosophiae.
        Berlin: Emil Felber, 1909.

        This is another printed version of the dissertation
        listed above.

25.   Fischer, Olga. "A Comparative Study of
        Philosophical Terms in the Alfredian and
        Chaucerian Boethius." **Neophilologus** 63
        (1979): 622-39.

        Fischer compares the philosophical terms used by
        Alfred and Chaucer in the **Consolatio**
        translations. After an initial appreciation of the
        differences in sources and intentions, Old English,
        in the hands of Alfred, is shown to be an adequate

vehicle for Boethian concepts, but Middle English, in the hands of Chaucer, required many loan words.

26. Fisher, John H., ed. **The Complete Poetry and Prose of Geoffrey Chaucer.** New York: Hold, Rinehart and Winston, 1977.

The edition of the **Boece** contained in this volume is based primarily on MS Cambridge Ii. 3.21 (I). The glosses at the bottoms of pages containing text make this a very readable edition.

27. Flügel, Ewald. "Kleinere Mitteilungen aus Handschriften." **Anglia: Zeitschrift für englische Philologie** 14 (1892): 463-501.

Section III of this article gives extracts from the text of an Elizabethan **Consolatio** translation by John Bracegirdle (Add. MS 11401).

28. Frieshammer, Johann. **Die sprachliche Form der Chaucerschen Prosa: ihr Verhältnis zur Reimtechnik des Dichters sowie zur Sprache der alteren Londoner Urkunden.** Studien zur Englischen Philologie. Halle: Max Niemeyer Verlag, 1910.

The book treats the language of Chaucer's four prose works. It presents a thorough study of the linguistic aspects of Chaucer's prose and of its effects upon the history of the language. It is not a study of the aesthetics of prose style.

29. Furnivall, F.J., ed. **Chaucer's** Boece **Englisht from Anicii Manlii Severini Boetii** Philosophiae Consolationis **Libri Quinque.** Chaucer Society, no. 75 (first series). 1886.

Reprint. New York: Johnson Reprint Corporation, 1967.

This is the second editing of Chaucer's **Boece** to be published by the Chaucer Society. It is an edition of MS. Ii. 3.21., including a glossary to the text.

30.   Gleason, Mark J. "Clearing the Fields: Towards a Reassessment of Chaucer's Use of Trevet in the **Boece**." In **The Medieval Boethius: Studies in the Vernacular Translations of** De Consolatione Philosophiae, edited by Alastair J. Minnis, 89-105. Woodbridge, Suffolk: D.S. Brewer, 1987.

Gleason discusses Chaucer's use of Trevet's commentary, discovering that the work was used as a scholarly tool in the poet's effort to understand the many diverse aspects of Boethius' complex work.

31.   Green, Richard L. "'The Port of Peace': Not Death But God." Modern Language Library of Liberal Arts. Indianapolis: Bobbs-Merrill, 1962.

Green identifies a poem from Carleton Brown's **Religious Lyrics of the Fifteenth Century** as John Walton's translation of Boethius' **Consolatio**, Book III, meter 10. This helps to clarify certain previous misinterpretations of the poem.

32.   Griffith, Richard R. Review of **Chaucer According to William Caxton: Minor Poems and Boece,** edited by Beverly Boyd. **Studies in the Age of Chaucer** 2 (1980): 151-3.

This review is favorable in terms of Boyd's
scholarship and accuracy. A question is raised,
however, as to whether a facsimile edition with
notes might not be more useful than a reprint.

33.   Hammond, Eleanor Prescott. "Boethius: Chaucer:
        Walton: Lydgate." **Modern Language Notes**
        41 (1926): 534-5.

        Two brief notes comprise this article: one adds
        items to Jefferson's list of Chaucer's
        mistranslations, the other shows direct influence
        of the **Consolatio** on John Lydgate.

34.   Herzig, Marie Jacobus. "The Early Recension and
        Continuity of Certain Middle English Texts in the
        Sixteenth Century." Ph.D. diss., University of
        Pennsylvania, 1973.

        Herzig uses the **Consolatio**, along with the
        Lydgate Canon, Piers Plowman, and the
        Book of Saint Albans, to demonstrate the
        literary continuity between the sixteenth century
        and the earlier medieval period.

35.   Hollander, John. "'Moedes or Prolaciouns' in
        Chaucer's **Boece." Modern Language Notes**
        71 (1956): 397-9.

        One word which Chaucer adds to the **Boece** that
        does not appear in the Latin text is **prolaciouns**
        in the phrase "moedes or prolaciouns." This
        mistaken gloss indicates that Chaucer knew more
        about fourteenth-century music than is usually
        believed.

36.   Houghton, Walter E., Jr. "English Translations of
        Boethius's **De Consolatione Philosophiae**

in the Seventeenth Century." Ph.D. diss., Yale
University, 1931.

As the title indicates, this is a study of the
Consolatio translations in England in the
seventeenth century.

37.   ----------. "S.E.M.--'Translator' of Boethius,"
Review of English Studies 7 (1931): 160-7.

After pointing out that the work by "S.E.M." is
no translation at all, but rather England's first
Latin edition with a study, Houghton identifies
"S.E.M." as Sir Edward Spencer (Spencer, Edward,
Miles or of Middlesex).

38.   Jefferson, Bernard L. **Chaucer and the**
Consolation of Philosophy **of Boethius.** 1917.
Reprint. New York: Haskell House, 1965.

This is still the basic work on the subject of
Boethius and Chaucer. The first chapter treats the
strengths and weaknesses of Chaucer's translation.
It offers a catalogue of Chaucer's possible sources,
his inaccuracies in translating the Latin, and his
linguistic treatment of the **Consolatio.**

39.   Koch, John. "Chaucer's Boethiusübersetzung: ein
Beitrag zur Bestimmung der Chronologie seiner
Werke." **Anglia: Zeitschrift für englische
Philologie** 46 (1922): 1-51.

After some introductory material, the author
presents a significant twenty-five page, book-by-
book summary of the **Consolatio** and its
influences on Chaucer's works. The analysis leads
to a re-evaluation of the dates assigned to certain
of Chaucer's works.

40.   Kottler, Barnet. "Chaucer's **Boece** and the Late
       Medieval Textual Tradition of the **Consolatio
       Philosophiae**." Ph.D. diss., Yale University,
       1953.

       In response to Silk's dissertation (Silk 1930),
       Kottler agrees that the Cambridge MS Ii. 3.21. is
       the closest Latin text to Chaucer's **Boece** found
       thus far, but maintains that there are enough
       variant readings to warrant a further search for **the**
       Latin text used by Chaucer. Other manuscripts of
       the fourteenth-century vulgate tradition of the
       Consolatio cannot be dismissed.

41.   ----------. "The Vulgate Tradition of the
       Consolatio Philosophiae in the Fourteenth
       Century." **Mediaeval Studies** 17 (1955): 209-
       14.

       The critical editions of the **Consolatio** are based
       primarily on about eighty-four manuscripts from
       the ninth, tenth, and eleventh centuries. The more
       than three hundred manuscripts surviving from the
       eleventh to the fifteenth centuries are generally not
       considered in critical studies. Vulgate readings
       developed in the fourteenth century, and this article
       indicates the importance of these late medieval
       developments for such translators as Jean de Meun
       and Chaucer.

42.   Krapp, George Philip, ed. **The Rise of
       English Literary Prose**. 1915. Reprint. New
       York: Frederick Ungar, 1963.

       The introduction contains an especially good
       statement on Chaucer's use of prose. The medium
       for entertaining literature in the fourteenth century
       was verse. Prose was for practical or documentary

purposes. Chaucer's use of prose follows this convention.

43.   Langhans, Victor. "Die Datierung der Prosastücke Chaucers." **Anglia: Zeitschrift für englische Philologie** 53 (1929): 235-68.

The article assigns Chaucer's **Boece** to c.1380, before he had written his major works, but after the **Book of the Duchess** (1364) and the **Parliament of Fowls** (1374). Langhans indicates that Chaucer's acquaintance with the **Consolatio** prior to 1380 was indirect, from his reading the **Roman de la Rose**. Due to Chaucer's use of the content of the **Consolatio**, his translation is important in dating the "Melibeus": material from the **Consolatio** is so conspicuous by its absence that it had to have been written before Chaucer wrote his **Boece**.

44.   Langlois, Ernest. "La Traduction de Boèce par Jean de Meun." **Romania** 42 (1913): 331-69.

Langlois identifies the French prose **Consolatio** translation (represented by MS BN fr. 1097) as the work of Jean de Meun. Quotations from the manuscript contained in this article substantiated Chaucer's indebtedness to Jean's translation in preparing his **Boece**.

45.   Liddell, Mark. H. "Chaucer's Translation of Boece's **Boke of Comfort** (Announcement of Chaucer's Use of the French Translation in His Own Translation of Boethius)." **Academy** 1 (1895): 227.

Taking MS BN fr. 1097 as representative of Jean de Meun's **Consolatio** translation, Liddell shows that Chaucer was indebted to Jean in preparing his **Boece**.

46. ----------. "One of Chaucer's Sources." **The Nation** 64 (1897): 124-5.

Liddell claims that, in addition to Jean de Meun's **Consolatio** translation, Chaucer also availed himself of a Latin commentary in preparing his **Boece**. Liddell suggests that it was the commentary attributed to Thomas Aquinas, the Pseudo-Aquinas, which both Chaucer and Jean de Meun used as a reference.

47. Liddell, Mark H., H.F. Heath, W.S. McCormick, A.W. Pollard, eds. **The Works of Chaucer** (The Globe Edition). London: Macmillan, 1908.

Some of the introductory observations here are important for studies of the **Boece**.

48. Lowes, John Livingston. "Chaucer's **Boethius** and Jean de Meun." **Romanic Review** 8 (1917): 383-400.

Basing his study on quotations made available by Langlois in 1913, Lowes demonstrates that Chaucer had relied on the Jean de Meun translation in preparing his **Boece**. Most convincing is the evidence from parallel phrases found in both translations. The use of similar glosses is questionable since any evidence might come from a mutual source.

49. Machan, Tim William. "Chaucer the Philologist: the **Boece**." Ph.D. diss., University of Wisconsin, 1984.

Machan takes the stand that Chaucer produced his
Boece not as literary prose but as a close
translation of the text. In his efforts, Chaucer
proves himself to be "a successful translator and a
skilled philologist."

50.   ----------. **"Forlynen:** a Ghost Word
Rematerializes." **Notes and Queries** 31 (1984):
22-4.

This note responds to Mark Science's earlier note
(Science 1923) on the appearance of **forlynen** in
the **Boece**. Machan finds that no emendation is
necessary in Chaucer but that emendation is
necessary in the texts produced by his editors.

51.   ----------. **Techniques of Translation:
Chaucer's** Boece. Norman, Okla.: Pilgrim
Books, 1985.

This is the published version of the study which
began as Machan's dissertation listed above.

52.   ----------. "Glosses in the Manuscripts of Chaucer's
Boece." In **The Medieval Boethius:
Studies in the Vernacular Translations
of** De Consolatione Philosophiae, edited by
Alastair J. Minnis, 125-38. Woodbridge, Suffolk:
D.S. Brewer, 1987.

In this article, Machan looks at the glosses upon
Chaucer's text, as opposed to the glosses which
Chaucer put into his text. He classifies the
various types of glosses by function, concluding
that, if a glossing tradition indeed existed, it was
limited and it probably did not originate with
Chaucer.

53. ----------. "Editorial Method and Medieval
Translations: The Example of Chaucer's **Boece**."
**Studies in Bibliography: Papers of the
Bibliographical Society of the
University of Virginia** 41 (1988): 188-96.

In this article, Machan complains that the concept
of "canon" too narrowly limits scholarly interest
in the field of medieval literary studies. For
editors of medieval texts, the concept of "textual
identity" should include the author's intention and
the attitude of the "original audience" toward the
work.

54. Minnis, Alistair. "Aspects of the Medieval French
and English Traditions of the **De Consolatione
Philosophiae**." In **Boethius: His Life,
Thought and Influence**, edited by Margaret
Gibson, 312-61. Oxford: Basil Blackwell, 1981.

This article is very helpful in understanding the
complexity of the problem of Chaucer's
dependence on commentaries (primarily Trevet's)
in preparing his **Boece**.

55. ----------. "'Glosynge is a glorious thyng': Chaucer
at Work on the **Boece**." In **The Medieval
Boethius: Studies in the Vernacular
Translations of** De Consolatione
Philosophiae, edited by Alastair J. Minnis, 106-
24. Woodbridge, Suffolk: D.S. Brewer, 1987.

In this article, Minnis concludes that Chaucer had
three texts at hand as he produced his
Consolatio translation: 1) an unglossed copy of
Jean de Meun's translation, 2) a Vulgate copy of
the **Consolatio** with glosses from the Remigian
commentary of the late 800s, and 3) a copy of
Trevet's commentary.

56.   Morris, Richard, ed. **Chaucer's** Boece **Englisht from Boethius's** De Consolatione Philosophiae. Chaucer Society, no 76 (first series). London: N. Trübner, 1886.

This is the editing of Chaucer's **Boece** prepared for the Chaucer Society. It is based on Addit. MS 10340. The introduction contains a thematic study of the influence of the **Consolatio** on Chaucer's works in general. The edition also contains a glossarial index to the text.

57.   Pace, George B. and Linda E. Voigts. "A 'Boece' Fragment." **Studies in the Age of Chaucer** 1 (1979): 143-50.

In the **Fragmenta Manuscripta**, a collection of manuscripts purchased in 1968 by the University of Missouri-Columbia, there is a fragment of Chaucer's **Boece** on one side and a non-corresponding fragment of the Latin **Consolatio** on the other. The article describes the fragment and many of its possible affinities.

58.   Patch, Howard Rollin. **The Tradition of Boethius: A Study of His Importance in Medieval Culture.** New York: Oxford University Press, 1935.

Chaucer's **Consolatio** translation is described as "workmanlike and eminently useful."

59.   Peck, Russell A. **Chaucer's** Romaunt of the Rose **and** Boece, Treatise on the Astrolabe, Equatorie of the Planetis, **Lost Works, and Chaucerian Apocrypha: an Annotated Bibliography, 1900 to 1985.** The Chaucer Bibliographies. Toronto: University of Toronto Press, 1988.

This is a very complete bibliography to all the works listed in the title.

60. Petersen, Kate O. "Chaucer and Trivet." **PMLA**, 18 (1903): 173-93.

Petersen makes a case for Trevet's commentary as the single commentary consulted by Chaucer in preparing his **Boece**. Trevet incorporates most of the glosses from the Pseudo-Aquinas which are found in Chaucer. This explains why critics such as Liddell (1897) had suggested the Pseudo-Aquinas as a source for the **Boece**.

61. Robertson, D.W., Jr. "Pope and Boethius." In **Classical, Mediaeval and Renaissance Studies in Honor of Berthold Louis Ullman**, edited by Charles Henderson, Jr. Vol. 2, 505-13. Rome: Edizioni de Storia e Letteratura, 1964.

Robertson asserts here that Pope's early translation of the **Consolatio**, Book III, meter 9, indicates early Boethian influence which helps explain later parallels between ideas in the **Consolatio** and the **Essay on Man**. These parallels reinforce the thesis that the **Essay on Man** is basically a traditional work.

62. Robinson, F.N., ed. **The Works of Geoffrey Chaucer**, 2nd ed. Cambridge, Mass.: Riverside Press, 1957.

This is one of the major editions of the complete works of Chaucer, including the **Boece**.

63. Root, Robert. **The Poetry of Chaucer**. 1934. Reprint. Gloucester, Mass.: Peter Smith, 1957.

This volume contains information useful to understanding Chaucer's prose as well as his poetry.

64.   Saintsbury, George. **A History of English Prose Rhythm**. 1912. Reprint. Bloomington: Indiana University Press, 1967.

One of the examples of Middle English prose analyzed by Saintsbury is Chaucer's **Consolatio** translation.

65.   Schlauch, Margaret. "Chaucer's Prose Rhythms." **PMLA** 65 (1950): 568-89.

Chaucer's knowledge of the medieval doctrine of **cursus** is evidenced by his use of the word **cadence** in his **Hous of Fame**. But analysis shows that he adapted the concept to his needs. His most mannered prose style is reserved for lyrical and emotional passages. His style in the **Boece** and the "Melibeus" is his most adorned.

66.   ----------. "The Art of Chaucer's Prose." In **Chaucer and Chaucerians**, edited by D.S. Brewer, 140-63. London: Thomas Nelson, 1966.

Schlauch takes exception to the view that Chaucer's prose is of poor quality. The prose works are examined for artistic merit and use of rhetorical devices. They are found not to be mannered, but to use cadences and appropriate alliteration which make them, including his **Boece**, worthy of notice.

67.   Science, Mark. "A Suggested Correction of the Text of Chaucer's **Boethius**." **London Times Literary Supplement**, 22 May 1923, 199-200.

In comparing John Walton's translation to
Chaucer's **Boece**, Science decided that the word
which translates the Latin **degenere** in Chaucer's
text should be emended.

68.   Shirley, Peggy Faye. "Fals Felicite and Verray
Blisfulnesse: Alfred and Chaucer Translate
Boethius's **Consolation of Philosophy.**"
Ph.D. diss., University of Mississippi, 1977.

In comparing Alfred's translation of the
Consolatio with that made by Chaucer, Shirley
concludes that Alfred's emphasis was on the
education of his audience while Chaucer's was on
accuracy in understanding the text. The differences
are reflections of the temperaments of the
translators and of their times.

69.   Silk, Edmund Taite. "Cambridge MS Ii. 3.21. and
the Relation of Chaucer's **Boethius** to Trivet and
Jean de Meung." Ph.D. diss., Yale University,
1930.

The Cambridge University Library MS Ii. 3.21.
contains Chaucer's **Boece**, the Latin
Consolatio with many interpolations from
Trevet as well as marginal and interlinear
annotations from Trevet. The Latin text is very
close to Chaucer's translation and it may represent,
according to Silk, the text tradition Chaucer used.
The article emphasized the indebtedness of Chaucer
to the commentaries as opposed to Jean de Meun.

70.   Skeat, Walter W., ed. **The Complete Works
of Geoffrey Chaucer.** Oxford University
Press, 1894-7. Reprint. London: Oxford
University Press, 1933.

These volumes contain one of the earlier editings
of Chaucer's **Boece.**

71.   Stewart, Hugh Fraser. **Boethius: An Essay.**
       London: 1891. Reprint. New York: Burt Franklin,
       1974.

       Stewart's treatment of Chaucer's use of Boethius
       refutes, first of all, the notion that the **Boece** is
       an early work. It also argues, referring to
       Chaucer's errors, that he "was no Latin scholar at
       all." Stewart is unique in pointing out that
       Chaucer and Notker share certain errors which they
       inherited from a similar manuscript tradition.

72.   Tatlock, John S.P. **A Concordance to the
       Complete Works of Geoffrey Chaucer
       and the Romaunt of the Rose.** Carnegie
       Institute of Washington, no. 353. Concord,
       Mass.: Rumford Press, 1927.

       This work is included because of its usefulness to
       studies of Chaucer's **Boece.**

73.   Thynne, William, ed. **Chaucer's Works.** N.p.:
       n.p., 1532.

       After Caxton's, this is the oldest printed edition of
       Chaucer's **Boece.**

74.   van de Vyver, A. "Les Traductions du De
       Consolatione philosophiae de Boèce en
       littérature comparée." **Humanisme et
       Renaissance** 6 (1939): 247-73.

       This article accepts c.1380 as the date for
       Chaucer's **Boece.** It puts Chaucer's translation
       into the context of the whole European tradition of
       Consolatio translations.

75.   Wimsatt, James. "**Samson Agonistes** and the
        Tradition of Boethius." **Renaissance Papers**
        n.v (1972): 1-10.

        After mentioning many pieces of literature
        strongly influenced by the **Consolatio,** Wimsatt
        demonstrates that Milton's play also echoes many
        aspects of Boethius' last work. This is partly an
        effort to emphasize the elements of medieval
        tragedy in the play.

76.   Witcutt, W.P. "Chaucer's Boëthius." **American
        Review** 8 (1936/1937): 61-70.

        This is an appreciation of Boethius' philosophical
        system and of Chaucer's translation of it into
        English. Witcutt expresses the hope that the
        Boethian system might bring sanity to the
        children of our own materialistic age.

The Influence of Chaucer's **Boece**;
Other Middle
English **Consolatio** Translations

Problems pertaining to the influence of Chaucer's **Boece** and
problems concerning the other Middle English **Consolatio** translations
are closely related. Other than Chaucer's, the major Middle English
Consolatio translation is John Walton's, and Walton relied heavily
upon the **Boece** while preparing his verse rendering of 1410. Walton's
work has been appropriately studied in relationship to Chaucer's;
unfortunately, the originality and quality of Walton's verses have been
frequently overlooked. Walton's translation will be discussed after a
preliminary discussion of the scholarship on the influence of Chaucer's
Consolatio translation.

Because Chaucer produced his translation before writing many of
his major works, a case could be made that all Boethian influence found in
his works subsequent to 1380 derives directly from the **Boece**. Such a
situation does not exist, for example, for Jean de Meun, who wrote his
Consolatio translation after he had finished his most famous creative
work, the **Roman de la Rose**. For Chaucer, however, it is difficult to
limit or define the problem of influence properly. In an article, Averil
Gardner says:

> This influence of Boethius on Chaucer's works appears in two
> ways. More superficially it appears in his Balades, in which he
> has either taken one Boethian idea with very little, or no, change
> and presented it in elegant verse; or has used it as a preliminary
> to which he can append some comment of his own. More subtly
> and interestingly, the influence appears in Chaucer's longer
> works, most notably **Troilus and Criseyde, The Knight's
> Tale**, and **The Wife of Bath's Tale**, in which, to a varying
> extent, Boethian ideas connected with the mood and plot are

completely incorporated and become the central theme. (Gardner 1971, 31)

Gardner's article is a good general introduction to this study because it helps readers to understand the full range of effects the **Consolatio** had on Chaucer. Within this range, a difference in approaches exists.

Bernard Jefferson, in his book (Jefferson 1917), takes a direct approach to the problem of influence studies: he lists lines from Chaucer's works along with the corresponding passages in the **Consolatio**. His work is a useful catalogue to which new material may be added whenever it is noted. James Smith accepts such a straightforward approach; however, in a cautionary article (Smith 1972), he warns that Chaucer's borrowings of words or phrases from Boethius does not necessarily indicate their "Boethian" meaning. Their context in Chaucer may imply any number of changes in meaning, altering the original significance of the lines.

In many articles and books a more subtle approach than Jefferson's is taken. For example, Peter Elbow suggests, in a book (Elbow 1965), that Chaucer learned from his reading and translating of the **Consolatio** a pattern of thinking which structured some of his later works. He maintains that Chaucer's method of reconciling oppositions was developed from Boethius's method of transcendence. In like manner, Theodore Stroud, in an article (Stroud 1951), concludes that Chaucer's plot in **Troilus and Criseyde** represents a quest similar in shape to that in Boethius' **Consolatio**: the hero is given a glimpse of the truth at the end of the poem. Such influence as this is not easily isolated and examined in single passages from a text.

Focusing on a more specific aspect of Boethian philosophy, Robert Shorter, in an article (Shorter 1965), describes the influence upon the **Troilus** of the theory of knowledge which Boethius outlines in the **Consolatio**; the palinode of the **Troilus** is found to be essential in converting the tragedy into a comedy. Gareth Dunleavy observes, in an article (Dunleavy 1967), that the theme of a wounded Boethius comforted by Lady Philosophy constantly recurs throughout Chaucer's works.

As to genre, though the word **Consolatio** is part of its title, Boethius' last work is not necessarily a part of the mainstream of consolation literature. Michael Means, in a book (Means 1972), defines the genre of the **De Consolatione Philosophiae** in terms of instruction rather than of consolation. The figure of the superior being

(Lady Philosophy) teaching a student (Boethius) is not unusual in medieval English literature. Jean Louise Carrière, in her dissertation (Carrière 1975), comes to the same conclusion, that the **Consolatio's** main purpose is instruction rather than comfort. She traces its unique pattern of instruction in the English literature of the fourteenth century.

Catalogues of passages are undoubtedly important in determining direct influence from the **Boece**. If the phrasing of passages from a text is very close to a corresponding passage in the **Boece**, its source is fairly certain. Critics, however, who choose a more subtle approach to the problem of influence base it on a deeper level of textual structure than critics who present lists of isolated passages. Chaucer translated the **Consolatio**, and in doing so, he learned much--he thoroughly internalized an entire philosophical system, a way of comprehending the operations of the world: these deeper dimensions of influence must necessarily be considered. As stated earlier, however, listings here are confined to studies of the direct influence of Chaucer's translation on subsequent texts, excluding studies of indirect Boethian influence. As a sampling of such studies, see [(Bloomfield 1970) (Lepley 1977/1978) (Schauber and Spolsky 1977) (de Vries 1970)].

One extremely important problem of medieval literary criticism undeniably derives from Chaucer's **Boece**; it originates in a gloss upon a prose passage of the **Consolatio**. Chaucer translates the words of Lady Philosophy:

> What other thing bewaylen the cryings of tragedyes but oonly the dedes of Fortune, that with an unwar stroke overtorneth realms of grete noblye? (Glose. Tragedye is to seyn, a dite of a prosperite for a tyme that endeth in wrecchednesse.) (Fisher 1977, 833)

Having borrowed the term from the French, Chaucer was the first English writer to use the word **tragedy**. The narrator of the **Troilus** even refers to his story as a tragedy. Thus, Chaucer's famous gloss from **Boece** II, prose ii, has become a catch phrase to characterize medieval tragedy, particularly Chaucerian tragedy.

Walter Clyde Curry, in a book (Curry 1960), discusses Chaucerian tragedy in the **Troilus** as resulting ultimately from the Boethian world system of the **Consolatio**. A sense of destiny dominates the action, and it is conflict with this destiny which creates the tragic effect in the poem. Unfortunately, Curry's interpretation asserts that the epilogue is a weak addition to the story, contributing nothing to the tragedy. D.W. Robertson, Jr. addresses the problem in one of his articles (Robertson 1952). He sees the tragedy of Troilus as more complex than a simple mechanical "fall of famous men." Behind the Boethian structure of the story lie the theological concepts of St. Augustine: the tragic fall of Troilus becomes, then, representative of the Fall of Man. He sees Chaucer's concept of tragedy as depending upon Augustinian Christianity for its deeper significance. A reconciliation between the de casibus type of tragedy (tragedy as the fall of famous men) and the type of tragedy described by Robertson (tragedy as the Fall of Man) is attempted by Paul Ruggiers in one of his articles (Ruggiers 1973/1974). The two extremes, exemplified in Chaucer by "The Monk's Tale," on the one hand, and the **Troilus,** on the other, allow an intermediate spectrum of tragic possibility throughout Chaucer's other works. Chaucer was consciously a master of both types.

Monica McAlpine, first in her dissertation (McAlpine 1973) and then in her book (McAlpine 1978), maintains that Chaucer was being ironic when his narrator calls the **Troilus** his "tragedy." She sees Chaucer's definition of tragedy as derived from Boethius, but the tragedy in the **Troilus** is that of Criseyde, not Troilus. This is a revolutionary interpretation.

I mention in this context one of my own articles (Kaylor 1992) in which I trace Chaucer's use of the word **Tragedy.** I conclude that the **Troilus** is a tragedy and that Troilus is the tragic hero.

To summarize, the problem of tragedy in Chaucer results from the poet's encounter with and translation of the **Consolatio.** It is one area in which direct influence can be assumed.

The Middle-English **Consolatio** translation by John Walton--a verse rendering based on Chaucer's prose, the original Latin text, and Trevet's commentary--demands particular attention. The same problems preoccupying critics of the **Boece** and the other medieval translations of Boethius' last work also trouble critics of Walton's work. The range of scholarship includes general studies, studies of manuscripts and editions, and textual analyses.

Unlike Chaucer, Walton was a relatively obscure figure even in his own time. We know little more about him today than Thomas

Warton did in 1871. In his **History of English Poetry**, Warton writes:

> I can assign only one poet to the reign of Henry IV, and this a
> translator of Boethius . . . . His name is John Walton. He was
> Canon of Osney, and he died subdean of York. (Warton 1871,
> vol. 3, 39)

Walton completed his translation in 1401 for his patron, Elizabeth
Berkeley. The work was first printed in 1525 at the monastery of
Travestock in Devonshire, and of that edition, three copies are still extant.
These, in sum, are the facts we have.

The usual general studies on Boethian translations are also useful
for Walton: Hugh Fraser Stewart's **Essay** (Stewart 1891), Howard Patch's
book (Patch 1935), and the chapter on Walton from Eleanor Prescott
Hammond's book (Hammond 1969) should be consulted first, since they
are the best introductions to the subject; Frederick Fehlauer's dissertation
and its subsequent printed version [(Fehlauer 1908) (Fehlauer 1909)] and
Guy Bayley Dolson's dissertation (Dolson 1926) are useful for putting
Walton's verse translation into its appropriate historical and generic
framework in the English tradition; and A. van de Vyver's article (van de
Vyver 1939) places Walton's work within the context of all European
Consolatio translations.

The first study of Walton's translation was Hermann Cossack's
dissertation (Cossack 1889), and it was also a first step toward
establishing a critical edition. It presents a comparison of Walton's verse
translation with Chaucer's prose rendering, and it includes the few facts
known about the translator's life and the manuscripts of the translation.
For the first mention of the possibility of Walton's having consulted
Chaucer's **Boece** in preparing his own translation, see Bernard ten Brink's
Geschichte der englischen Literatur (ten Brink 1912, 228-29).
Building on Cossack's work, K. Schümmer, in a careful and detailed study
(Schümmer 1914), draws the affiliations between all the manuscripts of
Walton's work as well as the edition of 1525. Again, this scholarship
was necessary preparation for any critical edition of the translation. That
critical edition appeared in 1927, prepared by Mark Science for the Early
English Text Society (Science 1927). Later, a previously unknown, odd
manuscript was found by Richard Dwyer and described in an article

(Dwyer 1973). The article contains enough variant readings to be considered a version. It does not necessitate any changes in the critical edition, but it does, along with the several manuscripts considered in Science's edition and the very early published version, indicate the popularity Walton's work enjoyed in the fifteenth and sixteenth centuries.

Several works which belong to the general category of textual studies on Walton's translation deserve to be mentioned here. They offer great variety in approach. For example, Richard Green recognized a controversial poem in Carlton Brown's **Religious Lyrics of the Fifteenth Century** to be an extract from Walton's translation (Book III, meter x) (Green 1954). His discovery helped solve certain problems of interpretation which had developed, and the existence of these mistaken interpretations can stand a warning for critics who judge material without regard for its proper context. In an article (Thomson 1964), Patricia Thomson compares Wyatt's work with the corresponding sections of Walton's translation. Her conclusion is that, whereas Walton had relied heavily on Chaucer's prose translation, Wyatt had not. Eleanor Prescott included Walton in her study of English verse (Prescott 1969); Walton appears in her book in the company of Chaucer and Surrey. Rita Copeland studies Walton's **Consolatio** translation in order to discuss the importance of rhetoric as a tool of interpretative translation (Copeland 1987); the article includes a summary of Walton's use of Chaucer and of commentaries in coming to understand and translate the Latin text.

An article by Alistair Minnis (Minnis 1981) presents a good summary of the importance of the Latin commentaries to Walton's verses as well as of their importance for Chaucer's prose translation. The subject of commentaries is often neglected in studies of the medieval **Consolatio** translations; therefore, such articles as Minnis' are valuable additions to the scholarship. Finally, as pointed out above, Walton's translation is too often treated merely as an interesting versification of Chaucer's **Boece**. My own article (Kaylor 1983) attempts to treat Walton's work as an important and independent part of the European tradition of **Consolatio** translations.

A substantial body of criticism exists on the subject of John Walton's translation, but still, his is a relatively neglected work, worthy of more critical attention. Unfortunately, the brightness of Walton's verses is overshadowed by the prose work of the greatest poet of the age, Geoffrey Chaucer. I.R. Johnson, however, in an article (Johnson 1987) argues convincingly that Walton's translation has much more merit than earlier critics were willing to admit. Johnson studies Walton's use of the Orpheus story in particular, showing how both Chaucer's **Boece** and Trevet's commentary were used in producing a lucid verse translation of the Latin text. Walton's translation is also treated in a dissertation by William Joseph Fahrenbach (Fahrenbach 1975). He discusses it along with seven other translations from classical literature. He proves that all eight translations have themes relevant to the vernacular audience of the time. He emphasizes the timeliness of Walton's translation.

Only one other Middle English translation of Boethius' last work has been found. It is completely obscure, being mentioned almost in passing by Fehlauer in his survey of medieval English **Consolatio** translations (Fehlauer 1909). He writes: "MS Auct. F.3.5., in der Bodleian Library, enthält eine Prosaübersetzung, die als von der Chaucerschen verschieden bezeichnet wird" (Fehlauer 1909, 3). Fehlauer gives no further information, and no critic seems to have followed up on the hint. These, then--Chaucer's **Boece**, Walton's verse translation, and the obscure work in the Bodleian Library--are the Middle English **Consolatio** translations.

From the several Renaissance translations, the one by Queen Elizabeth I deserves to be mentioned as a final note in this chapter. An edition was prepared by Caroline Pemberton (Pemberton 1899), but it was given rather negative comment by Geoffrey B. Riddehough (Riddehough 1946).

List of Relevant Titles

1. Bloomfield, Morton W. "The Miller's Tale--An UnBoethian Interpretation." In **Medieval Literature and Folklore Studies: Essays in Honor of Francis Lee Utley**, edited by Jerome Mandel and Bruce A. Rosenberg, 205-11. New Brunswick: Rutgers University Press, 1970.

    "The Knight's Tale" and the "Reeve's Tale" are set in an rational universe compatible with that described by Boethius in the **Consolatio**. Underlying the "Miller's Tale," however, is a

universe in which Fortune is not an instrument of
the Highest Good.

2.   ten Brink, Bernard. **Geschichte der
       englischen Literatur,** edited by Alois Brandl.
       Vol 2, 228-29. Strassburg: Karl Trübner, 1912.

       This entry contains the first mention of Chaucer's
       Boece as a source of Walton's translation.

3.   Carrière, Jeanne Louise. "Boethian Narrative
       Structure in Fourteenth-Century English
       Literature." Ph.D. diss., University of California
       at Los Angeles, 1975.

       Carrière first establishes the uniqueness of the
       structure of the **Consolatio** in the context of
       Classical consolation literature: its purpose is seen
       to be instructional rather than pure consolation.
       Then, the same pattern is studied in the
       Confessio Amantis, the **Pearl,** the **Book of
       the Duchess,** the **Parliament of Fowls,** and
       the **Troilus.**

4.   Copeland, Rita. "Rhetoric and Vernacular
       Translation in the Middle Ages." **Studies in the
       Age of Chaucer** 9 (1987): 41-75.

       Using Chaucer's **Boece** and Walton's
       Consolatio translation as subjects, Copeland
       studies medieval translation in terms of rhetoric
       and rhetoric's function as an interpretative tool.

5.   Cossack, Hermann. **Über die altenglische
       metrische Bearbeitung von Boethius,** De
       Consolatione Philosophiae. Ph.D. diss.,
       Universität Leipzig, 1889. Leipzig: Max
       Hoffmann, 1889.

This is the first study of Walton's **Consolatio** translation. The few facts known about Walton's life are presented here along with manuscript information. This dissertation presents primarily, however, a comparison of Walton's work with Chaucer's **Boece**.

6.   Curry, Walter Clyde. **Chaucer and the Medieval Sciences**. 1926. Reprint. New York: Barnes and Noble, 1960.

Curry points out that the **Troilus** is dominated by a sense of destiny which derives ultimately from the **Consolatio**. He asserts that both Boethius and Chaucer see the universe governed by God through various agents such as the stars. It is conflict with the forces of destiny which establishes the tragedy of Troilus. Chaucer's epilogue, however, is found to be weak, adding nothing to the tragic effect.

7.   Dolson, Guy Bayley. "The **Consolation of Philosophy** in English Literature." Ph.D. diss., Cornell University, 1926.

Dolson places Walton's **Consolatio** translation within the context of all occurrences of **Consolatio** influence upon English literature. It contains no comparative analysis, but the information is useful.

8.   Dunleavy, Gareth W. "The Wound and the Comforter: the Consolations of Geoffrey Chaucer." **Papers on Language and Literature** 3 (1967, Summer Supplement): 14-27.

Apart from the often noted concepts of "gentilnesse," "trouth," and the "elusiveness and

fickleness of power, fame, and fortune," Chaucer
shows repeated interest in a motif Dunleavy calls
"the wound and the comforter." According to the
article, the wounded Boethius and the comforting
Lady Philosophy appear in many guises
throughout Chaucer's works.

9.   Dwyer, Richard A. "The Newberry's Unknown
        Revision of Walton's Boethius." **Manuscripta**
        17 (1973): 27-30.

        In a fifteenth-century English miscellany
        manuscript in the Newberry Library is a revision
        of the John Walton translation of the
        Consolatio. It is unique due to erasure and
        rewriting in the manuscript and certain readings in
        the later portion of the text.

10.   Elbow, Peter. **Oppositions in Chaucer.**
        Middletown, Conn.: Wesleyan University Press,
        1965.

        Elbow studies the method of transcendence
        described by Boethius in the **Consolatio,** and he
        suggests that Boethius' way of thinking influenced
        Chaucer's reconciliation of opposites in his
        poetry. Chaucer learned Boethius' method at least
        in part through translating the **Consolatio.**

11.   Fahrenbach, William Joseph. "Vernacular
        Translations of Classical Literature in Late-
        Medieval Britain: Eight Translations Made
        Directly from Latin Between 1400 and 1525."
        Ph.D. diss., University of Toronto, 1975.

        Walton's **Consolatio** translation and seven other
        late medieval translations from Classical literature
        are studied. All eight works are seen to treat

topics relevant to the vernacular audience of the time.

12. Fehlauer, Friedrich. **Die englischen Übersetzungen von Boethius'** De Consolatione Philosophiae. Ph.D. diss., Albertus-Universität zu Königsberg: Hartungsche Buchdruckerei, 1908.

Fehlauer devotes about fourteen pages of his study to Walton's translation. In these, he summarizes scholarship on the subject.

13. ----------. **Die englischen Übersetzungen von Boethius'** De Consolatione Philosophiae. Berlin: Emil Felber, 1909.

This is a printed version of the dissertation listed above.

14. Fisher, John H., ed. **The Complete Poetry and Prose of Geoffrey Chaucer.** New York: Holt, Reinhart and Winston, 1977.

This is one of the modern editions of Chaucer's works, which includes the **Boece.**

15. Gardner, Averil. "Chaucer and Boethius: Some Illustrations of Indebtedness." **University of Capetown Studies in English** 2 (1971): 31-8.

Gardner indicates specific instances of Chaucer's indebtedness to the **Consolatio.** This is a good general introduction to the subject.

16. Green, Richard L. "'The Port of Peace': Not Death But God." **Modern Language Notes,** 69 (1954): 307-9.

Green notes in this article that a lyric cited in
Carleton Brown's **Religious Lyrics of the
Fifteenth Century** is in fact a piece quoted
from John Walton's translation of the
Consolatio.

17.   Hammond, Eleanor Prescott. **English Verse
       Between Chaucer and Surrey.** New York:
       Octagon Books, 1969.

       This book contains a chapter on Walton's
       Consolatio translation. It consists of a brief,
       general introduction to Walton and his work and
       gives many examples of verses from the text.
       Notes at the end of the article are helpful both as
       aids to the Middle English of the text and to an
       appreciation of Walton's types of verses.

18.   Jefferson, Bernard L. **Chaucer and the**
       Consolation of Philosophy **of Boethius.** 1917.
       Reprint. New York: Haskell House, 1965.

       This is the most comprehensive study of
       Chaucer's **Boece.** It is also important as a study
       of **Consolatio** influence on Chaucer's works.

19.   Johnson, I.R., "Walton's Sapient Orpheus." In
       **The Medieval Boethius: Studies in the
       Vernacular Translations of** De Consolatione
       Philosophiae, edited by Alastair J. Minnis, 139-
       68. Woodbridge, Suffolk: D.S. Brewer, 1987.

       Johnson, examining Walton's treatment of the
       story of Orpheus (**Consolatio,** Book III, meter
       12) in order to determine his translation methods,
       concludes that Walton did not simply versify
       Chaucer but that he used Chaucer's **Boece** in his
       effort to render the **Consolatio** as lucidly as

possible. To this purpose, he also made great use of Trevet's commentary.

20. Kaylor, Noel Harold, Jr. "John Walton's 1410 Verse Translation of the **De Consolatione Philosophiae** in the Context of Its Medieval Tradition." **Fifteenth-Century Studies** 6 (1983): 121-48.

   In this article, Walton is placed within the context of all medieval **Consolatio** translations.

21. ----------. "Chaucer's Use of the Word **Tragedy**: A Semantic Analysis." In **Language and Civilization**, edited by Claudia Blank. Vol. 2, 431-44. Frankfurt: Peter Lang Verlag, 1992.

   A semantic analysis indicates that the **Troilus** is Chaucer's tragedy and that Troilus is the tragic hero of the work.

22. Lepley, Douglas L. "The Monk's Tale." **Chaucer Review** 12 (1977/1978): 162-70.

   Lepley attempts to refute arguments which claim that the Monk's tragedies are philosophically unsound in Boethian terms. Lepley shows that the tales teach philosophy's lesson of true felicity. The Monk, according to the article, does not despair at the meaninglessness of creation as has been claimed.

23. McAlpine, Monica Ellen. "A Boethian Approach to the Problems of Genre in Chaucer's **Troilus and Criseyde**." Ph.D. diss., University of Rochester , 1973.

   McAlpine maintains that Chaucer derives his definition of tragedy from Boethius and Boccaccio.

By her interpretation, the story of Troilus is a
comedy and that of Criseyde is a tragedy.

24.   ----------. **The Genre of** Troilus and Criseyde.
Ithaca: Cornell University Press, 1978.

This book develops further the thesis of
McAlpine's dissertation which is listed above.

25.   Means, Michael H. **The Consolatio Genre in
Medieval English Literature.** University of
Florida Humanities Monograph, no. 3.
Gainesville, Fla.: University of Florida Press,
1972.

Means first defines the genre of the **Consolatio**
as a work of instruction rather than of consolation;
he then studies individual works as examples of
this thesis.

26.   Minnis, Alistair. "Aspects of the Medieval French
and English Traditions of the **De Consolatione
Philosophiae.**" In Boethius: **His Life,
Thought and Influence**, edited by Margaret
Gibson, 312-61. Oxford: Basil Blackwell, 1981.

Minnis indicates places where Walton relied not
only on Chaucer's **Boece** as the source for his
own translation, but also upon direct reference to
Trevet's commentary.

27.   Patch, Howard Rollin. **The Tradition of
Boethius: A Study of His Importance in
Medieval Culture.** New York: Oxford Press,
1935.

This is one of the major general studies on the
European **Consolatio** tradition.

28. Pemberton, Caroline, ed. **Queen Elizabeth's Englishings of Boethius,** De Consolatione Philosophiae; **Plutarch,** De Curiositate; **Horace,** De Arte Poetica **(part).** Early English Text Society, no. 113. London: Kegan Paul, Trench, Trübner, 1899.

   This is the critical edition of the **Consolatio** translation made by Elizabeth I in 1593. A brief introduction describes Queen Elizabeth's literary interests and the circumstances under which she translated the work.

29. Prescott, Eleanor. "John Walton's Boethius-Translation." In **English Verse Between Chaucer and Surrey,** 39-52. New York: Octagon Books, 1969.

   Prescott includes a section on Walton's **Consolatio** translation in this survey of English verse.

30. Riddehough, Geoffrey B. "Queen Elizabeth's Translation of Boethius' **De Consolatione Philosophiae.**" **Journal of English and Germanic Philology** 45 (1946): 88-94.

   Riddehough points out many inadequacies in the EETS edition of Queen Elizabeth's translation of the **Consolatio.** The errors include uncertainty in rules of sixteenth-century English and weaknesses in Latin which allow oversight of many of Elizabeth's mistranslations. Riddehough is dissatisfied both with the EETS edition and with Elizabeth's work as a translator.

31. Robertson, D.W., Jr. "Chaucerian Tragedy." **Journal of English Literary History** 19 (1952): 1-37.

Robertson takes the position that the "fall" of
Troilus recapitulates the "Fall of Man." This is
basically a study of Augustinian structures
operating in the **Troilus.**

32.   Ruggiers, Paul G. "Notes Towards a Theory of
        Tragedy in Chaucer." **Chaucer Review** 8
        (1973/1974): 89-99.

        Ruggiers emphasizes the complexity of range in
        Chaucerian tragedy. At one extreme is "The
        Monk's Tale," illustrating the fall of great men.
        At the other extreme is a poem like the **Troilus**
        which illustrates Chaucer's Christian view of
        Providence. Between these extremes, Chaucer's
        other works exhibit a spectrum of tragic
        possibilities.

33.   Schauber, Ellen and Ellen Spolsky. "The
        Consolation of Alison: the Speech Acts of the
        Wife of Bath." **Centrum** 5 (1977): 20-34.

        Schauber examines the Wife of Bath in terms of
        various speech acts. In this context, it is
        important to compare her, not to other women
        characters such as Constance, Griselda or Dorigen,
        but rather as a negative version of Lady
        Philosophy of the **Consolatio** by Boethius.

34.   Schümmer, K. **John Waltons metrische
        Übersetzung der** Consolatio Philosophiae:
        **Untersuchung des
        Handschriftenverhältnisses und Probe
        eines kritischen Textes.** Bonner Studien zur
        englischen Philologie, no. 6. Bonn: Peter
        Hanstein, Verlagsbuchhandlung, 1914.

The affiliations are drawn for all the manuscripts and the 1525 edition of Walton's translation. This work is preliminary to any future editings.

35.   Science, Mark, ed. **Boethius:** De Consolatione Philosophiae. John Walton, trans. Early English Text Society, no. 170. London: Oxford University Press, 1927.

This is the critical edition of John Walton's text. The introduction gives manuscript information, historical data, and stylistic analysis.

36.   Shorter, Robert Newland. "Boethian Philosophy as the Informing Principle in Chaucer's **Troilus and Criseyde.**" Ph.D. diss., Duke University, 1965.

Shorter analyzes the **Troilus** in terms of Boethius' theory of knowledge. The problematic epilogue is shown to be essential in treating the tragedy of Troilus as a comedy.

37.   Smith, James. "Chaucer, Boethius and Recent Trends in Criticism: A Lecture Delivered at the University of Bristol." **Essays in Criticism** 22 (1972): 4-32.

Smith advises critics to treat Chaucer's frequent use of unacknowledged quotation with caution. Their significance must remain questionable, and unguarded interpretation results in "ventriloquism" on the part of the critic.

38.   Stewart, Hugh Fraser. **Boethius: An Essay.** London: 1891. Reprint. New York: Burt Franklin, 1974.

In his treatment of the verse translation of the **Consolatio** from 1410, Stewart, too, identifies Johannes Capellanus as John Walton. He praises his work and indicates its indebtedness to Chaucer's **Boece**.

39.   Stroud, Theodore A. "Boethius' Influence on Chaucer's **Troilus**." **Modern Philology** 49 (1951): 1-9.

This critic emphasizes the allegorical dimension of the **Troilus**, representing, according to Stroud, a philosophical quest based on the model of the **Consolatio**.

40.   Thomson, Patricia. "Wyatt's Boethian Ballade." **Review of English Studies** 15 (1964): 262-67.

Thomson compares Wyatt's translation of some Boethian meters to Walton's full translation of the **Consolatio**. Whereas Walton (Wyatt's contemporary) relied heavily on Chaucer's **Boece**, Wyatt probably did not.

41.   de Vries, F.C. "In Chaucer's Workshop: Two Boethian Passages in **Troilus and Criseyde** (a synopsis)." **Australasian Universities Language and Literature Association** [Proceedings and Papers of the Thirteenth Congress] 13 (1970): 383-5.

This is a synopsis article on the two famous Boethian passages from the **Troilus**. It presents them as versifications of prose passages from Chaucer's **Boece**. The use of vocabulary and versification in the former show greater clarity.

42. van de Vyver, A. "Les Traductions du **De Consolatione philosophiae** de Boèce en littérature comparée." **Humanisme et Renaissance** 6 (1939): 247-73.

John Walton's verse translation of the **Consolatio** is given brief mention here as part of the larger European tradition of **Consolatio** vernacularizations. There is also a useful list of all post-1500 English translations of the **Consolatio**.

43. Warton, Thomas. **History of English Poetry from the Twelfth to the Sixteenth Century,** edited by W.C. Hazlitt. Vol. 3, 38-40. London: 1871. Reprint. Hildesheim: Georg Olms, 1968.

Warton refers to John Walton as the only poet of the reign of Henry IV. In about five sentences, he summarizes all facts known about the life of Walton.

CHAPTER VI

CONCLUSION

Boethius stated the case for a rational universe whose forces operate ultimately for the good as clearly and concisely as any writer before or since. As evidenced by its many medieval translations, his statement in the **Consolation of Philosophy**, in the form of the dialogue between Boethius (the character in the work) and Lady Philosophy, became a periodic fascination for the medieval mind: it was translated two dozen times into various vernaculars at various periods of vernacular development during the Middle Ages.

The primary function of this annotated bibliography, beyond its usefulness as a compilation of factual data, is to promote the medieval **Consolatio** translations as a valuable area for comparative studies. Comparative studies have been made by Olga Fischer and Peggy Faye Shirley on Alfred and Chaucer, between whose translations no direct influence exists, but such comparative studies are rare. Olga Fischer's comparative study of Alfred's and Chaucer's philosophical vocabulary is a particularly good example of the potential value such studies have; her work leads to a greater appreciation of Anglo-Saxon as a vehicle for philosophical concepts. But generally, criticism has tended to cross the boundaries of national literatures primarily where direct influence has been established between translations. For example, comparative studies exist for Jean de Meun and Chaucer because the latter used the work of the former in producing his own **Consolatio** vernacularization. Even within linguistic traditions, comparative studies have been limited to cases of direct influence; included among these are studies of Chaucer and

John Walton. Instances of direct influence between translations have been noted, and as indicated by the work of Fischer and Shirley, comparative studies are needed in areas other than that of influence.

One of the more fruitful fields for studies of indirect influence (in this case, influence through the commentaries, vitae, and other elements of the medieval Consolatio tradition) has been developed in the work of Pierre Courcelle. His study of the medieval commentaries on the Consolatio has helped to bind the entire European tradition into one fabric. The commentaries were universally consulted by the medieval translators and material was often lifted directly from them and incorporated into the translations, so much work remains to be done on the use of the commentaries in the production of those translations which constitute the European Consolatio tradition.

Boethius formulated his ideas as a propositional, or formal, logical system which he undoubtedly considered to be both complete and consistent. The popularity of his work indicates that the medieval audience also looked at it that way. Because of its systematic structure, the Consolatio appeals in all ages to a human longing for order and certainty. Today we know, however, that no propositional system can be both complete and consistent, but medieval people did not have Gödel's famous mathematical theorem of 1931, so they did not know that the philosophical system formulated in the Consolatio could offer no genuine certainty. A study of the medieval Consolatio tradition is an exploration into medieval attitudes toward the rational foundation of the universe. Philosophically, the translations offer a wide spectrum of medieval thought, varying from Alfred's doubt and uncertainty to Chaucer's faith. This philosophical dimension has been considered in the reception studies made of Alfred's translation, and Anne Payne's King Alfred and Boethius, or Ingeborg Schröbler's Notker III von St. Gallen als Übersetzer und Kommentator von Boethius' De Consolatione Philosophiae, are examples of the type of work that can be done. Critical foundations have thus been laid for further reception studies in each of the vernacular Consolatio traditions and for the European tradition as a whole, and these will surely appear. In our age, which seeks probability instead of Providence as the ruling force in the universe, studies on the medieval reception of the Consolatio will be valuable as explorations into a mentality which has become foreign to us.

The scholarly work in each linguistic tradition has thus far concentrated on the translation by one major literary, political, or scholarly figure: Alfred, Notker, Jean de Meun, and Chaucer. This is understandable, but it is also unfortunate because worthy translations have remained in obscurity. For example, John Walton's verse translation has too long been overshadowed by Chaucer's endeavor at literal translation, and Walton's work is a worthy, although less influential, translation. In the French tradition, several translations have been disregarded because Jean de Meun's name is not attached to them. Many critics come to consider the **Consolatio** tradition from other fields of literary research where their primary interest focuses on the translator's accomplishments in areas other than translation. Much work remains to be done on these neglected translators whose major literary contribution has been the production of their translations.

Editions of several medieval translations are lacking, though some are currently in various stages of completion. Printed editions of all the translations would facilitate the work of critics interested in the tradition as a whole. Furthermore, the lack of critical editions of such works as Trevet's commentary greatly slows the development of scholarship on the tradition.

The **Consolatio** tradition has another dimension common to all medieval literary traditions: the discovery of manuscripts continues to alter our understanding and interpretation of the translations. Thus, work on inventories and descriptions of manuscripts necessitates a periodic re-evaluation of existing critical editions.

On a related issue, the search should continue for lost manuscripts of such attested translations as the Middle High German work by Peter von Kastl. These translations might eventually be found, and their discovery would be significant.

Therefore, this annotated bibliography, which contains well over three hundred entries, is offered as a guide both to the work which has been accomplished and as an indication of the work that remains to be done on the European tradition of medieval **Consolatio** translations.

BIBLIOGRAPHY

Amsel, G. "Eine Erwähnung Catulls bei Notker." **Rheinisches Museum für Philologie** 43 (1888): 309.

Arngart, O. "Three Notes on King Alfred's Boethius." **English Studies: A Journal of English Language and Literature** 28 (1947): 74-80.

Assmann, Bruno. **Die Handschriften von Exeter, Metra des Boethius, Salomo und Saturn, die Psalmen**. Bibliothek der angelsächsischen Poesie, no. 3. Leipzig: n.p., 1898.

Atkinson, Keith. "A Critical Edition of the Medieval French Prose Translation of **De Consolatione Philosophiae** of Boethius Contained in the MS 898 of the Bibliothèque municipale, Troyes." Ph.D. diss., University of Queensland, Australia, 1976.

----------. Review of **Boethian Fictions: Narratives in the Medieval French Versions of the** Consolatio Philosophiae, by Richard A. Dwyer. **Medium Aevum** 47 (1978): 141-4.

----------. "Some Further Confirmations and Attributions of Manuscripts of the Mediaeval French Boethius." **Medium Aevum** 47 (1978): 22-9.

----------, ed. "An Early Fourteenth-Century French Boethian Orpheus." **Parergon: Bulletin of the Australian and New Zealand Association for Medieval and**

Renaissance Studies 26 (1980) (special issue: entire issue).

----------. "Le Dialecte du Boèce de Troyes 898 à propos d'une édition récente." Romania 102 (1981): 250-9.

----------. "A Fourteenth-Century Picard Translation-Commentary of the Consolatio Philosophiae." In The Medieval Boethius: Studies in the Vernacular Translations of the De Consolatione Philosophiae, edited by Alastair J. Minnis, 32-62. Woodbridge, Suffolk: D.S. Brewer, 1987.

Atkinson, Keith and Glynnis M. Cropp. "Trois traductions de la Consolatio Philosophiae de Boèce." Romania 106 (1985): 198-232.

Bach, Werner. Die althochdeutschen Boethiusglossen und Notkers Übersetzung der Consolatio. Ph.D. diss., Martin-Luther-Universität Halle-Wittenberg 1934. Würzburg: Buchdruckerei Richard Mayr, 1934.

Baldinger, Kurt. Review of Eine altfranzösische Übersetzung der Consolatio Philosophiae des Boethius (Handschrift Troyes No. 898), by Rolf Schroth. Zeitschrift für romanische Philologie 94 (1978): 181-5.

Barnes, Jonathan. "Boethius and the Study of Logic." In Boethius: His Life, Times and Influence, edited by Margaret Gibson, 73-89. Oxford: Basil Blackwell, 1981.

Barrett, Helen M. Boethius: Some Aspects of His Times and Works. Cambridge: n.p., 1940. Reprint. New York: Russell and Russell, 1965.

Baur, Arthur. Das Adjektiv in Notkers Boethius unter besonderer Berücksichtigung seines

Verhältnisses zur lateinischen Vorlage. Zurich:
Ernest Lang, 1940.

Beaumont, Jacqueline. "The Latin Tradition of the **De
Consolatione Philosophiae**." In **Boethius: His
Life, Thought and Influence**, edited by Margaret
Gibson, 278-305. Oxford: Basil Blackwell, 1981.

Behaghel, Dietrich. **Literaturblatt für germanische und
romanische Philologie** 54 (1933/1934): n.pp.

Benson, Larry D., ed. **The Riverside Chaucer**. 3rd ed. Boston:
Houghton Mifflin, 1987.

Bertoni, Giulio. "Des estats du siecle." **Zeitschrift für
romanische Philologie** 34 (1910): 368-9.

----------. **Notice sur deux manuscrits d'une traduction
française de la** Consolation de Boëce **conservés à
la Bibliothèque cantonale de Fribourg
(Suisse)**. Fribourg, Switzerland: Imprimerie Saint-Paul,
1910.

Bieler, Ludwig, ed. **Boethii Philosophiae Consolatio**.
Corpus Christianorum, Series Latina, no. 94. Turnholti,
Belgium: Typographi Brepols Editiones Pontificii, 1957.

Blake, N.F. "Caxton and Chaucer." **Leeds Studies in English**
n.s. 1 (1967): 19-36.

Bloomfield, Morton W. "The Miller's Tale--An UnBoethian
Interpretation." In **Medieval Literature and
Folklore Studies: Essays in Honor of Francis
Lee Utley**, edited by Jerome Mandel and Bruce A.
Rosenberg, 205-11. New Brunswick: Rutgers University
Press, 1970.

Bolender, Herbert. "Notkers **Consolatio**-Rezeption als
widerspruchsfreie Praktik: eine Hypothese." **Beiträge**

zur Geschichte der deutschen Sprache und
Literatur 102 (1980): 325-38.

Bolli, Ernst. **Die verbale Klammer bei Notker:
Untersuchung zur Wortstellung in der
Boethius-Übersetzung.** Das Althochdeutschung von
St. Gallen, no. 4. Berlin: Walter de Gruyter, 1975.

Bolton, Diane K. "The Study of The Consolation of
Philosophy in Saxon England." **Archives
d'histoire doctrinale et littéraire du moyen âge**
64 (1977): 33-78.

----------. "Illustrations in Manuscripts of Boethius' Works." In
Boethius: His Life, Thought and Influence,
edited by Margaret Gibson, 428-37. Oxford: Basil
Blackwell, 1981.

Bolton, W.F. "Boethius, Alfred, and Deor Again." **Modern
Philology: A Journal Devoted to Research in
Medieval and Modern Literature** 69 (1971/1972):
222-7.

----------. "The Alfredian Boethius in 'Ælfric's Lives of Saints I.'"
Notes and Queries 217 (1972): 406-7.

----------. "How Boethian is Alfred's Boethius?" In **Studies in
Earlier Old English Prose,** edited by Paul E.
Szarmach, 153-68. Albany: State University of New
York Press, 1986.

Bolton-Hall, Margaret. "A Critical Edition of the Translation of
Boethius's Consolation of Philosophy Contained in
the Manuscript: Vienna Nat. Lib. Lat. 2642." Ph.D.
diss., University of Queensland, 1988.

Bömer, A. "Fragmente einer gereimten deutschen Boethiusübersetzung."
**Zeitschrift für deutsches Altertum und deutsche
Literatur** 50 (1908): 149-58.

Borinski, Ludwig. **Der Stil König Alfreds: Eine Studie zur Psychologie der Rede.** Leipzig: Bernard Tauchnitz, 1934.

Boyd, Beverly, ed. **Chaucer According to William Caxton: Minor Poems and Boece.** Lawrence, Kansas: Allen Press, 1978.

Braune, Wilhelm. **Althochdeutsches Lesebuch,** edited by E.A. Ebbinghaus. Tübingen: Max Niemeyer Verlag, 1969.

Braungart, Georg. "Notker der Deutsche als Bearbeiter eines lateinischen Schultextes: Boethius **De Consolatione Philosophiae." Zeitschrift für deutsche Philologie** 106 (1987): 2-15.

ten Brink, Bernard. **Geschichte der englischen Literatur,** edited by Alois Brandl. Vol 2, 228-29. Strassburg: Karl Trübner, 1912.

Browne, George Forest. **King Alfred's Books.** London Society for Promoting Christian Knowledge. New York: Maxmillian, 1920.

Brunel, Clovis. "Fragment d'un ms. de la traduction Catalane de la **Consolatio** de Boèce." **Romania** 76 (1955): 522-4.

Brunet, Gustave. **La France littéraire au XVème siècle ou catalogue raisonné des ouvrages en tous genres imprimés en langue française jusqu'à l'an 1500.** Geneva: Slatkine Reprints, 1967.

Caldwell, John. "**De Institutione Arithmetica** and the **De Institutione Musica." In Boethius: His Life, Thought and Influence,** edited by Margaret Gibson, 135-54. Oxford: Basil Blackwell, 1981.

Cappuyns, M. "Boèce." In Dictionnaire d'histoire et de géographie ecclésiastique. Vol. 9, 347-80. Paris: Librairie Letouzey et Anê, 1937.

Cardale, J.S. King Alfred's Anglo-Saxon Version of Boethius' De Consolatione Philosophiae. London: n.p., 1829.

Carrière, Jeanne Louise. "Boethian Narrative Structure in Fourteenth-Century English Literature." Ph.D. diss., University of California at Los Angeles, 1975.

Caxton, William. Chaucer's Boece. N.p.: n.p., c.1478.

Chadwick, Henry. "Introduction." In Boethius: His Life, Thought and Influence, edited by Margaret Gibson, 1-12. Oxford: Basil Blackwell, 1981.

Cipriani, Lisi. "Studies in the Influence of the Romance of the Rose upon Chaucer." PMLA 22 [n.s., 25] (1907): 552-95.

Clark, James Midgley. The Abbey of St. Gall as a Centre of Literature and Art. Cambridge: University Press, 1926.

Cline, James M. "Chaucer and Jean de Meun: De Consolatione Philosophiae." Journal of English Literary History 3 (1936): 170-81.

Cohn, Martin. "Die Rolle der Metra des Boethius im Streit um die Datierung der Denkmäler der angelsächsischen Poesie." Ph.D. diss., Schlesische Friedrich-Wilhelms-Universität, Breslau, 1922.

Cohn, Norman. The World View of a Thirteenth-Century Parisian Intellectual: Jean de Meun and the Roman de la Rose. Newcastle upon Tyne: University of Durham, 1961.

Coleman, Evelyn S. "Die Lehnbildungen in Notkers
    Übersetzung." In Festschrift für Taylor Starck,
    edited by Werner Betz, Evelyn S. Coleman, and Kenneth
    Northcott, 106-29. The Hague: Moulton and Co., 1964.

----------. "Bibliographie zu Notker III von St. Gallen," In
    Germanic Studies in Honor of Edward Henry
    Sehrt, edited by Frithjov Andersen Raven, Wolfram K.
    Legner, and James Cecil King, 61-76. Miami Linguistic
    Series, no. 1. Coral Gables, Fla.: University of Miami
    Press, 1968.

Conlee, John W. "A Note on Verse Composition in the Meters
    of Boethius." Neuphilologische Mitteilungen
    71 (1970): 576-85.

Coolidge, John S. "Boethius and 'That Last Infirmity of Noble
    Mind.'" Philological Quarterly 42 (1963): 176-82.

Cooper, Lane. A Concordance of Boethius: the Five
    Theological Tractates and the Consolation of
    Philosophy. Mediaeval Academy of America Publication,
    no. 1. Cambridge, Mass.: Mediaeval Academy of
    America, 1928.

Copeland, Rita. "Rhetoric and Vernacular Translation in the
    Middle Ages." Studies in the Age of Chaucer 9
    (1987): 41-75.

Cossack, Hermann. Über die altenglische metrische
    Bearbeitung von Boethius, De Consolatione
    Philosophiae. Ph.D. diss., Universität Leipzig, 1889.
    Leipzig: Max Hoffmann, 1889.

Courcelle, Pierre. "Étude critique sur les commentaires de la
    Consolation de Boèce (IXe-XVe siècles)." Archives
    d'histoire doctrinale et littéraire du moyen âge
    4 (1939): 5-140.

----------. La Consolation de philosophie dans la tradition littéraire: antécédents et postérité de Boèce. Paris: Études Augustiniennes, 1967.

Crabbe, Anna. "Literary Design in the De Consolatione Philosophiae." In Boethius: His Life, Thought and Influence, edited by Margaret Gibson, 237-74. Oxford: Basil Blackwell, 1981.

Crespo, Roberto. "Jean de Meun traduttore della Consolatio Philosophiae de Boezio." Atti della Academia della Scienza de Torino: Classe de Scienze morali, Storiche e Filologiche 103 (1969): 71-170.

----------. "Il prologo alla traduzione della Consolatio Philosophiae di Jean de Meun e il Commento di Guglielmo d'Aragona." In Romanitas et Christianitas: Studia Iano Henrico Waszink AD Kal. Nov. A. 1973, 13 lustra complenti oblata, edited by Boer, et al., 55-70. Amsterdam: North-Holland Publishing, 1973.

Cropp, Glennis M. "La Traduction française de la Consolatio Philosophiae de Boèce: encore un manuscrit." Romania 90 (1969): 258-70.

----------. "A Checklist of Manuscripts of the Medieval French Anonymous Verse-Prose Translation of the Consolatio of Boethius." Notes and Queries 224 (1979): 294-6.

----------. "Quelques manuscrits méconnus de la traduction en prose de la Consolatio Philosophiae par Jean de Meun." Scriptorium 33 (1979): 260-6.

----------. " Two Historical Glosses in Le Livre de Boece de la Consolacion." New Zealand Journal of French Studies 2 (1981): 5-20.

----------. "Additional Manuscripts of the Medieval French Anonymous Verse-Prose Translation of the **Consolatio** of Boethius." **Notes and Queries** 227 [n.s. 29] (1982): 292-4.

----------. "Le Prologue de Jean de Meun et **Le Livre de Boece de Consolacion**." **Romania** 103 (1982): 278-98.

----------. "Les Manuscrits du **Livre de Boece de Consolacion**." **Revue d'histoire des textes** 12/13 (1982/1983): 263-352.

----------. "An Unnoticed Manuscript of a Medieval French Verse Translation of the **Consolatio** of Boethius." **Notes and Queries** 229 [n.s. 31] (1984): 156-8.

----------. "Les Gloses du **Livre de Boece de Consolacion**." **Le Moyen Age** 42 (1986): 367-81.

----------. "**Le Livre de Boece de Consolacion**: From Translation to Glossed Text." In **The Medieval Boethius: Studies in the Vernacular Translations of** De Consolatione Philosophiae, edited by Alastair J. Minnis, 63-88. Woodbridge, Suffolk: D.S. Brewer, 1987.

----------. "**Le Livre de Boece de Consolacion**: Revision of the Translation in Some Later Manuscripts." **Parergon** n.s. 9 (1991): 17-20.

Curry, Walter Clyde. **Chaucer and the Medieval Sciences.** 1926. Reprint. New York: Barnes and Noble, 1960.

Dedeck-Héry, Venceslas Louis. "Un Fragment inédit de la traduction de la **Consolation** de Boèce par Jean de Meun." **Romanic Review** 27 (1936): 110-24.

----------. "Jean de Meun et Chaucer, traducteurs de la **Consolation** de Boèce." **PMLA** 52 (1937): 967-91.

----------. "The Manuscripts of the Translation of Boethius' **Consolatio** by Jean de Meung." **Speculum** 15 (1940): 432-43.

----------. "Le **Boèce** de Chaucer et les manuscrits français de la **Consolatio** de Jean de Meun." **PMLA** 59 (1944): 18-25.

----------, ed. "Boethius' **De Consolatione** by Jean de Meun." **Mediaeval Studies** 14 (1952): 165-275.

Delisle, Léopold. "Anciennes traductions françaises de la **Consolation** de Boëce conservées à la Bibliothèque Nationale." **Bibliothèque de l'école des Chartes** 34 (1873): 5-32.

Denomy, Alex J. "The Vocabulary of Jean de Meun's Translation of Boethius' **De Consolatione Philosophiae**." **Mediaeval Studies** 16 (1954): 19-34.

Dolch, Alfred Karl. **Notker-Studien Teil I und II: lateinisch-althochdeutsches Glossar und althochdeutsch-lateinisches Wörterverzeichnis zu Notkers Boethius** De Consolatione Philosophiae **Buch I**. Ottendorfer Memorial Series of Germanic Monographs, no. 16. Leipzig: Buchdruckerei Robert Noske, 1952.

----------. **Notker-Studien Teil III: Stil- und Quellenprobleme zu Notkers Boethius und Martianus**. Ottendorfer Memorial Series of Germanic Monographs, no. 16. Leipzig: Buchdruckerei Robert Noske, 1952.

----------. "Quellenprobleme zu Notkers Boethius." In **Germanic Studies in Honor of Edward Henry Sehrt**, edited by Frithjov Andersen Raven, Wolfram K. Legner and James Cecil King, 77-82. Miami Linguistic Series, no. 1. Coral Gables, Fla.: University of Miami Press, 1968.

Dolson, Guy Bayley. "I.T.--Translator of Boethius." **American Journal of Philology** 42 (1921): 266.

----------. "Boethius' Consolation of Philosophy in English Literature During the Eighteenth Century." **Classical Weekly** 15 (1922): 124-6.

----------. "Imprisoned English Authors and the **Consolation of Philosophy** of Boethius." **American Journal of Philology** 43 (1922): 168-9.

----------. "Southey and Landor and the **Consolation of Philosophy** of Boethius." **American Journal of Philology** 43 (1922): 356-8.

----------. "The **Consolation of Philosophy** of Boethius in English Literature." Ph.D. diss., Cornell University, 1926.

----------. "Did Caxton Translate the **De Consolatione Philosophiae** of Boethius?" **American Journal of Philology** 47 (1926): 83-6.

Donaghey, Brian S. "The Sources of King Alfred's Translation of Boethius's **De Consolatione Philosophiae**." **Anglia: Zeitschrift für englische Literatur** 82 (1964): 23-57.

----------. "Alexander Pope's and Sir William Trumbull's Translations of Boethius." **Leeds Studies in English** n.s. 1 (1967): 71-82.

----------. "Another English Manuscript of an Old French Translation of Boethius." **Medium Aevum** 42 (1973): 38-41.

----------. "Nicholas Trevet's Use of King Alfred's Translation of Boethius, and the Dating of his Commentary." In **The Medieval Boethius: Studies in the Vernacular**

Translations of De Consolatione Philosophiae, edited by Alastair J. Minnis, 1-31. Woodbridge, Suffolk: D.S. Brewer, 1987.

Donner, Morton. "Derived Words in Chaucer's Boece: the Translator as Wordsmith." Chaucer Review 18 (1984): 187-203.

Donoghue, Daniel. "Word Order and Poetic Style: Auxiliary and Verbal in The Meters of Boethius." Anglo-Saxon England 15 (1986): 167-196.

Dunleavy, Gareth W. "The Wound and the Comforter: the Consolations of Geoffrey Chaucer." Papers on Language and Literature 3 (1967, Summer Supplement): 14-27.

Duval, M. Amaury. "Simon de Fresne." In Histoire littéraire de la France. Vol. 18, 822-24. Paris: Firmin Didot, 1835.

Dwyer, Richard A. "Another Boèce." Romance Philology 19 (1965): 268-70.

----------. "Old French Translations of Boethius' Consolatio Philosophiae in the National Library of Wales." National Library of Wales Journal 14 (1966): 486-8.

----------. "Manuscripts of the Medieval French Boethius." Notes and Queries 216 (1971): 124-5.

----------. "The Newberry's Unknown Revision of Walton's Boethius." Manuscripta 17 (1973): 27-30.

----------. "The Appreciation of Handmade Literature." Chaucer Review 8 (1974): 221-40.

----------. "Bonaventura da Demena, Sicilian Translator of
        Boethius." **French Studies** 28 (1974): 129-33.

----------. "The Old French Boethius: Addendum." **Medium
        Aevum** 43 (1974): 265-6.

----------. **Boethian Fictions: Narratives in the Medieval
        French Versions of** the Consolatio Philosophiae.
        Mediaeval Academy of America, no. 83. Cambridge,
        Mass.: Mediaeval Academy of America, 1976.

Eckhardt, Caroline D. "The Medieval **Prosimetrum** Genre (from
        Boethius to **Boece**)." **Genre** 16 (1983): 21-38.

Ehrismann, Gustav. "Notker III (Labeo) von St. Gallen." In
        **Handbuch des deutschen Unterrichts in höheren
        Schulen.** Vol. 6, pt. 1, **Die althochdeutsche
        Literatur,** 416-58. Munich: C.-H. Beck'sche
        Verlagsbuchhandlung, 1932.

Elbow, Peter. **Oppositions in Chaucer.** Middletown, Conn.:
        Wesleyan University Press, 1965.

Exter, Otto. **Beon und Wesen in Alfreds Übersetzung des
        Boethius, der Metra und der Soliloquien.** Ph.D.
        diss., Christian-Albrechts-Universität zu Kiel, 1911.
        Kiel: H. Fiencke, 1911.

Fäh, Laurenz. **Die Sprache der altfranzösischen
        Boëtius-Übersetzung, enthalten in dem Ms.
        365 der Stadtbibliothek Bern.** Freiburg (Schweiz):
        Buchdruckerei Gebrüder Fragnière, 1915.

Fahrenbach, William Joseph. "Vernacular Translations of Classical
        Literature in Late-Medieval Britain: Eight Translations
        Made Directly from Latin Between 1400 and 1525."
        Ph.D. diss., University of Toronto, 1975.

Fehlauer, Friedrich. **Die englischen Übersetzungen von Boethius'** De Consolatione Philosophiae. Ph.D. diss., Albertus-Universität zu Königsberg, 1908. Königsberg: Hartungsche Buchdruckerei, 1908.

----------. **Die englischen Übersetzungen von Boethius'** De Consolatione Philosophiae. Berlin: Emil Felber, 1909.

Fischer, Olga. "A Comparative Study of Philosophical Terms in the Alfredian and Chaucerian Boethius." **Neophilologus** 63 (1979): 622-39.

Fisher, John H., ed. **The Complete Poetry and Prose of Geoffrey Chaucer.** New York: Holt, Reinhart and Winston, 1977.

Flügel, Ewald. "Kleinere Mitteilungen aus Handschriften." **Anglia: Zeitschrift für englische Philologie** 14 (1892): 463-501.

Ford, Susan Chappell. "Poetry in Boethius' **Consolation of Philosophy.**" Ph.D. diss., Columbia University, 1967.

Förster, Max. "Zum altenglischen Boethius." **Archiv für das Studium der neueren Sprachen und Literaturen** 106 (1901): 342-3.

Fox, Samuel. **Alfred's Anglo-Saxon Version of the Meters of Boethius: With an English Translation and Notes.** London: n.p., 1835.

----------. **King Alfred's Anglo-Saxon Version of Boethius** De Consolatione Philosophiae **With a Literal English Translation, Notes, and Glossary.** London, 1864. Reprint. New York: AMS, 1970.

Fraeger, Franz. **Studien zur Sprache von Notkers Boethius.** Programm des königlichen humanistischen Gymnasium in Landshut für das Studienjahr 1905/1906. Landshut: Joseph Thomann'sche Buch und Kunstdruckerei, 1906.

Frakes, Jerold Coleman. **"Fortuna in the Consolatio:** Boethius, Alfred and Notker." Ph.D. diss., University of Minnesota, 1982.

----------. "Die Rezeption der Neuplatonischen Metaphysik des Boethius durch Alfred und Notker." **Beiträge zur Geschichte der deutschen Sprache und Literatur** 106 (1984): 51-74.

Friedman, Albert B. "Jean de Meun an Englishman?" **Modern Language Notes** 65 (1950): 319-25.

Frieshammer, Johann. **Die sprachliche Form der Chaucerschen Prosa: ihr Verhältnis zur Reimtechnik des Dichters sowie zur Sprache der alteren Londoner Urkunden.** Studien zur Englischen Philologie. Halle: Max Niemeyer Verlag, 1910.

Furnivall, F.J., ed. **Chaucer's Boece Englisht from Anicii Manlii Severini Boetii** Philosophiae Consolationis **Libri Quinque.** Chaucer Society, no. 75 (first series). 1886. Reprint. New York: Johnson Reprint Corporation, 1967.

Furrer, Dieter. **Modusprobleme bei Notker: die modalen Werte in den Nebensätzen der** Consolatio-Übersetzung. Das Althochdeutsche von St. Gallen: Texte und Untersuchungen zur sprachlichen Überlieferung St. Gallens vom 8. bis zum 12. Jahrhundert, no. 2. Berlin: Walter de Gruyter, 1971.

Gabriel, Astrik L. "The Source of the Anecdote of the Inconstant
    Scholar." Classica et Mediaevalia 19 (1958):
    152-76.

Gardner, Averil. "Chaucer and Boethius: Some Illustrations of
    Indebtedness." University of Capetown Studies in
    English 2 (1971): 31-8.

Gibbon, Edward. The History of the Decline and Fall of
    the Roman Empire, edited by J.B. Bury. Vol. 4.
    London, 1909. Reprint. New York: AMS, 1974.

Gibson, Margaret, ed. Boethius: His Life, Thought and
    Influence. Oxford: Basil Blackwell, 1981.

----------. "The Opuscula Sacra in the Middle Ages." In
    Boethius: His Life, Thought and Influence,
    edited by Margaret Gibson, 214-34. Oxford: Basil
    Blackwell, 1981.

Giles, J.A. The Whole Works of Alfred the Great. 2 vols.
    London, 1858. Reprint. New York: AMS, 1969.

Gleason, Mark J. "Clearing the Fields: Towards a Reassessment of
    Chaucer's Use of Trevet in the Boece." In The
    Medieval Boethius: Studies in the Vernacular
    Translations of De Consolatione Philosophiae, edited
    by Alastair J. Minnis, 89-105. Woodbridge, Suffolk:
    D.S. Brewer, 1987.

Godden, Malcolm. "King Alfred's Boethius." In Boethius: His
    Life, Thought and Influence, edited by Margaret
    Gibson, 419-24. Oxford: Basil Blackwell, 1981.

Graff, E.G. Althochdeutsche Übersetzung und
    Erläuterung der von Boethius verfassten fünf
    Bücher De Consolatione Philosophiae. N.p.: n.p.,
    1837.

Grafton, Anthony. "Epilogue: Boethius in the Renaissance." In
    Boethius: His Life, Thought and Influence,
    edited by Margaret Gibson, 410-15. Oxford: Basil
    Blackwell, 1981.

Green, Richard L. "'The Port of Peace': Not Death But God."
    Modern Language Notes, 69 (1954): 307-9.

Grein, Christian C.W.M. **Bibliothek der angelsächsischen
    Poesie**. 2 vols. Göttingen: n.p., 1858.

----------. "Zur Textkritik der angelsächsischen Dichter."
    Germania 10 (1865): 416-29.

Griffith, Richard R. Review of **Chaucer According to
    William Caxton: Minor Poems and Boece**,
    edited by Beverly Boyd. **Studies in the Age of
    Chaucer** 2 (1980): 151-3.

Gröber, Gustav. "Erbauliche und theologische Prosa." In
    Grundriss der romanischen Philologie. Vol. 2,
    1025-6. Strassburg: Trübner, 1902.

Hammond, Eleanor Prescott. "Boethius: Chaucer: Walton:
    Lydgate." **Modern Language Notes** 41 (1926):
    534-5.

----------. **English Verse Between Chaucer and Surrey**.
    New York: Octagon Books, 1969.

Handschuh, Doris. **Konjunktionen in Notkers
    Boethius-Übersetzung**. Ph.D. diss., Universität
    Zürich, 1964. Zurich: Juris-Verlag, 1964.

Hartmann, K.A. Martin. "Ist König Alfred der Verfasser der
    alliterierenden Übertragung der **Metra des Boethius?**"
    Anglia: Zeitschrift für englische Philologie 5
    (1882): 411-50.

Hattemer, Heinrich H. **Denkmale des Mittelalters.** St. Gallens altteutsche Sprachschätze. Vol. 3, 7-255. St. Gallen: Druck und Verlag von Scheitlin und Zollikofer, 1844-1849.

Herzig, Marie Jacobus. "The Early Recension and Continuity of Certain Middle English Texts in the Sixteenth Century." Ph.D. diss., University of Pennsylvania, 1973.

Hoek, Jacobus Martinus. **De Middelnederlandse vertalingen van Boethius'** De Consolatione Philosophiae. Ph.D. diss., Amsterdam, 1943. Harderwijk: Drukkerij-Uitgeverij "Flevo," 1943.

Hoffmann, Paul Th. **Der Mittelalterliche Mensch: Gesehen aus Welt und Umwelt Notkers des Deutschen.** Gotha: Verlag Friederich Andreas Perthes, 1922.

Hollander, John. "'Moedes or Prolaciouns' in Chaucer's **Boece."** **Modern Language Notes** 71 (1956): 397-9.

Houghton, Walter E., Jr. "English Translations of Boethius's **De Consolatione Philosophiae** in the Seventeenth Century." Ph.D. diss., Yale University, 1931.

----------. "S.E.M.--'Translator' of Boethius," **Review of English Studies** 7 (1931): 160-7.

Hubbard, Frank G. "The Relation of the 'Blooms of King Alfred' to the Anglo-Saxon Translation of Boethius." **Modern Language Notes** 9 (1894): 161-71.

Huet, M. Gédéon. "La première édition de la **Consolation** de Boèce en néerlandais." In **Mélanges Julien Havet,** edited by Ernest Leroux, 501-69. Paris: n.p., 1895.

Hündgen, Franz, ed. **Das altprovenzalische Boëthiuslied unter Beifügung einer Übersetzung, eines**

Glossars, erklärender Anmerkungen sowie grammatischer und metrischer Untersuchung. Oppeln: Eugen Frank's Buchhandlung, 1884.

Jack, R. Ian. "The Significance of the Alfredian Translations." **Australasian Universities Language and Literature Association** 13 (1971): 348-61.

Jefferson, Bernard L. **Chaucer and the** Consolation of Philosophy **of Boethius.** 1917. Reprint. New York: Haskell House, 1965.

Jellinek, M.H. "Althochdeutsch PHAFFO--Gothic PAPA." **Zeitschrift für deutsches Altertum und deutsche Literatur** 69 (1932): 143-4.

Johnson, I.R., "Walton's Sapient Orpheus." In **The Medieval Boethius: Studies in the Vernacular Translations of** De Consolatione Philosophiae, edited by Alastair J. Minnis, 139-68. Woodbridge, Suffolk: D.S. Brewer, 1987.

Joukovsky-Micha, Françoise. "La Notion de 'vaine gloire' de Simund de Freine à Martin le Franc (Part 1)." **Romania** 89 (1968): 1-30.

----------. "La Notion de 'vaine gloire' de Simund de Freine à Martin le Franc (Part 2)." **Romania** 89 (1968): 210-39.

Jourdain, M. Charles. "Des Commentaires inédits de Guillaume de Conches et de Nicolas Triveth sur **La Consolation de la philosophie** de Boèce." **Notices et extraits des manuscrits de la Bibliothèque Nationale** 20 (1862): 40-82.

Karg-Gasterstädt, Elizabeth. "Notker Labeo." In **Die deutsche Literatur des Mittelalters: Verfasserlexikon,** edited by Wolfgang Stammler and Karl Langosch. Vol. 5, 775-90. Berlin: n.p., 1955.

Kaylor, Noel Harold, Jr. "An Addition to the Checklist of
Manuscripts of the French Anonymous Verse-Prose
Translation of the **Consolation** of Boethius." **Notes
and Queries** 226 (1981): 196-7.

----------. "John Walton's 1410 Verse Translation of the **De
Consolatione Philosophiae** in the Context of Its
Medieval Tradition." **Fifteenth-Century Studies** 6
(1983): 121-48.

----------. "The Medieval Translations of Boethius' **Consolation
of Philosophy** in England, France, and Germany: An
Analysis and Annotated Bibliography." Ph.D. diss.,
Vanderbilt University, 1985.

----------. "Peter von Kastl: Fifteenth-Century Translator of
Boethius." **Fifteenth-Century Studies** 18 (1991):
133-142.

----------. "Chaucer's Use of the Word **Tragedy**: A Semantic
Analysis." In **Language and Civilization**, edited by
Claudia Blank. Vol. 2, 431-44. Frankfurt: Peter Lang
Verlag, 1992.

Keightley, Ronald G. "Boethius in Spain: A Classified Checklist
of Early Translations." In **The Medieval Boethius:
Studies in the Vernacular Translations of** De
Consolatione Philosophiae, edited by Alastair J. Minnis,
169-87. Woodbridge, Suffolk: D.S. Brewer, 1987.

Kelle, Johann. Review of **Die Schriften Notkers und seiner
Schule**, ed. by Paul Piper. **Zeitschrift für
Deutsches Altertum** 9 (1883), 313-29.

----------. "Die philosophischen Kunstausdrücke in Notkers
Werken." **Abhandlung der königlichen
bayerischen Akademie der Wissenschaften** 18
(1888): 1-58.

----------. "Über die Grundlage, auf der Notkers Erklärung von Boethius **De Consolatione Philosophiae** beruht." **Sitzungsberichte der königlichen bayerischen Akademie der Wissenschaften,** nv. (1896), 349-56.

----------. **Die rhetorischen Kunstausdrücke in Notkers Werken.** Munich: Verlag der königlichen Akademie, 1899.

Kern, J.H. "A Few Notes on the **Metra of Boethius** in Old English." **Neophilologus** 8 (1923): 295-300.

Kiernan, Kevin S. "Deor: the Consolations of an Anglo-Saxon Boethius." **Neuphilologische Mitteilungen** 79 (1978): 333-40.

Kirkby, Helen. "The Scholar and His Public." In **Boethius: His Life, Thought and Influence,** edited by Margaret Gibson, 44-69. Oxford: Basil Blackwell, 1981.

Kirshner, Harold. "The Nature Vocabulary of Notker Labeo: a Study in Early German Scientific Terminology." Ph.D. diss., New York University, 1963.

Klaeber, Fr. "Notes on Old English Prose Texts." **Modern Language Notes** 18 (1903): 241-7.

Koch, John. "Chaucer's Boethiusübersetzung: ein Beitrag zur Bestimmung der Chronologie seiner Werke." **Anglia: Zeitschrift für englische Philologie** 46 (1922): 1-51.

Koeppel, E. "Zur Chronologie der Übersetzungen des Königs Alfred." **Anglia: Zeitschrift für englische Philologie** (Beiblatt) 19 (1908): 330-3.

Kottler, Barnet. "Chaucer's **Boece** and the Late Medieval Textual Tradition of the **Consolatio Philosophiae.**" Ph.D. diss., Yale University, 1953.

----------. "The Vulgate Tradition of the Consolatio Philosophiae in the Fourteenth Century." **Mediaeval Studies** 17 (1955): 209-14.

Krämer, Ernest, ed. **Die altenglischen** Metra des Boethius. Bonner Beiträge zur Anglistik, no. 8. Bonn: P. Hanstein's Verlag, 1902.

Krapp, George Philip, ed. **The Paris Psalter and the Meters of Boethius.** New York: Columbia University Press, 1932.

----------. **The Rise of English Literary Prose.** 1915. Reprint. New York: Frederick Ungar, 1963.

Krawutschke, Alfred. **Die Sprache der Boëthius-Übersetzung des Königs Alfred.** Ph.D. diss., Friederich-Wilhelms-Universität zu Berlin, 1902. Berlin: Julius Driesner, 1902.

Langford, John Alfred. **Prison Books and Their Authors.** London: William Tegg, 1861.

Langhans, Victor. "Die Datierung der Prosastücke Chaucers." **Anglia: Zeitschrift für englische Philologie** 53 (1929): 235-68.

Langlois, Charles Victor. "La Consolation de Boèce, d'après Jean de Meun et plusieurs autres." In **La Vie en France au moyen âge.** Vol. 4, **La Vie spirituelle,** 269-326. Paris: Librairie Hachette, 1928.

----------. Les Manuscrits de Rome: Vat. 4788." **Notices et extraits des manuscrits de la Bibliothèque Nationale et autres bibliothèques** 33 (1889): 261-5.

Langlois, Ernest, ed. Le Roman de la Rose par Guillaume de Lorris et Jean de Meun. 5 vols. Société des Textes Français. Paris: Firmin Didot, 1912.

----------. "La Traduction de Boèce par Jean de Meun." Romania 42 (1913): 331-69.

Leicht, Alfred. "Ist König Ælfred der Verfasser der alliterierenden Metra des Boethius?" Anglia: Zeitschrift für englische Philologie 6 (1883): 126-70.

----------. "Zur angelsächsischen Bearbeitung des Boethius." Anglia: Zeitschrift für englische Philologie 7 (1884): 178-202.

Lepley, Douglas L. "The Monk's Tale." Chaucer Review 12 (1977/1978): 162-70.

Leroux, Ernest. Catalogue général des manuscrits français de la Bibliothèque Nationale. Vol. 1, 301-2. Paris: Librairie Ernest Leroux, 1931.

Lewry, Osmund. "Boethian Logic in the Medieval West." In Boethius: His Life, Thought and Influence, edited by Margaret Gibson, 90-134. Oxford: Basil Blackwell, 1981.

Liddell, Mark H. "Chaucer's Translation of Boece's 'Boke of Comfort' (Announcement of Chaucer's Use of the French Translation in His Own Translation of Boethius)." Academy 1 (1895): 227.

----------. "One of Chaucer's Sources." The Nation 64 (1897): 124-5.

Liddell, Mark H., H.F. Heath, W.S. McCormick, A.W. Pollard, eds. The Works of Chaucer (The Globe Edition). London: Macmillan, 1908.

Lindahl, Niels. "Vollständiges Glossar zu Notkers Boethius **De Consolatione I.**" Ph.D. diss., Uppsala, 1916.

Louis, Réné. "Esquisse d'une biographie de Jean de Meun, Continuateur du **Roman de la Rose** de Guillaume de Lorris." In **Études ligériennes d'histoire et d'archéologie médiévale**, 257-65. Paris: Publications de la Société, 1975.

Lowes, John Livingston. "Chaucer's **Boethius** and Jean de Meun." **Romanic Review** 8 (1917): 383-400.

Lucas, Robert H. "Mediaeval French Translations of the Latin Classics to 1500." **Speculum** 45 (1970): 225-53.

Luginbühl, Emil. **Studien zu Notkers Übersetzungskunst.** Das Althochdeutsche von St. Gallen, no. 1. Berlin: Walter de Gruyter, 1970.

McAlpine, Monica Ellen. "A Boethian Approach to the Problems of Genre in Chaucer's **Troilus and Criseyde.**" Ph.D. diss., University of Rochester, 1973.

----------. **The Genre of** Troilus and Criseyde. Ithaca: Cornell University Press, 1978.

Machan, Tim William. "Chaucer as Philologist: The **Boece.**" Ph.D. diss., University of Wisconsin, 1984.

----------. "**Forlynen:** a Ghost Word Rematerializes." **Notes and Queries** 31 (1984): 22-4.

----------. **Techniques of Translation: Chaucer's** Boece. Norman, Okla.: Pilgrim Books, 1985.

----------. "Glosses in the Manuscripts of Chaucer's **Boece.**" In **The Medieval Boethius: Studies in the Vernacular Translations of** De Consolatione

Philosophiae, edited by Alastair J. Minnis, 125-38. Woodbridge, Suffolk: D.S. Brewer, 1987.

----------. "Editorial Method and Medieval Translations: The Example of Chaucer's **Boece**." **Studies in Bibliography: Papers of the Bibliographical Society of the University of Virginia** 41 (1988): 188-96.

Mair, John. "The Text of the **Opuscula Sacra**." In **Boethius: His Life, Thought and Influence**, edited by Margaret Gibson, 206-13. Oxford: Basil Blackewll, 1981.

Markland, Murray F. "Boethius, Alfred, and Deor." **Modern Philology** 66 (1968/1969): 1-4.

Matthews, John. "Anicius Manlius Severinus Boethius." In **Boethius: His Life, Thought and Influence**, edited by Margaret Gibson, 15-43. Oxford: Basil Blackwell, 1981.

Matzke, John E. "The Anglo-Norman Poet Simund de Freine." **Transactions and Proceedings of the American Philological Association** 33 (1902): xc.

----------, ed. "Le Roman de Philosophie." In **Les Oeuvres de Simund de Freine**, 1-60. Société des Anciens Textes Français. Paris: Firmin Didot, 1909.

Means, Michael H. **The Consolatio Genre in Medieval English Literature**. University of Florida Humanities Monograph, no. 3. Gainesville, Fla.: University of Florida Press, 1972.

Mermier, Guy. "**Boeci**: An English Translation of the Old Provencal [sic] Fragment with a Preface and Notes." In **Contemporary Readings of Medieval Literature**, edited by Guy Mermier, 21-35. Ann Arbor: University of Michigan Press, 1989.

Metcalf, Allan A. "The Poetic Language of the Old English
    Meters of Boethius." Ph.D. diss., University of
    California at Berkeley, 1966.

----------. "On the Authorship and Originality of the **Meters of
    Boethius."** Neuphilologische Mitteilungen 71
    (1970): 185-7.

----------. **Poetic Diction in the Old English** Meters of
    Boethius. Indiana University, Series Practica, no. 50. The
    Hague: Moulton, 1973.

Meyer, Paul. Review of "Anciennes traductions françaises de la
    Consolation du Boëce conservées à la Bibliothèque
    Nationale" [**Bibliothèque de l'École des Chartes**,
    vol. 34], by Léopold Delisle. Romania 2 (1873): 271-3.

----------, ed. **Recueil d'anciens textes bas-latin,
    provençaux et français, accompagné de deux
    glossaires.** Paris: F. Vieweg, 1877.

Migne, J.P., ed. **Boetii, Opera Omnia.** Patrologiae Latinae,
    nos. 63-64. Turnholti, Belgium: Typograhi Brepols
    Editores Pontificii, n.d.

Minio-Paluello, Lorenzo. "Boethius." In **Dictionary of
    Scientific Biography.** Vol. 2, 228-36. New York:
    Charles Scribners' Sons, 1970.

Minnis, Alastair J. "Aspects of the Medieval French and English
    Traditions of the **De Consolatione Philosophiae."**
    In **Boethius: His Life, Thought and Influence,**
    edited by Margaret Gibson, 312-61. Oxford: Basil
    Blackwell, 1981.

---------- ed. **The Medieval Boethius: Studies in the
    Vernacular Translations of the** De Consolatione
    Philosophiae. Woodbridge, Suffolk: D.S. Brewer, 1987.

----------. "'Glosynge is a glorious thyng': Chaucer at Work on the **Boece**." In **The Medieval Boethius: Studies in the Vernacular Translations of** De Consolatione Philosophiae, edited by Alastair J. Minnis, 106-24. Woodbridge, Suffolk: D.S. Brewer, 1987.

Mommert, Michael. **Konrad Humery und seine Übersetzung der** Consolatio Philosophiae: **Studien zur deutschen Boethius-Tradition am Ausgang des Mittelalters.** Ph.D. diss., Westfälische Wilhelms-Universität, 1965. Münster: Westfälische Wilhelms-Universität, 1965.

Morris, Richard, ed. **Chaucer's** Boece **Englisht from Boethius's** De Consolatione Philosophiae. Chaucer Society, no. 76 (first series). London: N. Trübner, 1886.

Myrvaagnes, Naomi Suconick. "A Stylistic Study of the Old English **Meters of Boethius.**" Ph.D. diss., New York University, 1970.

Naaber, August. **Die Quellen von Notkers:** Boethius De Consolatione Philosophiae. Ph.D. diss., Königliche Westfälische-Wilhelms-Universität zu Münster in Westfalen, 1911. Borna-Leipzig: Buchdruckerei Robert Noske, 1911.

Nagel, Franz. **Die altfranzösische Übersetzung der** Consolatio Philosophiae **des Boëthius von Renaut von Louhans.** Ph.D. diss., Friederichs-Universität Halle-Wittenberg, 1890. Halle: Ehrhardt Karras, 1890.

----------. "Die altfranzösische Übersetzung der **Consolatio Philosophiae** des Boëthius von Renaud von Louhans." **Zeitschrift für romanische Philologie, 15** (1891): 1-23.

Napier, A. "Bruckstück einer altenglischen Boethiushandschrift."
    **Zeitschrift für deutsches Altertum und
    deutsche Literatur** 31 (1887): 52-4.

Naumann, Hans. **Notkers Boethius: Untersuchung Über
    Quellen und Stil.** Quellen und Forschung zur Sprach-
    und Culturgeschichte der Germanischen Völker, no. 121.
    Strassburg: Karl J. Trübner, 1913.

Ostberg, K. "Interpretations and Translations of
    Animal/Animans in the Writings of Notker Labeo."
    **Beiträge zur Geschichte der deutschen Sprache
    und Literatur: Tübingen** 81 (1959): 16-42.

----------. "The 'Prologi' of Notker's Boethius Reconsidered."
    German Life and Letters 16 (1962/1963): 256-65.

Otten, Kurt. **König Alfred's Boethius.** Studien zur englischen
    Philologie, no. 3 (neue Folge). Tübingen: Max Niemeyer
    Verlag, 1964.

Pace, George B. and Linda E. Voigts. "A 'Boece' Fragment."
    Studies in the Age of Chaucer 1 (1979): 143-50.

Page, Christopher. "The Boethian Metrum 'Bella bis quinis': a
    New Song from Saxon Canterbury." In **Boethius: His
    Life, Thought and Influence**, edited by Margaret
    Gibson, 306-11. Oxford: Basil Blackwell, 1981.

Palmer, Nigel F. "Latin and Vernacular in the Northern European
    Tradition of the **De Consolatione Philosophiae.**"
    In **Boethius: His Life, Thought and Influence**,
    edited by Margaret Gibson, 362-409. Oxford: Basil
    Blackwell, 1981.

Parks, M.B. "A Note on MS Vatican Bibl. Apost., lat. 3363." In
    Boethius: His Life, Thought and Influence,
    edited by Margaret Gibson, 425-7. Oxford: Basil
    Blackwell, 1981.

Paris, Paulin. "Jean de Meun, traducteur et poète." In **Histoire littéraire de la France** 28 (1881): 391-439.

Patch, Howard Rollin. **The Tradition of Boethius: A Study of His Importance in Medieval Culture.** New York: Oxford University Press, 1935.

Payne, F. Anne. **King Alfred and Boethius: An Analysis of the Old English Version of the** Consolation of Philosophy. Madison/Milwaukee: University of Wisconsin Press, 1968.

Peck, Russell A. **Chaucer's** Romaunt of the Rose **and** Boece, Treatise on the Astrolabe, Equatorie of the Planetis, **Lost Works, and Chaucerian Apocrypha: an Annotated Bibliography, 1900 to 1985.** The Chaucer Bibliographies. Toronto: University of Toronto Press, 1988.

Peiper, Rudolfus. **Anicii Manlii Severinii Boethii** Philosophiae Consolationis, **Libri Quinque, accedunt eiusdem atque incertorum** Opuscula Sacra. Lipsiae: Aedibus B.G. Teubneri, 1871.

Pemberton, Caroline, ed. **Queen Elizabeth's Englishings of Boethius,** De Consolatione Philosophiae; **Plutarch,** De Curiositate; **Horace,** De Arte Poetica (part). Early English Text Society, no. 113. London: Kegan Paul, Trench, Trübner, 1899.

Petersen, Kate O. "Chaucer and Trivet." **PMLA** 18 (1903): 173-93.

Pez (Pezius), Bernard. **Thesaurus Anecdotorum Novissimus.** Vol. 4, xxiv and 273-636. Augsburg: Augustae Vindelicorum and Gracii, 1723.

Pingree, David. "Boethius' Geometry and Astronomy." In **Boethius: His Life, Thought and Influence,**

edited by Margaret Gibson, 155-61. Oxford: Basil
Blackwell, 1981.

Piper, Paul, ed. **Die Schriften Notkers und seiner Schule.**
Germanischer Bücherschatz, no. 8-?. Freiburg und
Tübingen: Akamdemische Verlagsbuchhandlung von
J.C.B. Mohr, 1883.

Pompen, Fr. A. Review of **King Alfred's Books,** by Bishop
G.F. Browne. **English Studies** 5 (1923): 130-32.

Proppe, Katherine. "King Alfred's **Consolation of
Philosophy."** Neuphilologische Mitteilungen
74 (1973): 635-48.

Prescott, Eleanor. "John Walton's Boethius-Translation." In
English Verse Between Chaucer and Surrey, 39-
52. New York: Octagon Books, 1969.

Quichert, J. "Jean de Meung et sa maison à Paris." **Bibliothèque
de l'école des Chartes** nv. (1880): 46-52.

Rabotine, Vladimir. **Le Boëce provençal: étude
linguistique.** Ph.D. diss., Strasbourg, 1930.
Strasbourg: Librairie Universitaire d'Alsace, 1930.

Rädle, Fidel and F.J. Worstbrock. "Boethius, Anicius Manlius
Severinus." In **Die deutsche Literatur des
Mittelalters: Verfasserlexikon,** edited by Kurt
Ruh, et al. Vol. 1, 908-28. Berlin: Walter de Gruyter,
1978.

Ralph, Dorothy Marie. "Jean de Meun, the Voltaire of the Middle
Ages." Ph.D. diss., University of Illinois at Urbana,
1940.

Rand, E.K. Review of **The Abbey of St. Gall as a Centre
of Literature and Art,** by James Midgley Clark.
Speculum 2 (1927): 354-56.

Rawlinson, Christopher. **King Ælfred's** Consolation of
    Philosophy. Oxford: n.p., 1698.

Raynaud, Gaston and Anatole de Montaiglon. "Des estats du
    siecle." In **Recueil général et complet des**
    Fabliaux des XIIIè et XIVè siècles .Vol. 2, 264-
    8. 1877. Reprint. New York: Burt Franklin, 1877.

Raynouard. [An edition of the Old Provençal **Boëce.**] N.p.: n.p.,
    1813-1817.

Reiche, Rainer. "Unbekannte Boethiusglossen der Wiener
    Handschrift 271." **Zeitschrift für deutsches**
    Altertum und deutsche Literatur 99 (1970): 90-5.

Reiss, Edmund. "The Fall of Boethius and the Fiction of the
    Consolatio Philosophiae." Classical **Journal** 77
    (1981): 37-47.

Review of **Die altfranzösische Übersetzung der** Consolatio
    Philosophiae **des Boethius von Renaut von**
    Louhans, by Franz Nagel. **Romania** 20 (1891), 329-
    30.

Riddehough, Geoffrey B. "Queen Elizabeth's Translation of
    Boethius' **De Consolatione Philosophiae.**" **JEGP:**
    Journal of English and Germanic Philologie 45
    (1946): 88-94.

de Rijk, L.M. "On the Chronology of Boethius' Works of Logic,
    Part I." **Vivarium** 2 (1964): 1-49.

de Rijk, L.M. "On the Chronology of Boethius' Works of Logic,
    Part II." **Vivarium** 2 (1964): 125-62.

Robertson, D.W., Jr. "Chaucerian Tragedy." **Journal of**
    English Literary History 19 (1952): 1-37.

----------. "Pope and Boethius." In **Classical, Mediaeval and Renaissance Studies in Honor of Berthold Louis Ullman**, edited by Charles Henderson, Jr. Vol. 2, 505-13. Rome: Edizioni de Storia e Letteratura, 1964.

Robinson, F.N., ed. **The Works of Geoffrey Chaucer**, 2nd ed. Cambridge, Mass.: Riverside Press, 1957.

Root, Robert. **The Poetry of Chaucer**. 1934. Reprint. Gloucester, Mass.: Peter Smith, 1957.

Roti, Grant C. "Anonymous in Boetii Consolationem Philosophiae Commentarius ex Sangallensis Codice." Ph.D. diss., State University of New York at Albany, 1979.

Ruggiers, Paul G. "Notes Toward a Theory of Tragedy in Chaucer." **Chaucer Review** 8 (1973/1974): 89-99.

Saintsbury, George. **A History of Criticism and Literary Taste in Europe**. Vol. 1, **Classical and Medieval Criticism**. New York: Dodd, Mead, 1900.

----------. **A History of English Prose Rhythm**. 1912. Reprint. Bloomington: Indiana University Press, 1967.

Schauber, Ellen and Ellen Spolsky. "The Consolation of Alison: the Speech Acts of the Wife of Bath." **Centrum** 5 (1977): 20-34.

Schepss, Georg. **Handschriftliche Studien zu Boethius** De Consolatione Philosophiae. Programm der Königlichen Studien-Anstalt Würzburg. Würzburg: CK der Thein'schen Druckerei, 1881.

----------. "Zu König Alfreds 'Boethius.'" **Archiv für das Studium der neueren Sprachen und Literaturen** 94 (1895): 149-60.

Schlauch, Margaret. "Chaucer's Prose Rhythms." **PMLA** 65 (1950): 568-89.

----------. "The Art of Chaucer's Prose." In **Chaucer and Chaucerians,** edited by D.S. Brewer, 140-63. London: Thomas Nelson, 1966.

Schmidt, Karl Heinz. **König Alfreds Boethius-Bearbeitung.** Ph.D. diss., Georg-August-Universität zu Göttingen, 1934. Göttingen: University Press, 1934.

Schmidt, Wieland. "Konrad Humery." In **Die deutsche Literatur des Mittelalters: Verfasserlexikon,** edited by Wolfgang Stammler. Vol. 2, 537-41. Berlin: Walter de Gruyter, 1936.

Schröbler, Ingeborg. "Interpretatio Christiana in Notkers Bearbeitung von Boethius' **Trost der Philosophie."** **Zeitschrift für deutsches Altertum und deutsche Literatur** 83 (1951): 40-57.

----------. **Notker III von St. Gallen als Übersetzer und Kommentator von Boethius'** De Consolatione Philosophiae. Hermaea Germanistische Forschung, no. 2 (neue folge). Tübingen: Max Niemeyer Verlag, 1953.

Schroth, Rolf. **Eine altfranzösische Übersetzung der** Consolatio Philosophiae **des Boethius (Handschrift Troyes Nr. 898): Edition und Kommentar.** Europäische Hochschulschriften, Reihe 8: Französische Sprache und Literatur, no. 36. Frankfurt: Peter Lang, 1976.

Schümmer, K. **John Waltons metrische Übersetzung der** Consolatio Philosophiae: Untersuchung des Handschriftenverhältnisses und Probe eines kritischen Textes. Bonner Studien zur englischen Philologie, no. 6. Bonn: Peter Hanstein Verlagsbuchhandlung, 1914.

Schwarze, Christoph. **Der altprovenzalische** Boeci.
     Forschungen zur romanischen Philologie, no. 12.
     Münster, Westfalen: Aschendorffsche
     Verlagsbuchhandlung, 1963.

Schwentner, Ernst. "Catull, Boethius, Notker."
     Germanisch-Romanische Monatsschrift 36
     (1955): 77-8.

Science, Mark. "A Suggested Correction of the Text of Chaucer's
     Boethius." London Times Literary Supplement,
     22 May 1923, 199-200.

----------, ed. **Boethius:** De Consolatione Philosophiae. John
     Walton, trans. Early English Text Society, no. 170.
     London: Oxford University Press, 1927.

Sedgefield, Walter John, ed. **King Alfred's Old English
     Version of Boethius** De Consolatione Philosophiae.
     1899. Reprint. Darmstadt: Wissenschaftliche
     Buchstellschaft, 1968.

----------, trans. **King Alfred's Version of the** Consolations
     of Boethius **Done into Modern English, With an
     Introduction.** Oxford: n.p., 1900.

Sehrt, Edward H. "Ze--Zuo in Notker." **JEGP: Journal of
     English and Germanic Philology** 35 (1936):
     331-6.

----------. Notker-Glossar: Ein althochdeutsch-
     lateinisch-neuhochdeutsches Wörterbuch zu
     Notkers des Deutschen Schriften. Tübingen: Max
     Niemeyer Verlag, 1962.

Sehrt, Edward H. and Wolfram K. Legner, eds.
     Notker-Wortschatz. Halle: VEB Max Niemeyer
     Verlag, 1955.

Sehrt, Edward H. and Taylor Starck, eds. **Notkers des Deutschen Werke**. Althochdeutsche Textbibliothek, nos. 32, 33, & 34. 1933-1934. Reprint. Halle: Max Niemeyer Verlag, 1966.

----------. "Zum Text von Notkers Schriften." **Zeitschrift für deutsches Altertum und deutsche Literatur** 71 (1934): 259-64.

----------. "Notker's Accentuation of the Prepositions **AN, IN, MIT**." **Modern Language Notes** 51 (1936): 81-6.

Shirley, Peggy Faye. "Fals Felicite and Verray Blisfulnesse: Alfred and Chaucer Translate Boethius's **Consolation of Philosophy**." Ph.D. diss., University of Mississippi, 1977.

Shorter, Robert Newland. "Boethian Philosophy as the Informing Principle in Chaucer's **Troilus and Criseyde**." Ph.D. diss., Duke University, 1965.

Silk, Edmund Taite. "Cambridge Ms. Ii. 3. 21. and the Relation of Chaucer's **Boethius** to Trivet and Jean de Meung." Ph.D. diss., Yale University, 1930.

Sisam, Kenneth. "The Authorship of the Verse Translation of Boethius's **Metra**." In **Studies in the History of Old English Literature**, 293-7. Oxford: Clarendon Press, 1953.

Skeat, Walter W., ed. **The Complete Works of Geoffrey Chaucer**. Oxford University Press, 1894-7. Reprint. London: Oxford University Press, 1933.

Smith, James. "Chaucer, Boethius and Recent Trends in Criticism: A Lecture Delivered at the University of Bristol." **Essays in Criticism** 22 (1972): 4-32.

Sonderegger, Stefan. **Althochdeutsch in St. Gallen. St. Gall**: Verlag Ostschweiz, 1970.

Sonnenburg, P. **Bemerkungen zu Notkers Bearbeitung des Boethius**. Programm des königlichen Gymnasiums zu Bonn, 1886/1887. Bonn: Universitäts-Buchdruckerei von Carl George, 1887.

Starck, Taylor. "Unpublished Old High German Glosses to Boethius and Prudentius." In **Medieval Studies in Honor of Jeremiah Denis Matthias Ford**, 301-17. Cambridge, Mass.: Harvard University Press, 1948.

Steinmeyer, Elias and Edward Sievers. **Die althochdeutschen Glossen**. 5 vols. Berlin: Wiedmann, 1879-1922.

Stevenson, William Henry, ed. **Asser's Life of King Alfred: Together With the Annals of Saint Neots**. Oxford: Clarendon Press, 1959.

Stewart, Hugh Fraser. **Boethius: An Essay**. London: 1891. Reprint. New York: Burt Franklin, 1974.

Stewart, Hugh Fraser, E.K. Rand, and S.J. Tester, eds./trans. **Boethius: Tractates, De Consolatione Philosophiae**. Cambridge, Mass.: Loeb Classical University Press, 1978.

Stone, Louise W. "Old French Translations of the **De Consolatione Philosophiae** of Boethius: Some Unnoticed Manuscripts". **Medium Aevum 6** (1937): 21-30.

Stroud, Theodore A. "Boethius' Influence on Chaucer's **Troilus**." **Modern Philology** 49 (1951): 1-9.

Tatlock, John S.P. **A Concordance to the Complete Works of Geoffrey Chaucer and the Romaunt**

of the Rose. Carnegie Institute of Washington, no.
353. Concord, Mass.: Rumford Press, 1927.

Tax, Petrus W., ed. **Boethius, De Consolatione Philosophiae:
Buch I/II.** Altdeutsch Textbibliothek, no. 94.
Tübingen: Max Niemeyer Verlag, 1986.

----------, ed. **Boethius, De Consolatione Philosophiae: Buch
III.** Altdeutsch Textbibliothek, no. 100. Tübingen: Max
Niemeyer Verlag, 1988.

Temple, Maude Elizabeth. "The Glossed **Boèce de
Consolation** of Jean de Meung: Medieval Prolegomena
to French Classic Rationalism." PMLA [Proceedings for
the 34th Annual Meeting of 1916] 32 (1917): xxviii.

Thomas, M. Antoine. "Jean de Sy et Jean de Cis." **Romania** 21
(1892): 612-15.

----------. "Jean de Meun ou de Meung." In **Encyclopédie des
sciences, des lettres et des arts (La Grande
Encyclopédie),** sv. Paris: H. Lamirault, c.1900.

----------. **Notice sur le manuscrit latin 4788 du
Vatican.** Paris: Imprimerie Nationale, 1917.

Thomas, M. Antoine and Mario Roques. "Traductions françaises de
la **Consolation Philosophiae** de Boèce." In
Histoire littéraire de la France 37 (1938): 419-506
and 542-7.

Thomson, Patricia. "Wyatt's Boethian Ballade." **Review of
English Studies** 15 (1964): 262-67.

Thynne, William, ed. **Chaucer's Works.** N.p.: n.p., 1532.

Traeger, Franz. **Studien zur Sprache von Notkers Boethius.**
Programm des königlichen humanistischen Gymnasium

in Landshut für das Studienjahr 1905/1906. Landshut: Jos. Thomann'sche Buch- und Kunstbucherei, 1906.

Twaddell, W.F. "A Main Clause With 'Final' Verb in Notker's Boethius." **JEGP: Journal of English and Germanic Philology** 31 (1932): 403-6.

Vayssière, M. August. "Renaud de Louens, poète franc-comtois du XIVe siècle (Part 1)." **Bulletin de la Société d'agriculture, sciences et arts de Poligny** 13 (1872/1873 and 1875): 345-56.

----------. "Renaud de Louens, poète franc-comtois du XVIe siècle (Part 2)." **Bulletin de la société d'agriculture, sciences et arts de Poigny** 17 (1876/1877): n.pp.

Vollmann, Benedikt. "Simplicitas divinae providentiae: zur Entwicklung des Begriffs in der antiken Philosophie und seiner Eindeutschung in Notkers Consolatio-Übersetzung." **Literaturwissenschaftliches Jahrbuch der Görres-Gesellschaft** 8 (1967): 5-29.

de Vooys, C.G.N. "De Middelnederlanse Boethius-vertaling van Jacob Vilt." **Tijdschrift voor Nederlandsche Taal- en Letterkunde** 60 (1941): 1-25.

de Vries, F.C. "In Chaucer's Workshop: Two Boethian Passages in Troilus and Criseyde (a synopsis)." **Australasian Universities Language and Literature Association** [Proceedings and Papers of the Thirteenth Congress] 13 (1970): 383-5.

van de Vyver, A. "Les Traductions du **De Consolatione philosophiae** de Boèce en littérature comparée." **Humanisme et Renaissance** 6 (1939): 247-73.

Warton, Thomas. **History of English Poetry from the Twelfth to the Sixteenth Century**, edited by W.C.

Hazlitt. Vol. 3, 38-40. London: 1871. Reprint. Hildesheim: Georg Olms, 1968.

White, Alison. "Boethius in the Medieval Quadrivium." In **Boethius: His Life, Thought and Influence,** edited by Margaret Gibson, 162-205. Oxford: Basil Blackwell, 1981.

Whitelock, Dorothy. "The Prose of Alfred's Reign." In **Continuations and Beginnings: Studies in Old English Literature,** edited by Eric Gerald Stanley, 67-103. London: Nelson, 1966.

Wimsatt, James. "Samson Agonistes and the Tradition of Boethius." **Renaissance Papers** n.v (1972): 1-10.

Witcutt, W.P. "Chaucer's Boëthius." **American Review** 8 (1936/1937): 61-70.

Wittig, Joseph S. "King Alfred's **Boethius** and its Latin Sources: A Reconsideration." **Anglo-Saxon England** 11 (1983): 157-98.

Wolfermann, Oskar. **Die Flexionslehre in Notkers althochdeutscher Übersetzung von Boethius:** De Consolatione Philosophiae, **ein Beitrag zur althochdeutschen Grammatik.** Altenburg: Oskar Bonde, 1886.

Wright, Thomas. **Biographia Britanica Literaria I.** London: n.p., 1842.

Wülfing, J.E. "Zum altenglischen Boethius: zwei Briefe von Cardale an Bosworth und von Bosworth an Fox." **Anglia: Zeitschrift für englische Philologie** 19 (1897): 99-100.

Wunderlich, Hermann. **Beiträge zur Syntax des Notker'schen Boethius.** Ph.D. diss., Friederich-

Wilhelm-Universität zu Berlin, 1883. Berlin:
Buchdruckerei von Gustav Schade, 1883.

Zimmermann, Otto. **Über den Verfasser der altenglischen**
Metren des Boethius. Ph.D. diss., Universität Greifswald,
1882. Greifswald: Julius Abel, 1882.

Zingarelli, Nicola. "Il **Boezio** Provenzale e la Leggenda di
Boezio." **Reciconti del reale Istituto Lombardo
di Scienze e Lettere** 53 (1920): 193-221.